The Mana of Mass Society

Chicago Studies in Practices of Meaning

A series edited by Andreas Glaeser, William Mazzarella, William Sewell, Kaushik Sunder Rajan, and Lisa Wedeen

Published in collaboration with the Chicago Center for Contemporary Theory http://ccct.uchicago.edu

RECENT BOOKS IN THE SERIES

The Sins of the Father: Germany, Memory, Method
by Jeffrey K. Olick

The Genealogical Science: The Search for Jewish Origins and the Politics of Epistemology
by Nadia Abu El-Haj

Questioning Secularism: Islam, Sovereignty, and the Rule of Law in Modern Egypt
by Hussein Ali Agrama

Political Epistemics: The Secret Police, the Opposition, and the End of East German Socialism
by Andreas Glaeser

The Politics of Dialogic Imagination: Power and Popular Culture in Early Modern Japan
by Katsuya Hirano

The Moral Neoliberal: Welfare and Citizenship in Italy
by Andrea Muehlebach

American Value: Migrants, Money, and Meaning in El Salvador and the United States
by David Pedersen

The Making of Romantic Love: Longing and Sexuality in Europe, South Asia, and Japan, 900–1200 CE
by William M. Reddy

Laughing at Leviathan: Sovereignty and Audience in West Papua
by Danilyn Rutherford

William
Mazzarella

The Mana
of Mass
Society

The University of Chicago Press
Chicago and London

The University of Chicago Press, Chicago 60637
The University of Chicago Press, Ltd., London
© 2017 by The University of Chicago
All rights reserved. No part of this book may be used or reproduced in any
manner whatsoever without written permission, except in the case of brief
quotations in critical articles and reviews. For more information, contact the
University of Chicago Press, 1427 E. 60th St., Chicago, IL 60637.
Published 2017
Printed in the United States of America

26 25 24 23 22 21 20 19 18 17   1 2 3 4 5

ISBN-13: 978-0-226-43611-1 (cloth)
ISBN-13: 978-0-226-43625-8 (paper)
ISBN-13: 978-0-226-43639-5 (e-book)
DOI: 10.7208/chicago/9780226436395.001.0001

Library of Congress Cataloging-in-Publication Data

Names: Mazzarella, William, 1969– author.
Title: The mana of mass society / William Mazzarella.
Other titles: Chicago studies in practices of meaning.
Description: Chicago ; London : The University of Chicago Press, 2017. |
Series: Chicago studies in practices of meaning | Includes bibliographical
references and index.
Identifiers: LCCN 2016058492 | ISBN 9780226436111 (cloth : alk. paper) |
ISBN 9780226436258 (pbk. : alk. paper) | ISBN 9780226436395 (e-book)
Subjects: LCSH: Mana. | Critical theory. | Anthropology—Philosophy. |
Mass media and anthropology.
Classification: LCC GN471.4 .M39 2017 | DDC 301.01—dc23
LC record available at https://lccn.loc.gov/2016058492

♾ This paper meets the requirements of ANSI/NISO Z39.48-1992
(Permanence of Paper).

Contents

Acknowledgments

The phrase "the mana of mass society" has been haunting me for a while. It first came to me in early 2004, when I dropped it, rather casually, into the conclusion of a lecture—thus conveniently excusing myself of the responsibility of any rigorous elaboration. It reappeared as a section heading in my second book, *Censorium*, where it framed a preliminary sketch of my reinterpretation of Émile Durkheim's theory of ritual as a theory of mass publicity—a central theme in the present book. Having now attained the declarative promise of an actual book title, I hope that these words will also agree to the exorcism that their full explication implies.

Although—or perhaps because—the questions that drive this book have, in one form or another, been with me since as long as I can remember, the manuscript itself emerged with startling, even explosive, speed during three intense bursts of writing in the summers of 2015 and 2016. Between the bursts, friends and colleagues were overwhelmingly generous in their critical engagements with various elements of the work. This is, unabashedly, a "theory book." But it is also in its half-masked way the most intimate academic text I've written. That so many of my interlocutors have understood this, that so many of them have sensed the resonance between "theory" and "experience"—in their own lives as much as in mine—has felt like a profound reward.

For their readings, commentaries, and suggestions, I want to thank Sneha Annavarapu, Josh Babcock, Greg Beckett, Christian Borch, Nusrat Chowdhury, Jean Comaroff, John Comaroff, Shannon Dawdy, Vincent Duclos, Maura Finkelstein, Dianna Frid, Leela Gandhi, Rohit Goel, Guangtian Ha, Jenna Henderson, Laura-Zoe Humphreys, Patrick Jagoda, Harini Kumar, Andrew Kunze, Amanda Lucia, Agnes Mondragón, Sarah Muir, Nancy Munn, Sasha Newell, Tejaswini Niranjana, Ray Noll, Eléonore Rimbault, Marshall Sahlins, Eric Santner, Jay Schutte, Kristen Simmons, Bhrigupati Singh, Emilio Spadola, Mick Taussig, Jeremy Walton, and Lisa Wedeen.

My coconspirators at the Chicago Center for Contemporary Theory have, over the years, given me an intellectual home. Respect and gratitude to—in addition to those already mentioned—Lauren Berlant, Bill Brown, Dipesh Chakrabarty, Andreas Glaeser, Patchen Markell, Joe Masco, Moishe Postone, Bill Sewell, Kaushik Sunder Rajan, and Anwen Tormey. Priya Nelson, my dynamic editor at the University of Chicago Press, somehow knew right away how to calm my anxieties and to help me believe in the broader plausibility of a project that, on some days, felt painfully idiosyncratic. As for the mana of everyday and thus extraordinary life, I have, crab-like as ever, approached it sideways, under cover of my disciplines. For Dianna Frid, no such subterfuge was necessary. Her presence and practice continues in so many ways to inspire my thinking about the Sirens' call, about wormholes, and about conceptual form as always-already immanent life.

Introduction

A Certain Rush of Energy

A certain rush of energy. This is what the sociologist Émile Durkheim [1] wrote in his 1912 masterpiece, *The Elementary Forms of Religious Life*: "The stimulating action of society is not felt in exceptional circumstances alone. There is virtually no instant of our lives in which a certain rush of energy fails to come to us from outside ourselves."[1] One of the names that Durkheim gave to this energy, this stimulating action of society, was *mana*—a Polynesian word meaning, roughly, supernatural force or efficacy. Although Durkheim's book was ostensibly concerned with "primitive" forms of *collective effervescence*, with the ritual assemblies of Australian Aborigines and Northwest Coast American Indians, it was in fact a meditation on what one could call the *vital energetics* of all human societies, from the smallest to the most complex, from face-to-face interactions to mass-mediated networks. Mana, Durkheim argued, was "at once a physical force and a moral power."[2] It was a name for that feeling of "genuine respect" that makes us "defer to society's orders."[3] It might be embodied in a chief's potency or in the aura of a sacred object. But it was also chronically unstable and leaky, perpetually and sometimes dangerously overflowing its containers: "Religious forces are so imagined as to appear always on the point of escaping the places they occupy and invading all that passes within their reach."[4]

This book picks up on Durkheim's provocation and asks what it would mean, for social theory, to imagine the mana that powers an Aboriginal ritual as substantially continuous with the mana that infuses an urban crowd or even, differently modulated, a television audience or an Internet public. It asks how one might theorize the mana of mass society in a world where a certain rush of energy is as likely to be found in consumer brand advertising as in totemic signs, as likely to power a fascination with charismatic politicians as an affiliation with traditional authorities. Is mana different when it comes to us with the curious blend of intimacy and impersonality so characteristic of public address?

Durkheim tended to presume that the "stimulating action of society" was unambiguously vitalizing, that it was the source not only of our sense of commitment to life in common but also of our moral faculties, even our very ability to think at all. But what about the mana of, say, racist or nationalist ideologies that offer their adherents a sense of common energy and solidarity at the cost of abjecting an other? Knowing what we now know about murderous forms of collective effervescence, from the centralized cults of fascism to the decentralized networks of global terror, do we need a different way to understanding the dynamic movement of what Durkheim's nephew, the polymath Marcel Mauss, called "the collective forces of society"?[5]

This book came together during a time of surging energies, light and dark. The energies of the worldwide Occupy movement, of the Arab Spring, and of Black Lives Matter. The energies of the migrant crisis in Europe, of gathering ecological catastrophe, of meandering militarism and the tense topology of terror. As I thought and wrote, I watched "that *mana* wave called Trump"[6] morph from improbable to inevitable and back . . . and back again. As one commentator observed: "He is not trying to persuade, detail, or prove: he is trying to thrill, agitate, be liked, be loved, here and now. He is trying to make energy."[7] Amid these surges, I pondered the questions that animate this book. What *powers* authority? What in us responds to it? How is *vital energy* turned into *social form*? Conversely, how do social forms activate new *vital potentials*? Why do certain times, people, places, and things feel *heightened* in relation to humdrum life? How are we to understand not just the *meanings* to which we find ourselves attached but also their *rhythms*? What is the social basis of commitment, engagement, identification, and desire? In short: how is it that we have not only meaning, but *meaning that matters*?

Thinking the mana of mass society means reconsidering Durkheim's theory of ritual and collective effervescence, but also Max Weber's discussions of authority and charisma and Karl Marx's ideas about fetishism and ideology. Mana, I will be suggesting, marks the spot where vitality and its relation to authority and experience is at once acknowledged and disavowed. As such, it helps to bring together classic topics in social theory with more recent debates around affect, sovereignty, immanence, and emergence. Crucially, this is not just a story about large-scale phenomena. Spectacle can too easily overshadow less blinding events. After all, as Durkheim wrote, "There is virtually no instant in our lives in which a certain rush of energy fails to come to us from outside ourselves." An important question for me in the pages that follow is how the mana of mass society connects the macro-forms of ritual, publicity, and display with the micro-dimensions of experience.

This means at least two things. First, it means exploring the relation between the exceptional and the everyday, a key Durkheimian theme. If certain occasions or practices—for example important rituals—have to be *special* and yet also have to sustain the rhythms of ordinary life, then how is that specialness both maintained and diffused? This turns out to be a crucial question in democratic theory as well as in consumer marketing. In an age when the people are sovereign, and yet the people are, by definition, not a single body in a particular place, how is this sovereignty to be ritually represented in such a way that it can focus energies and commitments and yet also appear as the immanent substance of the collective?[8] In marketing, brands do the work of "keeping-while-giving," of remaining proprietary repositories of heightened value, controlled by corporations, while at the same time being readily available for purchase.[9]

Second, Durkheim says that social energy comes to us "from outside ourselves," and one of my key preoccupations in this book is rethinking the relation between what is "inside" and what is "outside." Mana, I will be arguing, offers a handle on what the psychoanalyst Jacques Lacan called the *extimate*: that which is at once external and intimate, that which we experience, ambivalently, as part of the world that confronts us and yet at the same time as something that is palpably, intensely, at the very core of our sense of ourselves.[10] Again one can see how this plays out in both politics and marketing once one asks what, exactly, is activated by the charismatic leader or by the desirable brand? Where is it? Is it inside us or outside us? Does it lie in wait somewhere inside us, fully formed, waiting to find its perfect match in the outside world? Or is it in a fundamental sense *actualized* by the encounter with the leader or the brand that turns out to be "just what I always wanted" (except I didn't know I wanted it until the moment of encounter)? This sense of power as potentiality, of an efficacy that brings things into the world and makes them "work" is, as we shall see, one of the faces of mana.

Order and emergence: that is the double fascination of mana. Mana appears as a name for the transcendent force guaranteeing a moral order, a symbolic order, a cultural order. But it is also always a mark of excess, of the super-natural, the sur-plus, the "surcharge."[11] It is the efficacy that exceeds and overflows basic requirements. And yet somehow this very excessiveness, this way in which mana always seems to embody a "something more" at the heart of any given social order, makes it both instrumentally and aesthetically indispensable. It is this emergent property at the heart of order that links mana to notions of mass publicity,[12] both in the register of charismatic politics (as Max Weber knew) and in the register of the auratic aesthetics of artworks (as Theodor Adorno knew).

I devote quite a bit of space, particularly in the second half of this book, to thinking about politics as marketing and marketing as politics. We live in a time when the lessons of consumer marketing have become *doxa* among political strategists, and the figure of the consumer-citizen has become the most readily accessible shorthand for the democratic subject. Thinking the mana of mass society across politics and marketing, then, at one level merely acknowledges a social fact. As an interpretive strategy, though, it has the added advantage of allowing me to revisit those debates in critical theory and aesthetics that, for almost a century now, have speculated on the fate of human flourishing in a world where what Theodor Adorno and Walter Benjamin called the *mimetic faculty* — a sensuous, transformative ability to resonate with the world—has increasingly been harnessed by sovereign pretenders, whether political or commercial.

Constitutive Resonance: An Analytic of Encounter

Mimetic resonance may also be glossed as *constitutive resonance*, a term that I borrow from the philosopher Peter Sloterdijk.[13] A variation on the more familiar *elective affinity*, constitutive resonance suggests a relation of mutual becoming rather than causal determination. Not all people or things are capable of resonating with each other (and one of the first tasks of the would-be mana worker— whether politician or marketer or just garden-variety magician—is to figure out what resonates with what). But resonance, once established, is a source of both actualization and anxiety. I become myself through you, but I also lose myself in you. By the logic of constitutive resonance, if "I" and "you" can appear as "subject" and "object" then it is only by means of a shared field of emergence in which no such boundaries can be taken for granted.

Resonant encounters, then, are *erotic* in the ancient sense explored by Anne Carson: on the one hand, "this heightened sense of one's own personality ('I am more myself than ever before!')," and, on the other hand, a loss of self experienced as a crisis of physical and emotional integrity; Sappho called eros the "melter of limbs."[14] Resonant encounter is at once constitutive and destitutive. It's a way of thinking about the making and unmaking of selves and worlds, as well as of the attachments of selves to the worlds in which they can feel alive, usually by means of some ambivalent combination of affirmation and refusal. Sometimes the pursuit of constitutive resonance is self-consciously "sacred," such as in several recent ethnographic accounts of learning to hear and to receive the call of piety.[15] Sometimes, as in the second half of this book, constitutive resonance is experienced as a more "secular" seduction: how to negotiate the siren songs of political and commercial publicity.

This book is based on a deceptively simple assumption: *encounter is primary*. What might that mean? Social theorists often talk and write as if people inhabit given, more or less bounded social structures and identities that periodically come up against challenges to their coherence and integrity. From such a standpoint, difference appears from outside—an uncanny stranger or an inexplicable way of doing things. From that perspective, the important question is generally, how far must structure be stretched in order to make sense of this external intrusion?

But what if one turns this around? What if one starts with encounter rather than with structure? This may seem like a chicken-and-egg problem; surely, one always presupposes the other? Yes. Of course it's not as if people ever have encounters that are innocent of the contexts and histories that they bring to them. Nor is there any social structure free of more or less destabilizing encounters. So maybe I'm just proposing a different emphasis? Maybe I'm advocating paying attention to moments of difference rather than to structures of sameness? Not quite.

My premise is that it matters a great deal for how we understand key concepts like society, subjectivity, and ideology whether the inquiry starts with encounter or starts with structure. Again, it's not about choosing or valorizing one or the other. If the discussion starts with structure, then it's likely to become preoccupied with questions like "how is structure reproduced?" "How can we account for change?" Here, structure is the baseline and encounter is the potential interruption of structure. But if encounter is the starting point, then other kinds of questions appear. What resonates in the wake of the encounter? What doesn't? What is activated in an encounter such that it might feel like a moment of promise, of agitation, of potential, or of threat?

Rather than asking how structure is reproduced one might ask how it is that the world comes to seem structured at all. Given that, as Heraclitus observed, one can't step in the same river twice, it's really quite extraordinary that anyone is ever able to feel that they live in relatively continuous worlds and that they generally experience—or come to experience—encounter as iteration rather than as rupture or drift. What interests me is encounter as the resonant occasion and trigger for everything social theory understands as "identity," "culture," "desire," and so on; encounter as a moment of mimetic yielding that at the same time actualizes the intelligible differences that people then proceed to inhabit as "me" and "you," "ours" and "theirs."

Starting with encounter means starting with provocation—in two senses. On the one hand, provocation mobilizes categories so that sameness and difference can be managed. Social scientists are used to talking about the provocation of difference: how do people deal with difference? Where do they put it? How do they "place" unfamiliar things, making sense of them—even when they don't quite fit—in terms of familiar things? Such questions are of course fundamental to the operation of any kind of social life, from the smallest face-to-face relationships to the most extensive bureaucracies. Encounter provokes classification and routinization.

But the provocation of encounter may also be read as provocation—as, literally, a *calling forth*,[16] an activation, a prompt to becoming. Encounter doesn't just mean coming face to face with difference, the way an academic or a clerk might, and having to work out what to do with it. It also suggests a resonant (not necessarily pleasant) triggering of something unexpected: a potentiation, perhaps an actualization, but perhaps also a traumatic echo (in which case the constitutive aspect of the resonance is mediated by the scars of suffering). An encounter is what the philosopher J. G. Fichte called *Anstoss*: a trigger moment, an impact, an impetus, or an initiation. In any case, a moment whose affective tenor is not just one of a categorical challenge but also potentially one of fascination, seduction, identification, or desire.

Ritual—the central preoccupation of Durkheim's *Elementary Forms*—is a crucial category here, because it so palpably blends both senses of provocation: on the one hand, ritual involves *Anstoss*, a live calling forth of "the collective forces of society" in a manner that aspires to be at once impersonal and exquisitely intimate. On the other hand, ritual reproduces form through the repetitive affirmation of categories. This, too, is one of the faces of mana: the potentiality that is always unstable, leaky, unpredictable, and, at the same time, the substance that powers and authorizes a reigning social order, lending it the weight of the sacred. The fascination and the power of ritual is that it at once activates and routinizes encounter.

But if there is provocation, then what is provoked? If there is activation, then what is activated? What is the *material*, the substance on which all these processes go to work? Anthropologists (particularly on the American side of the pond) have long been in the habit of invoking "culture" in order to explain the patterned ways in which "the collective forces of society" move, as well as what I will gloss as the relatively predictable patterns of our *addressability* as individuals living in particular, meaningful worlds. Painfully aware of the compromised quality of the culture concept today—not least because of its hijacking by politics and marketing—I suggest an alternative concept, the *mimetic archive*: the residue, embedded not only in the explicitly articulated forms commonly recognized as cultural discourses but also in built environments and material forms, in the concrete history of the senses, and in the habits of our shared embodiment.

This residue, the mimetic archive, is preserved on two levels. On one level, it appears as incipient potential. On another level, it takes the form of all the explicitly elaborated discursive and symbolic forms through which the potentials of a mimetic archive have earlier been actualized, each actualization then proliferating and returning new potentials to the archive. Some of the archive is of course textual or signifies in other more or less overt ways. But by far the largest part of the archive exists virtually yet immanently in the nonsignifying yet palpably sensuous dimensions of collective life. In Deleuzian language, these immanent potentials are *infolded* as incipience. In a Benjaminian idiom, one could say that they are *innervated*. In a more directly anthropological register, one could invoke a figure like Marcel Jousse, a student of Marcel Mauss and Pierre Janet, who grounded both language and consciousness in the mimetic rhythms of the body. Memory, as Charles Hirschkind glosses Jousse, is built on "the reactivation of gestures, understood as the sensory sediments of prior perceptions." These sediments become the basis for "latent tendencies, dispositions toward certain kinds of action operating independently of conscious thought."[17]

Lauren Berlant writes of "a history of impacts held in reserve."[18] On that note I would like to stress two dimensions of the mimetic archive as I conceive it: its virtuality and its historicity. First, "impacts held in reserve" are, indeed, "latent." They are virtual potentialities that at once embed a history of encounters and lie in wait for the future encounters that will actualize them in new forms. "Reactivation," then, is not simply duplicative reenactment but always involves unpredictable transformations in the transition from the virtual to the actual. The virtuality of the mimetic archive is therefore inseparable from its historicity. On the one hand, the archive embeds latent histories of encounter; on the other hand, its actualization *is* constitutive resonance awakened between these embedded encounter-histories and the triggers of the present.

For this formulation I am, as in so many respects, indebted to Walter Benjamin, who wrote: "this dialectical penetration and actualization of former contexts puts the truth of all present action to the test. Or rather, it serves to ignite the explosive materials that are latent in what has been."[19] Pasts, collective and/or intimate, are only at one level the stories we tell ourselves. At another level, they are the potentials, embedded, perhaps, in some apparently trivial object, much like Proust's protagonist finds in his madeleine an unexpected and overwhelming sensuous prompt to the evocation of a whole world. Like Benjamin, I'm interested in constitutive encounter as a way of talking about how resonance—whether routinized or entirely surprising—makes and unmakes us through those decisive (although not always dramatic) moments of legibility that Benjamin called dialectical images:

> It's not that what is past casts its light on what is present, or what is present its light on what is past; rather, image is that wherein what has been comes together in a flash with the now to form a constellation. . . . Every present day is determined by the images that are synchronic with it: each 'now' is the now of a particular recognizability. In it, truth is charged to the bursting point with time. . . . For while the relation of the present to the past is purely temporal, the relation of what-has-been to the now is dialectical: not temporal in nature but figural.[20]

Crucially, there's no reason to assume that mimetic resonance necessarily points to liberation. Rather, the point is that mimesis, as Homi Bhabha has shown us, is as much a matter of discipline as it is about transformation—again, the two faces of mana.[21] I use the term *mimetic archive* strategically, then, not necessarily in a bid to replace the culture concept, but rather as a reminder of what that concept would have to be capable of in order to do what it must.

Settlement and Symptom

The Mana of Mass Society is by no means a work of intellectual history. It is far too interpretive and idiosyncratic to deserve such a dignified name. Instead, I take as my primary methodological tool the concept of *settlements*. I discuss three: the empiricist settlement (chapter 1), the primitive settlement (chapter 2), and the aesthetic settlement (chapter 3). The list of settlements could — and I hope will — be extended. I use the term to suggest the tension between the appearance of a negotiated, reasonable compromise and the violence of the settler whose stability of residence depends on the displacement and disavowal of the one that his presence silences. My basic premise is that each of these settlements marks a moment of encounter in social theory and the consequent attempt to resolve an unstable yet seductive relation of ambivalence. So: the empiricist settlement establishes a boundary between modern fieldwork-based anthropology and its speculative-comparative precursors; the primitive settlement separates "primitive" practices from "civilized" norms; and the aesthetic settlement makes a safe place for magic in one privileged location within civilization — art.

By attempting the purification, as Bruno Latour might say, of a pro-vocative encounter, each settlement establishes an extimate relation: it draws a line of demarcation that constitutes a coherent discipline by abjecting its intolerably intimate and thus also irreducibly constitutive other. And as with all extimacies, it generates an inescapable symptom. No sooner has the line of settlement been drawn than the repressed starts to return. What unites the three settlements that I discuss in this book is their common concern with mana. In each case, mana is the name for a "primitive" potentiality — of energy, of magic, of the sacred — that at once is and is not the same as parallel potentialities in "modern" societies. By the same token, in each case mana is, as we shall see, the recurrent symptom.

Much of what mana is, does, or could become will sound very familiar to present-day readers of affect theory.[22] Kathleen Stewart, in *Ordinary Affects*, writes: "Something huge and impersonal runs through things, but it's also mysteriously intimate and close at hand. At once abstract and concrete, it's both a distant, untouchable order of things and a claustrophobically close presence"[23] — and she could be invoking mana. Likewise, once one starts probing the mana symptom, it opens up onto something not altogether separable from what Terry Eagleton and W. F. Haug call the aesthetic: an ideological discourse that naturalizes domination *and* an emergent domain of palpable resonance that is both indispensable to power and refractory to its ambitions.[24]

Rather than treating mana as yet another variant of something already known, however, I want to give it the benefit of a provocative encounter—just as thinking aesthetics requires a different kind of historical sensing. Berlant puts it admirably: "too often we derive a sense of a time, place, and power through historical archives whose job it is to explain something aesthetic without thinking the aesthetic in the sensually affective terms that conventions of entextualization always code, perform, and release."[25] Because of the ways that mana haunts settled sites, then, I'm wagering that opening up those settlements may well also open up fresh ways of thinking affect and aesthetics.

Confessions of a Dialectical Vitalist

Perhaps this whole exercise is, in a way, motivated by a desire to revisit yet another settlement—the line that was drawn through anthropology in the mid-1980s right before my generation started studying it. This line, variably known as the "critique of representation" or, following the title of one of its key texts, *Writing Culture*, had the effect of demarcating a "before"—when anthropologists supposedly engaged in naively unreflexive modes of ethnographic description—and an "after"—when they were hip to critical theory, deconstruction, and a postcolonial politics of representation.[26] Hardly anyone really thought that it was as simple as all that, but the sense of a line having been drawn often did make our relation to the anthropological canon rather awkward. While we could certainly pretend that a genome sequencing lab or a television news production studio was a bit like a tribal village, ethnographic strategies developed for face-to-face societies were not in any obvious way very useful when it came to making sense of how even the most local field sites were now, thanks to increasingly ubiquitous electronic media, embroiled in translocal circuits of images, goods, and knowledge, as well as in real-time communication with far-flung people and places.

I write from the standpoint of my own specifically located experience as a graduate student at Berkeley in the early 1990s, still suffering from something like a time-travel hangover after having been an undergraduate at the University of Cambridge. Of course things played out differently in other places. But as I recall it, introductory graduate seminars on anthropological theory often manifested the before/after split. Some professors tried a simple chronological exposition, with the result that many students, bored and restless, dutifully waded through structural functionalism, kinship models, and structuralist analyses of myth, before, with an air of now being superbly deserving of dessert, devouring more recent articles on globalization, NGOs, and biosociality. Other professors started with the critique of representation before arcing back through classic works in the discipline. This strategy tended to have the effect of producing in many of us students a supercilious (and, it must be said, naively historicist) attitude toward earlier anthropologies, since we thought we already possessed the tools with which to diagnose their irretrievable outmodedness and incurable pathology. Either way, the "after" was where things were happening, and the "before" was something that, at best, provided raw material for narcissistically indignant denunciations of anthropology's colonial complicities.

To be sure, there were other students who took a more conservative path. Repelled by the posturing of their right-on peers, they saw themselves as custodians of a rich ethnographic heritage, one now at risk from the so-called navel-gazing theoreticism of the new, *soi-disant* "critical" anthropology. Only relatively few of us—most of the time I was not one—found ways of making the deeper anthropological heritage come alive in the present, not by insisting on the continued importance of small-scale village fieldwork (nothing wrong with that, obviously), but rather by exploring how emergent concerns in the present might activate hitherto unrealized potentials in the mimetic archive of the discipline. This book is my belated attempt at such an exercise. After a long and frequently fruitful detour through critical theory, thinking the mana of mass society feels like a homecoming more or less unencumbered by the cloying scent of nostalgia.

In an inaugural essay for *HAU*, the open access "journal of ethnographic theory" and book imprint, Giovanni Da Col and David Graeber lament the passing of a golden age of anthropology during which ethnographically derived concepts—totem, taboo, potlatch, mana— "were heated topics of intellectual debate; concepts that everyone, philosophers included, had to take seriously."[27] Today, they charge, anthropologists have been reduced to second-rate exegetes of concepts from European philosophy, "and no one outside anthropology really cares what we have to say about them."[28] Likewise, anthropologists, having fallen prey to "a colossal failure of nerve"[29] brought on in part by the critique of representation, have forgotten how to remind our fellow scholars of the long and deep conceptual archive we have to offer to areas of common concern: "Deleuzians and Speculative Realists write about the ontology and the elusiveness of *life* . . . and their reflections are gravely debated in other disciplines, without anyone even noticing the rich anthropological literature on *mana*."[30]

How could I not be sympathetic? Aren't Da Col and Graeber invoking something like what I have sketched above under the rubrics of encounter and constitutive resonance when they call for "a conversion of stranger-concepts that does not entail merely trying to establish a correspondence of meaning between two entities or the construction of heteronymous harmony between different worlds, but rather, the generation of a *disjunctive homonymity*, that destruction of any firm sense of place that can only be resolved by the imaginative formulation of novel worldviews"?[31] The project of *HAU* promises a renewal of an anthropology constitutively engaged with the concerns and imaginations of ordinary informants around the world rather than passively importing readymades from the Great Men of Theory. And I do sense a strong affinity between my own project in this book and Da Col and Graeber's allegiance to those "who, acknowledging the analogies between philosophy and anthropology, are careful enough to think about what makes the two distinctive, and at the same time, bold enough to create their own conceptual repertoire."[32]

At the same time, if my own book is a small contribution to this larger project of "return[ing] anthropology to its original and distinctive conceptual wealth,"[33] then it proceeds not by reinstalling a lost integrity but rather by reencountering the symptoms that mark the settlements that allowed, say, "anthropology" and "European philosophy" to begin appearing as distinct and autonomous projects. For there is a common mimetic archive here—an archive that is the condition of possibility for both anthropology and critical theory, an archive that lies half buried under the settlements that forced their separation. If "reading" a settlement symptom like mana is to help trigger new insights then it will not happen, I suspect, by means of an act of pure will, through a principled decision to correct the course of an anthropology that has drifted too far into dependence on outside centers of intellectual authority. Rather, the challenge, the opportunity, lies in acknowledging the resonant intimacy of that outside—its extimacy—and working back through a long genealogy of "almost-saying,"[34] of constitutive encounters that are already embedded in the sense making that has taken place between anthropologists, critical theorists, and psychoanalysts for a hundred years or more.

It is not unimportant to my engagement with mana that vitalism has made something of a comeback in anthropology—now most often, as Da Col and Graeber note, in a Deleuzian avatar. This renewed concern with the uncanny intimacy of impersonal processes of emergence has, moreover, been given a boost by a combination of posthuman and ecological engagements. While there is much that is urgent, rich, and sophisticated in these lines of inquiry, I have for some time been concerned that they often tend, as Slavoj Žižek notes, toward an undialectical (indeed, often proudly antidialectical) "preference for difference over sameness, for historical change over order, for openness over closure, for vital dynamics over rigid schemes, for temporal finitude over eternity.... For me, these preferences are by no means self-evident."[35]

In my book *Censorium* I admitted, in a coyly performative wording, that "I would not be altogether embarrassed, then, if someone accused me of being that rather peculiar monster: a 'dialectical vitalist.'"[36] Some months later, a friend and senior colleague accused me, more prosaically but not unsympathetically, of "wanting to have it both ways." On that score I remain unrepentant, if anything more insistent than ever. *The Mana of Mass Society* is, if not quite a manifesto of dialectical vitalism, then certainly an exercise in it. It's not a question for me of choosing "ethnographic theory" or "critical theory."

Rather, it's a question of how the particular road I have taken, by means of vehicles belonging to both, allows me to re-member them in ways that may illuminate the present.

The Ontological Need All Over Again

One example of what I mean by this re-membering is the object-ethics that I develop in these pages. Here, as ever, mana is the extimate symptom that marks a brittle settlement: in the case of the argument that I develop in chapter 3, the settlement that separates Adorno's aesthetic theory—which is fundamentally premised on constitutive resonance—from his furious denunciation of commodified cultural production. Thinking through this settlement, I realized that it offered something of an alternative perspective on what it means to be a human being, living in the world and theorizing that world—an alternative to much of what has appeared under the heading of the "ontological turn" that has brought anthropologists and philosophers into renewed conversation in recent years. My purpose here is neither to preempt chapter 3 nor to offer any kind of comprehensive review of an ontological turn that, in any case, is more of a resonant assemblage than a "position." My purpose, rather, is only to offer some very general framing thoughts about why an object-ethics can also be a subject-ethics—why thinking in more complex ways about encounters with objects doesn't have to involve falling back on zombie constructions like "The Enlightenment Subject" or "The Kantian Subject" (undead straw concepts that can be relied on to return eternally so that posthumanist critics can keep shooting them down, all the while not hearing what the undead, from behind their zombie makeup, are trying to say).

The global ecological crisis as well as the explosion in alter-phobic (racist, misogynistic, xenophobic, queer-phobic) violence presses upon us urgently. How are we to reconnect with a world—and with our own and each other's organic emplacements in that world—from which, the ontophiles tell us, the Kantian tradition has exiled us? The Kantian tradition insists that we cannot know the world *in itself*, only the representations of the world that our brains (and latterly our cultures) permit us. Consequently, the anti-Kantian critics claim, we have effectively allowed an ethic of epistemological modesty ("we can't ever be completely sure of our knowledge of the world") to slip into an attitude of violent and arrogant mastery ("because we are separated from the world we need to find ways of controlling it"). Likewise, in anthropology a pose of relativist modesty ("all any of us have is our culturally constructed perspectives on the world") has tended to slip into a kind of formalist universalism that permits difference only at the level of content ("anthropology is a master-survey of the range of cultural solutions to the universal natural predicament of being human").[37]

To remedy this supposed "Kantian catastrophe," a range of thinkers are trying to find ways of reversing what one might call the human sciences' epistemological humblebrag. The prize to be regained is, as the philosopher Quentin Meillassoux puts it, "the great outdoors"—the world out there in its ontological actuality.[38] Some of the more speculative variations on the enterprise are asking us to consider such enigmas as what it might be like to be a rock.[39] Anthropological exponents of the ontological turn have, however, tended toward comparatively more modest inquiries. Eduardo Viveiros de Castro, for example, calls for an anthropology that allows the "form of the matter" of our informants' discourse to reach into and transform the "matter of the form" of our conceptual work, an anthropology that is concerned with "determining the problems posed by each culture, not of finding solutions for the problems posed by our own."[40]

So far, so Georg Lukács, for didn't the great Marxist philosopher diagnose, in the early 1920s, that the problem with what he called the "reified" forms of bourgeois knowledge was that they assumed at once a universalizing and a contemplative relation to an external world that they were thereby unable to understand as anything but a series of contents or variables to be slotted into transcendent formal structures? As Lukács wrote of the bureaucratic imagination, which he took to be a paradigm of reified thought: "objectively all issues are subjected to an increasingly *formal* and standardized treatment and . . . there is an ever-increasing remoteness from the qualitative and material essence of the 'things' to which bureaucratic activity pertains."[41] And just as Viveiros de Castro calls for an anthropological opening to the ontological alterity—not just the "cultural content"—of other ways of apprehending and organizing life, so Lukács imagines a nonreifying relation to the world in which "actuality, content, matter reaches right into the form [of knowledge], the structures of the forms and their interrelations and thus *into the structure of the system itself.*"[42]

Whereas Lukács's critical aim is a dialectical overcoming of the antinomies of bourgeois thought, Viveiros de Castro seems to be defending a form of ethnographic encounter that transforms both anthropologists and their informants by leaving their preexisting differences suspended in a productive relation of integral nonidentity: "What would happen if the native's discourse were to operate within the discourse of the anthropologist in a way that produced reciprocal knowledge effects upon it?"[43] Such an opening sounds exemplary, of course—who's not in favor of being open? But just as the price of Lukács dialectical overcoming is a totalizing historical narrative in which there is only one destination (proletarian revolution), so Viveiros de Castro's opening continues to rely on a figure of bounded cultural difference ("determining the problems posed by each culture").

Must we end up with either unified destiny or integral islands? As Graeber points out in the course of a critical engagement with Viveiros de Castro and the ontological turn more generally: "Radical alterity applies [for the ontological theorists] only to relations between cultural worlds." By contrast, Graeber's own argument about a kind of Malagasy charm medicine called *fanafody* seems proximate to my own analytic of encounter. He suggests that the persistent Malagasy claim that *fanafody* is a quintessentially Malagasy practice has always been an outcome—and a negotiation—of encounter, such that the perceived Malagasy-ness of *fanafody* is fundamentally predicated on the routine incorporation of non-Malagasy elements. If I'm reading Graeber right—although he might well reject my terminology—*fanafody* is symptomatic of an ongoing and restless settlement. Rather than starting from the presumption of preconstituted, bounded cultural worlds, what would happen to the analysis if it started from the presumption that the making of such worlds and the discourses that defend them (us/them, ours/theirs) is a kind of immune reaction to pro-vocative encounters?[44]

Adorno wrote scathingly of the "ontological need" that seemed to beset the Heideggerians of his day, by which he meant a longing for an unmediated access to the world such that one might dwell in it "authentically." For Adorno, part of the problem with this ontological desire for immediacy was its erasure of the mediations that produce the actual, historical worlds that we all inhabit, its desire "to delete the transmissions instead of reflecting them."[45] Similarly, as Eduardo Kohn notes, the current ontological longing is in part a reaction to approaches ushered in by the critique of representation, "which draw attention to the constructed nature of anthropological representations and thus amplify the linguistic even as they incorporate more sophisticated analyses of power and history."[46] Unlike many current ontophiles, Kohn is careful to note that representations—language, symbolic systems—are themselves ontological problems. Nevertheless, his discussion remains organized around an opposition between the promise of ontological access and a long-hegemonic linguistic-symbolic-constructionist "humanist" or "cultural" approach to knowledge, which is based on "a sharp division between the world of signs and the world to which those signs refer without an account of how these worlds may be connected."[47] The ontological—and, crucially, the ecological—challenge, Kohn suggests, is "getting right this relationship of language to nonlanguage, especially via the route of the representational but not linguistic."[48]

Amid the indubitable urgencies of our global situation, Kohn offers two choices: either anthropologists acknowledge the integral difference of our informants' worlds (the ontological option), or they insist that there is no longer any outside to the global sameness machine of neocolonial domination: "Anthropology surely has a nostalgic relation to the kinds of alterity that certain historical forces (which have also played a role in creating our field) have destroyed. To recognize this is one thing. It is quite another to say that for this reason there is no longer any conceptual space 'alter' to the logic of this kind of domination. For this would be the final act of colonization, one that would subject the possibility of something else, located in other lived worlds, human and otherwise, to a far more permanent death."[49]

But surely these are not the only alternatives. Why should we have to choose between external alterity and internal uniformity? What if difference itself is immanently emergent? And what if the totality out of which it emerges is not so much a totalizing imperial machine as a network of encounters in which the logic of domination is not easily distinguishable from (but also not reducible to) that of the recognition of integral difference? What if the key problem is not how to establish ethical encounters between entities that must be allowed their difference, but rather one of attending to the long and ongoing making of difference as a response to/management of/disavowal of encounter?

Let me be clear. What I'm suggesting is neither that these differences "aren't real" nor that they are simply ideological media of some global system of governmentality. The worlds people produce and dismantle—by means of representations, discourses, and built environments—are artifacts as real and as vital as anything else they inhabit. And the fact that these worlds arise out of social relations that are not innocent of translocal power projects does not in any way automatically curtail their creative and transformative potential. My point is simply that we shouldn't have to choose between totalizing discourses of global capitalism/empire/governmentality/whatever on the one hand and quasi-essentializing discourses of cultural difference on the other.

I'm Still Here! (Or, What Enlightenment Subject?)

Mana, in one version, is the substance that holds worlds together and yet leaks out so as to blur the boundaries between one thing and another. Mana infuses and radiates from the people and objects that have the capacity to mark the boundaries of worlds and, above all, to be efficacious within and between those worlds. Mana is, as I noted at the outset, at once the palpable authority of canonical order and the volatile force that troubles order. As such, thinking mana means thinking the social ontology of objects.

But mana also needs to be considered from the side of the subject since, as Durkheim pointed out, mana feels, subjectively, like "genuine respect," like that which makes us "defer to society's orders."[50] Mana is, Durkheim says, the medium of collective morality; it's what makes a given social order feel necessary and legitimate. From a critical theory standpoint, one might say that mana is a medium of ideology, of subjectivation. Durkheim is quite explicit about what I would call the extimacy of mana qua ideology: "we readily conceive of it in the form of a moral power that, while immanent in us, also represents something in us that is other than ourselves."[51] At one level, my project in this book is to reconsider what mana might help to clarify about world making, especially in terms of the mediation of social energy and social form. But the question of world making has never been separable from the question of how worlds recruit and condition the subjects that come to understand themselves through, and thus also reproduce, those worlds. As the section titles of this book suggests, mana is as much a problem of the social in the subject as it is a problem of the subject in the social.

So here's something else I want to be clear about: it's because I take seriously the problem of how we might produce, recover, and cultivate ethical relations with our broader ecologies (human and nonhuman) that I think the allegedly catastrophic Enlightenment Subject is worth a longer look. In particular, I'd like to suggest that it would be helpful to think two dimensions of the subject together: the subject's resonant opening to others (what I will later call the subject's *addressability*), and the subject's susceptibility to ideological attachments and identifications. In making the case, I want to acknowledge my long and profound debt—to be sure, an ambivalent relation of allegiance and rebellion—to Max Horkheimer and Theodor Adorno's *Dialectic of Enlightenment*, a pro-vocative text if ever there was one.[52] But I would also note that what I'm offering in this book, especially in chapter 4, could be read as a modification of Louis Althusser's theory of interpellation (which is also a story of encounter and constitutive resonance)—the theory of how we become subjects, how we come to identify with the names and identities that give us ourselves.[53] As Peter Sloterdijk has observed, something remains to be understood here concerning why certain encounters cause us to resonate and not others:

> How can it be that for billions of messages, I am the rock on which their waves break without resonance, while certain voices and instructions unlock me and make me tremble as if I were the chosen instrument to render them audible, a medium and mouthpiece simply for their urge to sound? Is there not still a mystery of access to consider here? Does my accessibility to certain unrefusable messages not

have its dark 'reason' in an ability to reverberate that has not yet been adequately discussed?[54]

Present-day posthumanists and ontophiles are absolutely right to lament the radical gap that Enlightenment thinkers imposed between humans and nonhumans. A majority of canonical texts from the eighteenth and nineteenth centuries devote significant space to making the case for human exceptionality vis-à-vis all other animals, let alone other forms of life and nonlife. But as Horkheimer and Adorno point out, this "diremption" (violent tearing apart) of the human and the nonhuman didn't only lead moderns to reduce the entire field of the nonhuman to an object of (more or less successful) human mastery. Just as importantly, it also bequeathed to them a radically impoverished conception of the human itself. Central to Horkheimer and Adorno's story is the repression and co-optation of a human capacity for mimesis or constitutive resonance, such that modern humans exiled themselves into a position of alienated domination vis-à-vis natures both external and internal that allowed them to understand the world only insofar as they disavowed their mimetic continuity with it. One of the most remarkable things about the anthropological approach—participant observation—is the way it turns constitutive encounter into method, ambivalently both affirming and disavowing mimetic resonance.

One might add to this story another dimension that is all too frequently forgotten today. Many of the thinkers associated most paradigmatically with the Enlightenment were in fact not so much obsessed with how to master the world from a position of domineering externality (although that is how their thought often took practical form, once it was operationalized by political and commercial bureaucracies). Rather, they remained preoccupied with questions of affective resonance and human permeability. In the mid-eighteenth century, David Hume and Adam Smith tried, through the notion of "sympathy," to work out whether the human propensity for encounter-based mimetic response might be "scaled up" so as to provide a medium of moral orientation in a modern society of strangers.[55] A few decades later, Kant's third and final critique suggested that our capacity for aesthetic judgment provided a spontaneously sensuous foundation for human reason—an object-ethics preceding and subtending his subject-ethics.[56] (Does this point to another settlement? One for which "the Kantian catastrophe" is the symptom marking the spot where one part of Kant's thinking—his object-ethics—has to be disavowed in order to sustain the "injury," the "loss" that justifies the ontological turn?)

The first principle of Kant's aesthetic was, in/famously, his insistence that a true aesthetic judgment has to be absolutely noninterested—that we can only truly know beauty if our relation to the beautiful thing is completely free of any desire or instrumental motive. Much ink has been spilled on his apparently perverse demand. Is it even possible to separate desire from aesthetic pleasure? What kind of subject position, at once world embedded and world transcending, would that require? For the purposes of my discussion here, I only want to note one thing: Kant demands such a rigorous policing of desire because he's tenderly conscious of our susceptibility to ideological seduction precisely on the terrain of aesthetic pleasure.

As such, Kant sets up a way of thinking about subjectivity and ideology that will have profound ramifications all the way down to the present. On the one hand, we are resonantly, vitally porous to objects. On the other hand, *because* we are resonantly, vitally porous to objects we must constantly be on guard against the manipulative uses that interested parties might make of our porosity. Beauty, Kant says, makes the good society possible by pulling people together freely in sense and sensibility. But beauty is also the treacherous lure that politicians and churchmen use to lull us into surrendering our autonomous judgment—in Kant's terms, our capacity for enlightenment.[57] Here we have the matrix of most theories of ideology. The mana of mass society might be, as Durkheim claimed, a "moral power" of solidarity and reason. But it might also be the honeyed words of the charismatic leader inciting patriotic murder, a garden-variety discourse of prejudice in the naturalizing name of "values," or just an advertisement promising youth and vitality for the price of a purchase. The question then becomes: why should one have to imagine autonomy and resonance in a zero-sum way? Especially if Kant himself, *alias* Papa Enlightenment Subject, understood constitutive resonance—the basis of our experience of beauty—as the very condition of possibility for autonomous reason.

This book reads mana as an extimate symptom of the settlements that establish more or less coherently inhabitable worlds, both at the level of the worlds in which we live and at the level of how social theory divides up its objects. As an extimate symptom it feels at once like the thing that makes those worlds matter, that solicits affective attachment, and the thing that troubles their edges, that calls their coherence into question. A key premise of my argument in these pages will be that these two dimensions of the mana symptom are inextricable, in fact mutually constitutive. This has major implications for how we think about subjectivity, the ways in which we are addressable as subjects, and thus what it means for us to inhabit the worlds in which we live and in relation to which we become who we are.

My proposition will, in its general outlines, be familiar from Freud: subjectivity is itself a settlement, made and remade, arising out of an ongoing series of encounters. Because it's a settlement, it's a space of familiar attachments (including attachments to habits of rebelling against those attachments). And yet it's also symptomatic, constantly generative of uncanny intimations—in dreams, in unexpected associations, in recurrent contradictions—of what has been disavowed in order to produce the appearance of coherence and stability. Sloterdijk observes: "Half of normality consists of microscopic deviations from the norms."[58] And so it is with subjectivity. Just as the human eye, in order to maintain the subjective appearance of stable objects, constantly has to move ever so slightly from side to side, so we engage in the constant, exhausting yet largely unconscious, labor of producing and reproducing the stability of our sense of ourselves.

And yet at the same time—and this is the crucial point—the mana of a relation to a world (an inner world, an outer world) is double. It appears as an attachment to order and stability, yet that attachment would be impossible were it not for the simultaneous sense that it contains something that is not yet clear, that is not yet settled, that is at once seductive and threatening. As G. W. F. Hegel once remarked: "What through art or thinking we have before our physical or spiritual eye as an object has lost all absolute interest for us if it has been put before us so completely that the content is exhausted, that everything is revealed, and nothing obscure or inward is left over any more."[59]

Approaching the problem dialectically reveals that the mimetic excess that might be called mana does simultaneously constitutive and destitutive work vis-à-vis any given social order and, further, that both the constitutive and the destitutive dimensions of mana work are both part of the fascination (the mana) of a world. Jacques Derrida (whom I am hereby proud to induct into the Guild of Unwilling Dialecticians—better late than never) captures this effect beautifully, illustrating how precisely the *non*-closure that we sense in a discourse can often be what draws us further into its web. Here the plenitude of mana appears at the same time as an irresistible absence: "If a speech could be purely present, unveiled, naked, offered up in person in its truth, without the detours of a signifier foreign to it, if at the limit an undeferred *logos* were possible, it would not seduce anyone."[60]

The implications would seem to be significant. First and foremost, the need to move beyond the zero-sum drama of hegemony and resistance, of the co-opted versus the critical subject. What attaches us to worlds—to ideologies, to subject positions, to ways of being—is not a watertight and self-sufficient set of propositions that one might accept or reject, believe in or not believe in. Rather, it is, if anything, precisely the opposite. Worlds solicit identification and resonance—and thus also conflict—because of an unresolved lack that gives us a prompt for work, play, and desire. The Indian poet, scholar, and translator A. K. Ramanujan used to say that myths are like crystals: they grow where there's a flaw—in other words, a symptomatic gap that triggers the creative work of imagination and interpretation. It's the same with worlds; we need them because they need us. But this also means that resistance is not cleanly separable from attachment. Or to put it differently, that the weakness or vulnerability of an ideological formation is also its strength.

This is, obviously, not a Romantic position. There is no guarantee that the gaps, fissures, and internal contradictions of a worldview open onto resistance; they might just as well be the source of the fascination that draws us closer into the attachments that keep us in line. Difference and desire are built into power; they are the very conditions of its efficacy. And yet, as John Durham Peters notes, there is also something profoundly vitalizing in the knowledge that it's not just that our perspectives on the world will always be lacking but rather that vitally, generatively, *the world itself is lacking*:

> Perhaps the past cannot be tapped in its full immediacy because the present is not fully immediate. There are vast patches of unobserved reality silently lurking in every moment — at higher and lower levels of magnification, for different organs of sense, for minds quicker or slower than ours. Even for the most acute observer, descriptions might be incomplete, not only because of limited tools but because reality is lacking. Just as we often do not know what we mean when we speak, so the universe might not always be so sure of itself. The cosmos is structurally incomplete, as gap-ridden as its file. Such wonderful conditions these are! The universe generously accommodates our every new act, word, or thought. There is still plenty to do. It is open for new events; it is a container with a gracious void.[61]

Ticking Clock: Organization

My reappraisal of mana is by no means a nostalgic exercise (although it will no doubt offer the fetishist some incidental antiquarian pleasures!). Nor is it some reactionary appeal for a return to anthropological fundamentals. What motivates me is, rather, a sense of unexpected contemporaneity. With Walter Benjamin, I believe that elements of our pasts, once liberated from the historicist burden of having to culminate in the present, may, like sparks leaping across time, illuminate novel resonances between then and now. If the mana moment in one sense ended about a century ago, it is in another sense perhaps only now becoming intelligible. Just as Benjamin once wrote to his friend and sponsor Horkheimer of his ongoing attempts to make the Paris arcades of the nineteenth century release their profane illumination into his own historical present, I now write in the conviction that mana "has something to say to us only because it is contained in the ticking of a clock whose striking of the hour has just reached *our* ears."[62]

The *mana moment*, the period spanning roughly 1870 to 1920, saw, in Euro-American social thought, an undoing of the energetic settle-

ment that had produced the nineteenth-century bourgeois individual and his (yes, paradigmatically *his*) social forms. I will have
more to say about the mana moment in chapter 1. For now, it may
simply be relevant to suggest that the ticking of the mana clock may
have reached our ears today because we are all, once again, facing
the undoing, at a planetary level, of the energetic settlements that
have constituted long-reigning assumptions about the human and
the social. In both moments, the question was, and is: what can be
redeemed, carried over, translated, activated, so as to retheorize the
social rewards and risks of our vital powers? Perhaps a previously
impossible phrase—the mana of mass society—is now becoming intelligible.

In addition to this introduction, the book is organized into two
parts, "The Social in the Subject" and "The Subject in the Social,"
each comprising two chapters. The first two chapters deal predomi-
nantly with classic anthropological materials, as refracted through
critical-theoretical concerns. The second two, inversely, engage critical theory in light of the earlier anthropological readings.

Chapter 1, "Modern Savagery: Mana beyond the Empiricist
Settlement," offers a genealogy of the mana concept, the better to
show (a) that mana always pointed to an ambiguous kinship between
the energetics of so-called primitive ritual and those of so-called
modern or civilized powers, and (b) that the theoretical development of this insight was blocked by what I am calling the "empiricist settlement." The empiricist settlement was the consolidation,
around 1920, of the notion that legitimate anthropology consisted
paradigmatically of single-sited long-term fieldwork in (what had to
look like) a bounded, small-scale society, and the principle that all
social phenomena should be interpreted in terms of, and referred
back to, the social and cultural order of that bounded, small-scale
society. What the empiricist settlement most strenuously disavowed
was its relation to its immediate precursor, the speculative, compara-
tivist, and progressionist models of the so-called armchair anthropologists. Chapter 1, then, has two main conceptual aims. The first
is to push back beyond the empiricist settlement by interpreting its
symptoms and ask what might be worth redeeming from the speculative impulse that it so strenuously repressed. The second, by way
of a possible exemplification, is to move toward a fulfillment of the

lost promise embedded in a conception of mana that straddled the division between "primitive" and "modern" societies. What would it mean to speak of a mana of mass society? In what sense is the mana work of "primitive" magicians comparable to that of, say, "modern" orators or marketers?

The heart of chapter 2, "Ecstatic Life and Social Form: Collective Effervescence and the Primitive Settlement," is a reconsideration of Durkheim's classic theory of ritual, read as a theory of the social mediation of vital energy. I situate Durkheim's discussion in relation to a long-standing tendency in anthropology to render questions of vitality secondary to questions of intelligibility, such that the energetic dimensions of world making are at once acknowledged and disavowed. The conceptual core of chapter 2 is the question of the relation between immanence and transcendence in the making of social worlds, a question that I consider in light of apparently defunct anthropological debates about "primitive" versus "modern" forms of thought. Here, too, mana emerges as a symptom of a settlement: the primitive settlement, according to which "primitives" engage the world by participation, whereas "moderns" manage it by means of representation. The energy/form dialectic of Durkheim's ritual scenario offers me a way to point beyond the primitive settlement, but not before putting equal critical pressure on the primitivism of Durkheim's own anthropological imagination. I move toward the concerns of part II by rounding off chapter 2 with a consideration of the charismatic settlements that establish and undermine the worlds we inhabit—and, as such, the potentially troubling indistinction between ideological subjection and human flourishing.

Chapter 3, "Anxious Autonomy: The Agony of Perfect Addressability and the Aesthetic Settlement," moves the focus of my discussion from anthropology to critical theory, and from the social to the subject. The central concern of the chapter is to get to grips with a motif that structures critical-theoretical approaches to the seductions of ideology, from politics to marketing: the anxiety of the autonomous subject, who, at the limit, cannot distinguish being perfectly and completely recognized as *who he or she really is* from being perfectly and completely incorporated into an external order—that is to say, being completely extinguished as an autonomous and critically vigilant subject. I explore the current fascination with algorithmically organized precision-targeted forms of marketing that are, like Homer's Sirens, supposed only to sing the singular song of the individual they're addressing. I ask what might be made of the fact that subliminal manipulation is currently being reconceptualized as a desirable good. Having pushed the figure of manipulation to the limit, I then return to the locus classicus of the paranoid style in mass cultural analysis, Horkheimer and Adorno's essay on the culture industry, and proceed to suggest, against the prevailing tide, that it is precisely by way of Adorno's dialectical aesthetic theory that one can get beyond Adorno's debilitating (and completely undialectical) dismissal of mass culture. Here, too, a settlement is at stake: the aesthetic settlement that permitted otherwise "primitive" mana a place in the order of "civilization," as long as that place could be called "art." The work of the latter part of the chapter consists in showing how Adorno's autonomously critical subject requires a parallel conception of an autonomous aesthetic object, and in asking under what terms what Adorno calls the "primacy of the object" might be allowed to do what Adorno insisted it must not: inform a dialectical theory of the mana of mass society beyond the sequestered space of art.

Finally, chapter 4, "Are You Talking to Me? Eros and Nomos in the Mimetic Archive," offers a theory of self- and world-making through constitutive resonance. Pulling together the threads of chapters 1 through 3, chapter 4 makes a case for the mimetic archive as an alternative to (or possibly a revitalization of) a culture concept that has been compromised not least by its ready adoption by state and commercial interests. I argue that constitutive resonance can usefully be understood in terms of a dialectical play between eros (resonance, love) and nomos (order, law) and sketch the outlines of a theory of addressability—not only a theory of interpellation (how do we become the selves that we are in moments of encounter such that we experience that becoming as "fated") but also a theory of the vital co-constitution of inner and outer worlds, and of the inseparability of self-understanding and object-resonance. I conclude the chapter by returning to Durkheim's theory of the sacred and Weber's theory of charisma in order to ask how one might understand the *fractalized*, distributed forms of these capacities and these intensities once one considers their life beyond their spectacular and exceptional concentration in big rituals, monuments, or leaders. This becomes an occasion to reflect on some of the ways in which politics and marketing respond to a crisis in the self-representation of popular sovereignty by appearing, by means of constitutive resonance, to reconcile eros and nomos, love and law. Chapter 4 rounds off the book by returning to the question of how one might retheorize power and ideological interpellation starting from the ambivalent complicities and attachments of constitutive resonance.

Part I

The Social in the Subject

Chapter 1

Modern Savagery

Mana beyond the Empiricist Settlement

> We go on great journeys to see the things that we do not
> favour with our attention at home.[1]

A century ago, social scientists and scholars of comparative religion identified *mana* as a force powering the affirmation of collective ideals in religious ritual, the pursuit of instrumental ends in magical practice—and the blandishments of mass publicity. In *The Elementary Forms of Religious Life*, Émile Durkheim asked how the potential of mana, as harnessed in "primitive" ritual, might similarly be derived, on a much wider scale, from the energies of urban crowds.[2] Marcel Mauss and Henri Hubert had already left an important clue when they described ritual specialists as protopublicists, mana workers who draw on "the collective forces of society."[3] "It is public opinion," Mauss and Hubert wrote, "which makes the magician and creates the power he wields. Thanks to public opinion he knows everything and can do anything."[4] It fell to the inventor of modern fieldwork-based anthropology, Bronislaw Malinowski, to close the circle by directly comparing "primitive" magic to "modern" advertising.[5]

In *Coral Gardens and Their Magic*, Malinowski calls advertising "the richest field of modern verbal magic" and remarks that "the advertisements of modern beauty specialists, especially of the magnitude of my countrywoman Helena Rubinstein, or of her rival, Elizabeth Arden, would make interesting reading if collated with the formulae of Trobriand beauty magic."[6] Notably, the comparison is not intended to flatter anyone; Malinowski imagines the comparative research project that someone might undertake on these matters as an inquiry into "parallels between modern and primitive savagery."[7] His distaste for what he implicitly renders as atavistic survivals in modern mass publicity is entirely conventional, albeit also understandable given the European political climate at the time. He renders the magical dimensions of mass communication as tools of mass hypnosis energized by mob frenzy and, as such, as inherently inimical to the flourishing of liberal democracy:

> Modern political oratory would probably yield a rich harvest of purely magical elements. Some of the least desirable of modern pseudo-statesmen or gigantic politicanti have earned the titles of wizards or spell-binders. The great leaders such as Hitler or Mussolini have achieved their influence primarily by the power of speech, coupled with the power of action which is always given to those who know how to raise the prejudices and the passions of the mob. Moreover, the modern socialistic state, whether it be painted red, black or brown, has developed the powers of advertisement to an extraordinary extent. Political propaganda, as it is called, has become a gigantic advertising agency, in which merely verbal statements are destined to hypnotize foreigner and citizen alike into the belief that something really great has been achieved.[8]

I will have occasion to reflect in a moment on the ambiguous parallels between "the prejudices and the passions of the mob" as a persistent pejorative preoccupation and the generative, vitalizing, and sustaining power of "collective effervescence" in Durkheim's work. Malinowski acknowledges (and generally disparages) the importance of collective energies. Their effect is for Malinowski entirely a function of a kind of language use he calls "mystical" or "magical" and which might today be called performative: bringing about a state of affairs by invoking it in speech. For Malinowski, the use of such magical techniques in modern mass publicity is regressive in that it reconfuses the "magical" and "pragmatic" functions of language that the long march from savagery to civilization was supposed to have separated.[9] This is, of course, a normative discourse that is still widespread today: the assumption that the affective and mimetic dimensions of mass communication are, if not actually savage, then certainly incompatible with mature and responsible citizenship. But are there nonprejudicial ways of thinking magic and mass publicity together?

In his study of eros and magic in the European Renaissance, the historian of religion Ioan Couliano writes: "we would tend to say that . . . the actual magician and the prophet have now vanished. More probably, however, they have simply been camouflaged in sober and legal guises. . . . Nowadays the magician busies himself with public relations, propaganda, market research, sociological surveys, publicity, information, counterinformation and misinformation, censorship, espionage, and even cryptography—a science which in the sixteenth century was a branch of magic."[10] Like the ancient and Renaissance magicians, Couliano suggests, the modern publicity professional requires an exquisite understanding of the potentials for creating erotic resonances and bonds between people, images, and things that dwell in the form of potentially constitutive resonances in any social world.[11]

Two points need to be made here. First, Couliano is suggesting that the work of a publicity professional, like that of a magician, consists in identifying latent potentials that are immanent to relations between people, images, and things. These are the potentials that, when activated, can trigger desire and identification—a process of actualizing encounter that, in the introduction, I called, following Peter Sloterdijk, constitutive resonance.[12] The idea of constitutive resonance touches closely on what anthropologists during the mana moment identified, often prejudicially, as a tendency among primitive peoples to think in terms of concrete and sensuous *participation* rather than in terms of abstract and conceptual *representation*.

Second, being attentive to potentials for constitutive resonance is not at all the same thing as what more recent generations of anthropologists, some of whom have been able to translate their expertise into more or less profitable jobs in the publicity sector, would understand by the phrase "knowing the culture" of the individuals or the groups addressed by the magic spell, the State of the Union address, or the advertisement. Much remains to be clarified about the deep elective affinity—some would say the complicity—between culturalist anthropology, particularly in its 1970s structuralist mode, and the marketing science of positioning. For now, I will only hint at one of the most important outcomes of this elective affinity—namely, the paradoxical way in which it has obscured the decisive importance of, precisely, elective affinity to the mana work of both producing culture and making markets. For what are elective affinities? Max Weber adapted the phrase from Goethe to capture not pre-established equivalences or linear cause-effect relations but rather contingent yet germinal sympathies that, in an emergent way, allow both parties to the resonant relationship to *become themselves via each other* in a way that only retroactively creates the impression of a preexisting "pattern of culture."[13] Goethe borrowed the phrase from eighteenth-century chemistry. But the chemists were in turn adapting and "scientizing" long-standing esoteric traditions of attending to cosmic correspondences.

By invoking constitutive resonance as a way of thinking elective affinity, I want to stress, in particular, the *constitutive* face of the encounter. Some usages of the phrase "elective affinity" might imply two preexisting entities, whole unto themselves, which, by combining or existing in vibrant proximity to each other, contribute to each other's flourishing. By contrast, insisting on the constitutive dimension means that what we retroactively understand as separate elements that have entered into a relation of affinity could not, in fact, have become themselves without that resonant relation. So to reinterpret Weber's classic example along these lines, it is not that puritanism and capitalism each arrive fully formed in the world and then happen to find conveniently vitalizing support in the other. Rather, certain virtual potentials in a socially and historically locatable mimetic archive encounter and pro-voke each other so as to actualize as the formations that we will later recognize as "puritanism" and "capitalism." A relation of constitutive resonance involves, then, a striking combination of contingency and overdetermination.[14]

Couliano notes that while the development of modern natural science has largely, and, he thinks, rightly, overtaken magical attempts to control the nonhuman world, "nothing has replaced magic on its own terrain, that of intersubjective relationships."[15] The would-be sciences of this terrain of constitutive resonance, particularly as they apply to persuasion on a mass-mediated level—socioeconomic categorization, psychographic classification, and so on—remain woefully crude and approximate compared to the minutely elaborated esoteric prescriptions of ancient and early modern magicians.[16] And yet this is where social scientific explorations during the mana moment open up tantalizing possibilities. As R. R. Marett wrote at the dawn of the twentieth century, one of the meanings of mana is "the man who can exercise the magic of persuasion."[17]

"Communication" did not, as John Durham Peters has shown, take on its modern meaning until the last two decades of the nineteenth century—in other words, at the same time as mana was becoming a major scholarly preoccupation and the uneasy doubling of political and commercial engagement that we now know as mass publicity was moving into place.[18] The concept of communication, linked as it is to notions of communion and community, carries into its contemporary semantic space a dense archive of mystical and magical resonances. Peters notes that in the seventeenth century, "communication" commonly referred to what the Scholastic philosophers called *actio in distans*, a key problem in natural philosophy: how one body can influence another without touching it. This is how Mauss describes magical action: "Distance does not preclude contact. Desires and images can be immediately realized."[19] Such, too, are the dreams of close distance that thrive at the heart of mass communication: "evangelist Oral Roberts asked his listeners to place their hands on their radio sets as they listened from afar in their parlors to pray with him and receive a special blessing which he would send by touching the microphone through which he broadcast his sermon."[20]

Malinowski may have been the first to make a direct connection between "primitive" magic and "civilized" advertising. But it was also the triumph of Malinowski's empiricist ethnographic paradigm that helped to foreclose the speculative development of these early hints regarding the mana of mass society. Indeed, Malinowski specifically singled out mana—what he contemptuously dismissed as "the thin, fluid, ubiquitous mana"[21]—as the kind of fuzzy speculative concept that a properly grounded, properly empirical anthropological practice would have to reject.

Against this empiricist settlement, my task in this chapter is as follows: to follow up on these early intimations of vital resonances between "primitive" and "civilized" media of persuasion. I will do so by means of a genealogy of the mana concept that will allow me to refuse both of the canonical methods that anthropology has bequeathed: on the one hand, the kind of speculative universalizing discourse in which a concept like mana is made, in an unmediated way, to subsume all kinds of human practices from all kinds of unconnected locations; on the other hand, the empiricist insistence that a concept like mana may only be discussed in the context of those (Melanesian and Polynesian) societies in which it is a "native" term and in relation to which one may empirically specify "native" uses. The first method proliferates grand but ungrounded generalities. The second tends to amount to little more than "varied stories about how people in different places see and do things differently."[22]

My strategy, by contrast, is to interpret mana as a symptom of a series of encounters that had their roots in the historically simultaneous rise of mass-mediated societies in the Global North and the consolidation of colonial rule in the Global South. As a symptom, mana insists and obtrudes; it points to a problem of constitutive resonance that, for reasons at once political and intellectual, had at once to be acknowledged and disavowed.

And since mana is the symptom, the red thread, the lure, I might as well start there. So: what is, or was, mana?

What Was Mana?

One might be forgiven for retorting "what *wasn't* mana?" Mana, it seems, was all things to everyone. A kind of efficacious force, sometimes sacred, sometimes profane, that infused all things, ensuring not only fertility and life but also the prestige of the powerful and success in ventures ranging from farming to warfare. But even putting it this way is controversial. For every suggestion that mana was a force, expressible as a noun, others would claim that mana was something closer to a condition. A person, place, situation, or object might not so much have mana as be in a state of mana-ness. Mana was notoriously mobile; it had to be ritually accumulated; it might be transmitted—either deliberately or by (sometimes violent) accident—and it could be altogether lost. A subtle substance, if that is what it was, mana was invisible but palpable. Its presence and its action had to be inferred from its exceptional effects.

Mana quickly gained the status of a general concept. Among several other notions of supernatural efficacy with which it was often connected—for instance, American Indian terms like *orenda*, *wakan*, and *manitou*—mana became a name for the class of which it was at the same time a member. At the most general level, mana was "the ever present actuating force in things,"[23] a physical as well as a moral force,[24] a "divine psychic potency,"[25] "a state of efficacy, success, truth, potency, blessing, luck, realization"[26]—or maybe just the difference between the gardener who gets the bumper crop after using exactly the same inputs and techniques as his neighbor who does not: "Having done the part humans must do to win wars, catch fish, grow taro, give successful feasts, cure the sick, and conduct divinations, they waited to see whether the gods and spirits had done what they must do—the invisible complement of what humans do. . . . The stone or potion that 'works' magically looks the same as an ordinary stone or potion. The difference is invisible, a *potentiation* by the spirits."[27]

The missionary ethnologist Robert Codrington, who introduced mana into the ethnographic corpus toward the end of the nineteenth century,[28] presented it as a Melanesian name for a kind of omnipresent, supernatural efficacy that might be embodied in people and things, and could be recognized by results that would otherwise be inexplicable:

> The Melanesian mind is entirely possessed by the belief in a supernatural power or influence, called almost universally *mana*. This is what works to effect everything which is beyond the ordinary power of men, outside the common processes of nature; it is present in the atmosphere of life, attaches itself to persons or things, and is manifested by results which can only be ascribed to its operation. When one has got it he can use it and direct it, but its force may break forth at some new point; the presence of it is ascertained by proof.[29]

By the time Marcel Mauss and Henri Hubert published their *General Theory of Magic* in 1902-3, mana was not only the force powering religion as well as magic (Codrington had already described mana as "the active force in all [the Melanesians] do and believe to be done in magic, white or black"[30]) — it was a kind of universal vital substance, dwelling immanently in everything.

> This extraneous substance is invisible, marvelous, spiritual — in fact, it is the spirit which contains all efficacy and all life. It cannot be experienced, since it truly absorbs all experience. The rite adds it to things, and it is of the same nature as the rite. Codrington thought he could call it the supernatural, but then he more correctly says that it is only supernatural "in a way," that is to say, that *mana* is both supernatural and natural, since it is spread throughout the tangible world where it is both heterogeneous and ever immanent.[31]

A decade on from Mauss, Émile Durkheim described mana as the palpable expression of social energy tout court. In a passage at once more concise and, if possible, even more maximal, Durkheim wrote of mana that "enumeration cannot exhaust this infinitely complex notion. It is not a defined or definable power, the power to do this or that; it is Power in the absolute, without qualification or limitation of any kind."[32]

Inevitably, the scholarly sequitur to such sublime inflation was a firm earthward turn. Malinowski insisted that mana never amounted to much more than evidence of the most primitive metaphysical stuttering, and certainly not to anything like the universal life force "so brilliantly advocated and so recklessly handled" by the likes of Mauss, Durkheim, and Marett.[33] Others gave mana more play, but squabbled over the details. Was it natural, supernatural, secular, or sacred? Was it a "truly primitive conception,"[34] or perhaps a later philosophical development? Was it an inherently moral force or, instead, prior to or even beyond all morality? Could it originate in human beings or might they only and temporarily come to embody or harness it? Did the perpetuation of mana require regular ritual assembly or was mana the power that, in the first place, prompted people to gather together? Did Melanesians and Polynesians — or others who used similar terms — deploy it as a noun, an adjective, or a verb? Was mana a substance, a quality, or a relation?

The Mana Moment

A concept resonates because it actualizes historically situated potentials; it channels incipient urgencies that may, in a given time and
place, feel like both inclination and dread. Indeed, in the broad-
est sense, mana brought questions of potentiation, intensity, and
emergence to the fore, questions that opened a wormhole between
"primitive" magical and ritual action on the one hand and "modern"
practices of mass publicity on the other.

Intellectually, the mana moment (roughly 1870–1920) was a limi-
nal phase, a phase of transition between dominant paradigms. The
nineteenth-century social evolutionist paradigm of E. B. Tylor, James
Frazer, and others was still strong but beginning to waver as a more
empirically oriented field science took its first steps in the form of
ventures like the Cambridge Torres Straits expedition of 1898. At the
same time, the fully-fledged fieldwork paradigm, whose manifesto
Bronislaw Malinowski would provide in the form of the introduction to *Argonauts of the Western Pacific* (1922), was not yet in place.

Sociologically speaking, urban life in the Euro-American world
was undergoing a daemonic transformation. The ambiguous energies
of the *masses*, tensely oscillating between volatile crowd and rational
public, became at once the monogram and the stigma of modernity:
mass housing, mass labor, mass publicity, mass suffrage, mass production of everything from clothing and food to art and entertainment.[35] One gets a palpable sense of these transformations in films
like Walter Ruttmann's *Berlin: Symphony of a Great City* (1927) or in
the opening pages of Robert Musil's novel *The Man without Qualities*, where the author describes "a fine day in August 1913" in terms
of intensities that are manifest in the streetscape but irreducible to
its structural features, at once ritually rhythmic and synesthetically
open-ended:

> Automobiles shot out of deep, narrow streets into the shallows of
> bright squares. Dark clusters of pedestrians formed cloudlike strings.
> Where more powerful lines of speed cut across their casual haste they
> clotted up, then trickled on faster and, after a few oscillations, re-
> sumed their steady rhythm. Hundreds of noises wove themselves into
> a wiry texture of sound with barbs protruding here and there, smart

edges running along it and subsiding again, with clear notes splintering off and dissipating. By this noise alone, whose special quality cannot be captured in words, a man returning after years of absence would have been able to tell with his eyes shut that he was back in the Imperial Capital and Royal City of Vienna. Cities, like people, can be recognized by their walk. Opening his eyes, he would know the place by the rhythm of movement in the streets long before he caught any characteristic detail. It would not matter even if he only imagined that he could do this. We overestimate the importance of knowing where we are because in nomadic times it was essential to recognize the tribal feeding grounds.[36]

Imperial Capital, rhythm of movement, tribal feeding grounds: the urban sensorium of Europe during the mana moment was at once metaphorically and actually tied into new savageries, not least an accelerated new wave of rapaciously extractive European colonization, especially in the so-called scramble for Africa. Under such circumstances, it was hardly surprising that the confident, linear narratives of civilizational progress that had been so central to the nineteenth-century imagination should have become at once all the more urgent and all the more implausible. In those colonial territories moving toward national self-determination, mass energies were, in a different way, an ambivalent matter: a kind of protonational substance to be harnessed against the colonizer and an embarrassing sign of the very savagery that, by the terms of the white man's burden, served to legitimate the colonial enterprise.

Atavism, a key word of the mana moment, translated into the horrifying terms of savagery the anxious prospect that mass energies would not be properly harnessed and channeled into progress-enhancing projects. Into the industrial productivity of the laboring mass body, to be sure, but also, into what Robert Nye calls the new "pragmatic aesthetics" of epic romanticism and political oratory, the nationalist-mythical identifications of the patriotic body and the populist absorption, under charismatic leaders, of the mass qua sovereign democratic substance.[37] "Baudelaire," observes Walter Benjamin, "speaks of a man who plunges into the crowd as into a reservoir of electric energy."[38] Urban crowds, the human raw material of all such projects, appeared at once definitively modern and essentially savage. The other side of energetic enthusiasm was, of course, simmering political panic. Mana moment anthropologists like Frazer and Marett were, as George Stocking reminds us, driven to study "primitive" religion and ritual in no small part because of their anxiety about the "irrational" forces stirring, in the shape of urban "mobs," just underneath the surface of polite Edwardian society.[39]

The mana moment found Europe hurtling toward the decisive cataclysm of World War I. As such it was a period preoccupied with the ambiguities of a form of industrial progress that yielded, often in confusing proximity, technologies for the enhancement of life and for the mass production of death.[40] It was, likewise, a time of anxiety about the uncertain relations between sensuous capacity, aesthetic experience, and technical rationality. In a widely read pamphlet from the exhausted final year of World War I, Georg Simmel looks back at the "conflict of modern culture" that, at the end of the nineteenth century, had given birth to various cults of vitalism.[41] All these cults, Simmel suggests—in the arts, in philosophy, in interpersonal ethics, in religion—arose out of a palpable sense of disjuncture between the vital energies of European civilization and institutional forms that had proved inadequate to the vital demand. As an assemblage, they helped to give the early European twentieth century its distinctive tone: the pursuit, in modes both apocalyptic and affirmative, of "the direct revelation of life."[42] Hence expressionism in painting, pragmatism in philosophy, libertine ethics, and a turn to various occult modes of spirit communication, all of them teetering on the brink of the most charismatic corrective to what Weber called the "iron cage" (or carapace) of bureaucratic reason: the voluptuous ecstasy of war, fusing machine eros and machine thanatos, as in Marinetti and the Futurists' effervescent aestheticization of techno-violence.

The mana moment's aesthetic and philosophical fascination with the primitive other was part and parcel of this hunger for "the direct revelation of life"—vitality without the allegedly devitalizing mediation of concepts. Lucien Lévy-Bruhl, whose *How Natives Think* has long been held to exemplify the most prejudicial excesses of the speculative phase in anthropology, was under no illusions as to the periodically powerful lure of these vitalisms: "they promise that which neither a purely positive science nor any theory of philosophy

can hope to attain: a direct and intimate contact with the essence
of being, by intuition, interpenetration, the mutual communion of
subject and object, full participation and immanence, in short, that
which Plotinus has described as ecstasy."[43]

The mana moment combined elements of disenchanting evolu-
tionism with romantic projects of reenchantment.[44] Vitality walked
hand in hand with pathology. This intimacy takes literary form in the
morbid exaltation and exalted morbidity of life in the sanatoria of
prewar Europe, as conjured by Thomas Mann in *Magic Mountain*,
where pneumatic daydreams intermingle the optimism of humanis-
tic reason with a sublime cult of death, where X-ray plates provide
less perspicacity than spirit séances, and where history seems simultaneously to have stopped in its tracks and to be hurtling toward
disaster.[45] Psychoanalysis provided even greater scope for creative speculation than literary fiction during these years—witness
Sigmund Freud's *Totem and Taboo*, in which the uneasy proximity
between vitality and pathology is opened up by the figure of magical
thinking, which Freud characterizes as neurotic under modern conditions, but non-neurotic (albeit objectively delusional) in primitive
society.[46]

The speculative inflation of mana during these years had everything to do with the fascination of a concept that seemed capable of
mediating *and* of short-circuiting the distance between social order
and vital energy, between the primitive and the civilized, and between participation and representation. This was mana at its most
charismatic, described by Mauss as "a pure efficacy, which is, however, a localizable material substance at the same time as it is spiritual, that acts at a distance and yet through direct connection, if not
by contact, mobile and moving without moving itself, impersonal
and clothed in personal form, divisible and continuous."[47]

The Empiricist Settlement

As Europe struggled to emerge from the debris of the Great War,
the mana moment met its denouement in the shape of the empiricist
settlement. The empiricist settlement transformed anthropology,
around 1920, into a social science based on extended empirical field-

work, ideal-typically conducted in and on a single, small-scale social setting. The heirs of Malinowski in Britain and of Franz Boas in the United States dismantled the cloud castles that the likes of Tylor and Frazer had spun in the late nineteenth century out of fragments of anecdotal evidence gathered, pell-mell, from the most diverse locations and sources. As Malinowski's student and successor Raymond Firth stoutly declares: "Much of the obscurity and confusion has arisen through the fact that elaborate theoretical discussions have been constructed on the basis of inadequate factual data."[48]

A tone of soberly sardonic realism replaced earlier sublimities. Firth, for example, notes that mana, as a comparative concept in the anthropology of religion and magic, had drifted so far from any empirical basis as to bear little relation to native usage. Having "hammered away" at his Tikopia informants for evidence of mana as a general concept, Firth emerges wryly empty-handed: "all my inquiries for the *Ding an sich* came to nothing."[49] Mana, argues E. E. Evans-Pritchard, simply doesn't exist in the sense of the kind of "impersonal force — an almost metaphysical conception"[50] that had fired up Mauss, Marett, and Durkheim. Rather, Firth's Tikopians, it seems, always and only speak of mana as an aspect of particular things — "the mana of the rain, the mana of the crops" — or as a way of expressing the unusual efficacy of a person — "great was his mana . . . he spoke for rain — it rained at that moment."[51] As to the much-worried metaphysical conundrum about how mana could be at once an impersonal substance and a personal property, Firth suggests that it is really not much more complicated than being able to say, in English, that someone might *be* successful and *have* success.[52] Edmund Leach bequeaths a kind of empiricist motto: "Grand generalities of the impressionistic sort favoured by Frazer and his successors have no value at all. If anthropology can contribute anything to our understanding of religion it must be on the basis of research into local particulars, not on the basis of guesswork."[53] In retrospect, the mana craze came to look like the last gasp of a romantic urge to find mystical universals behind the vast and variegated parade of human difference.

The empiricist settlement largely reduced subsequent discussions of mana to scholastic exercises in cultural and linguistic specification, which, while impressively learned and sometimes absorbing, tended to exemplify Marshall Sahlins's bon mot about anthropology being "Talmudic exegesis by non-believers."[54] Clearly, speculative reconstruction of the purportedly universal origins of social phenomena à la Tylor, Frazer, and their contemporaries—what Evans-Pritchard characterized as "the scissors-and-paste method of compilation by the armchair scholars"—is questionable.[55] By contrast, the Malinowskian fieldwork paradigm rests on long-term first-hand participant observation and analysis based on comparisons not with fragmentary evidence from some entirely different place and time, but, ideally, with data on other institutions in the same social context. So, for example, instead of analyzing Maori utterances about mana alongside Iroquois statements about orenda, Maori mana talk might best be understood in relation to Maori patterns of social hierarchy or, perhaps, by comparison with similar institutions in other parts of Polynesia.[56]

By contrast, Marett, writing in 1908, is still able to poke gentle fun at the prospect of his evolutionary speculations being challenged by "some skeptical champion of the actual."[57] Marett is operating under the then-common assumption that "primitive" thought is, under its own steam, incapable of abstraction and generalization. Consequently, it falls to the scholar to assist in the self-birth of native concepts like mana by developing their immanent potentials for actualization. In a quasi-Hegelian way, Marett sees his task as the simulation of a situation in which native thought might have abstracted itself and thereby "somehow quickened into self-consciousness and self-expression."[58]

Undoubtedly, the universal aspirations of mana as a comparative concept often implied, if not a speculative science of the common basis of human experience, then a kind of Platonic ideal. Boas's student Alexander Goldenweiser, for example, defends the generalized use of the term *mana* on the circular grounds that even if words like *mana, wakan, orenda*, and so on do not in fact refer to exactly the same thing, the prevalence of "such concepts" across widely different ethnographic contexts nevertheless suggests a "pristine notion," widely prevalent in primitive societies, "containing the common care" of those various concepts—and mana is, according to Goldenweiser, a legitimate name for that notion.[59]

To be fair, an awareness of the dangers of mistranslation is part of some of the very earliest discussions of mana.[60] And Malinow-

ski, for all his brisk empiricism, hardly hesitates to leap from painstakingly documented particulars of Trobriand life to universalizing
assertions about human nature.[61] The consolidation of the empiricist
settlement may have required anthropologists to pay careful attention to the native's point of view. But it also, as Dominic Boyer and
Cymene Howe argue, installed a structural opposition, mediated by
anthropologists, between theory-generating metropolitan centers of
academic authority and the intimate life worlds of the field sites that
anthropologists mine. The self-proclaimed credo of the ethnographic
empiricists was, ostensibly, localist. But in fact, as any scholar knows,
intellectual prestige depends on achieving what Boyer and Howe call
transparticularity, "a study that speaks with other studies, a study that
operates as a cryptological key to a larger set of information or that
repatterns the light and shadow around some broader problem."[62]

To an anthropology committed to grounding all propositions in
the facts and nothing but the facts, the speculatively transparticu-
lar methodological tendencies of the mana moment are, for obvious reasons, problematic. But the sheer vehemence, the dispropor-
tionate affective intensity with which the anthropologists of the
empiricist settlement reject the mana moment leaves something to
be explained. The violent verve of Evans-Pritchard's attack on F. B.
Jevons's once-influential *Introduction to the History of Religion* (1896)
is the stuff of minor academic legend.[63] But equally significant, perhaps, is the tone of faux-perplexity that the empiricists tend to adopt
vis-à-vis their precursors.

Looking back at the mana moment from the 1980s, for example,
Edmund Leach muses that the "whole argument about the proper
specification of an entirely hypothetical original religion, which
went on for nearly seventy years, is strangely unreal,"[64] and, some
pages later, pronounces it "obvious that Tylor, Jevons, Frazer and the
rest were entirely preoccupied with superficial trivialities."[65] Both
Evans-Pritchard and Leach apparently find it worthwhile to write
extended and detailed accounts of an intellectual history from which
they claim to be able to salvage next to nothing of value. Both their
surveys drip with contemptuous incredulity at the thought that any
of the ideas they are describing could ever have been taken seriously
by intelligent people. One doesn't have to be a partisan of armchair
anthropology to get the uneasy feeling that these often-scathing nar-

ratives seem to treat Tylor, Frazer, and their contemporaries with much the same intellectual imperiousness and lack of ethnographic empathy of which they are at the same time being convicted.[66]

One might say that mana obtrudes as the itchy symptomal point in a ritual of academic recollection that otherwise largely amounts to flogging a very dead horse. It first makes an appearance relatively early in Evans-Pritchard's account, allowing him to lament the "disastrous results" of anthropologists having adopted it into their conceptual vocabularies with scant regard for what it actually meant to the peoples from whom they had learned the term.[67] It then reappears near the end, where Evans-Pritchard, while summing up, feels the need to single it out once more for special attention as an intolerable source of disorientation: "I will only draw passing attention again to the appalling fog of confusion, which lasted for many years and is not yet entirely dispersed, about the . . . concept of mana."[68]

Even decades after its glory years, then, mana was still making mischief despite its intellectual basis apparently being, in Evans-Pritchard's bluntly redolent phrase, "as dead as mutton."[69] How to interpret this zombie vitality of mana, this refusal to lie down and be still? And why, you might ask, am I so recklessly feeding the undead?

Feeding the Undead: A Methodological Apology

In his *Primitive Culture*, the Victorian anthropologist E. B. Tylor sought to draw a sharp line between the dead and the living, the past and the present. By means of a startling surgical simile, Tylor decreed that, for ethical reasons, anthropologists should concern themselves only with the cadavers of cultures past rather than attempt to struggle with the messy demands of living patients: "The ethnographer's course, again, should be like that of the anatomist who carries on his studies if possible rather on dead than on living subjects; vivisection is nervous work, and the humane investigator hates inflicting needless pain."[70] And yet no sooner had Tylor declared a principled triage between the dead and the living than he proceeded to justify the whole exercise in the name of a kind of eternal return: "The thing that has been will be; and we are to study savages and old nations to learn the laws that under new circumstances are working for good or ill in our own development."[71]

The empiricist settlement had little patience for such cosmically synthetic speculations and no time for such enigmatic transhistorical returns. And so the question inevitably arises: by intimating connections between mana and mass publicity, am I not as guilty of the kind of speculative comparison, based on superficial resonances and opportunistic juxtapositions, as that of anthropologists consigned to the dustbin of intellectual history a century ago? My answer, of course, is a resolute no. But why and in what ways, then, can the debates of the mana moment be expected to illuminate anything about the present?

One way of beginning to answer these questions is to recall Evans-Pritchard's deceptively straightforward prescription for anthropology after the empiricist settlement: "we have to account for religious [or any other anthropological] facts in terms of the totality of the culture and society in which they are found, to try to understand them in terms of what the *Gestalt* psychologists called the *Kulturganze*, or of what Mauss called *fait total*."[72] But what, in the case of mana, is the relevant "totality"? Apparently there are only two possible answers, one wrong (human understandings of extraordinary efficacy considered in universal terms) and one right (the bounded sociocultural orders in which "natives" use and understand the word). But what if the "totality of the culture and society" really at stake here is the transnational space of technological, imperial, and anthropological encounter that I am calling the mana moment? What if the "natives" attempting to harness and account for supernatural powers were, equally, the Euro-American contemporaries and compatriots of the late nineteenth- and early twentieth-century scholars to whom this elusive word, mana, seemed to glow so numinously?

My argument is *not* that mana was "really" all about concerns internal to a Victorian and Edwardian Euro-American world going through a series of wrenching transformations. Rather, the vitality of mana during the mana moment and its long zombie afterlife are symptomatic of a fact that the anthropologists who spearheaded the empiricist settlement recognized but, for reasons of disciplinary demarcation, were unable coherently to incorporate into their methodological tool kit—namely, that, as Jean and John Comaroff remark: "modernity was, almost from the start, a north–south collaboration—indeed, a world-historical production—albeit a sharply asymmetrical one."[73] In ways that this book explores in detail, the mana of "mana" is a symptom of this uneasy, asymmetrical, and only intermittently acknowledged collaboration.

A friend asked me, after a public presentation of some of this material, whether I shouldn't have started by inquiring into situated (by which he meant "native") usages of mana. Initially I was exasperated. Against the eternal avalanche of articles quibbling about the lexical and grammatical operations of mana in this or that corner of the Pacific, I sighed, I'm trying to open up another kind of question. But as I thought about our conversation later, I realized that this part of my project *is* in fact an inquiry into situated uses of mana. It's just that I am trying to highlight a *different set of situations*—ambivalent situations of encounter rather than the kind of reified cultural worlds that even the present wave of ontological anthropologists refers to as indigenous cosmologies. Encountering a term like mana is not so much valuable because it does what anthropology is popularly supposed to do, that is, "open us up to difference," as important as that undoubtedly is. Rather, encountering mana means retracing a history of other encounters, resonant provocations that have, for more than a century, sustained the ambivalently resonant play of identification and refusal between "the West and the Rest."

What interests me about a term like mana is not how one might adequately "translate" it or how anthropologists trained in the Global North might modify "their" cultural assumptions so as to get closer to another worldview in which mana would not look like something mysterious or irrational. The point for me is not to begin with the difference of cultural worlds and then find ways of thinking "across" or "with" that difference. The point is, rather, to recognize how the fascination of a term like mana discloses the moments of encounter that have prompted anthropologists, critical theorists, and administrators to construct the schemes of difference and similarity that have allowed them—provisionally, interpretively, but also often violently—to navigate and to manage our common worlds. To invoke the Lacanian term, then, mana marks the extimacy—the simultaneous and ambivalent externality and intimacy[74]—of an encounter that produced all the many ways of imagining and inhabiting the relation between an emergent Euro-American mass-mediated "civilization" and its "primitive" others.

Dark Matter

So what would a speculative redemption of mana, one attentive to the productive tensions between its classic articulation and the present, look like? What are the risks, what are the potential yields? Perhaps mana is nothing more than the dark matter of the social-theoretical imagination—the place, as Claude Lévi-Strauss insisted against Mauss—where anthropologists place a shape-shifting signifier because they simply don't know what is going on.[75] Perhaps the great convenience—and the great vacuity—of mana is that we see in it what we want to see but can't quite acknowledge, an image of ourselves disguised to the point of un/recognizability in a primitive mise-en-scène, and yet at the same time recuperated by way of familiar analogies.

This has certainly been a frequent line of critique (and one that has more recently been aimed at affect theory, to which the mana debates bear more than a passing resemblance and relevance). Once the mana moment was over—once "mana" had, as it were, lost its mana—the partisans of the empiricist settlement scrambled over one another to demonstrate that mana was nothing more than an ethnocentric projection of industrial thought-figures onto the primitive. The mana theorists' habit of reaching for electromagnetic metaphors and similes made this all too easy. Consider Marett's figuring of the range of mana, from quotidian to sacred, and its volatility, its "power to bless or to blast":[76] "*Mana* is always *mana*, supernatural power, differing in intensity—in voltage, so to speak—but never in essence,"[77] and "there is at work in every phase of [primitive] life a spiritual force of alternating current; the energy flowing not only from the positive pole [mana], but likewise from the negative pole [tabu] in turn."[78]

Or look at Durkheim, attempting to convey both the palpably physical compulsion of collective morality and the equally visceral dangers of transgression against the collective conscience. Electricity here becomes a way to analogize a force that Durkheim insists is all too real: "When I speak of these principles [such as mana] as forces, I do not use the word in a metaphorical sense; they behave like real forces. In a sense, they are even physical forces that bring about physical effects mechanically. Does an individual come into contact with them without having taken the proper precautions? He receives a shock that has been compared with the effect of an electrical charge."[79] The analogy also serves Durkheim to convey the intensity of collective effervescence in the heat of ritual assembly: "The very act of congregating is an exceptionally powerful stimulant. Once the individuals are gathered together, a sort of electricity is generated from their closeness and quickly launches them to an extraordinary height of exaltation."[80]

No one elaborates the electrical trope quite as extravagantly as E. S. Craighill Handy. Like Marett, Handy translates mana, across several pages of his *Polynesian Religion*, into positive and negative poles; imagines Polynesian creation myths in terms of a primordial "charging" impregnation of the negative pole by the positive; writes of the necessity of ritual "insulation of the transmitter and reservoir (the sacred chief or priest, for example) for his own protection"; characterizes food, clothing, and other physical media as "conductors"; distinguishes "kinetic," "static," and "latent" mana; and suggests that any individual, qua transmitter, can become "the center of a field of psychic magnetic influence."[81]

As Ulf Hannerz remarks, "whenever one takes an intellectual ride on a metaphor, it is essential that one knows where to get off."[82] This wisdom was, apparently, lost on those supercharged mana theorists who rode the metaphor all the way to the terminus.[83] We have already seen Firth drolly confessing in 1940 to having "hammered away" in vain at his Tikopian informants for evidence of the *Ding an sich*. By 1963, Rodney Needham is arguing that Durkheim's reliance on electromagnetic metaphors arises from his desire to lend scientific gravitas to his social theory, an argument subsequently echoed by Durkheim's biographer Steven Lukes.[84] Slightly later, Needham insists that the substantializing metaphorics of the mana moment writers—"a scientific idiom derived from physics: electromagnetism, hydraulics, mechanics"—mark a failure, on the part of a generation of anthropologists not obliged to hold their theories accountable to ethnographic and linguistic evidence, to transcend figures of thought "pervad[ing] the daily experience of technological civilizations."[85]

The empiricist boundary drawing culminates in a 1984 article by Roger Keesing. Like Needham, Keesing argues that the idea that mana was a substance or a thing was "an invention of Europeans, drawing on their own folk metaphors of power and the theories of nineteenth century physics."[86] Extending the point in explicitly culturalist terms, Keesing explains:

> The European error lay in inferring some substance-like medium, mana, the invisible element the spirits and gods gave or withheld, the universal medium of power and success. Pacific Islanders knew that what made a magical stone mana was not the same as what made a war canoe mana or a fishing expedition mana: different ancestors or gods conveyed different powers to different people in different (though unknown) ways. But with few exceptions, Pacific Islanders have been unsuccessful in explaining that to theologically minded Europeans, caught up in their own conventional metaphors of power, notions of a universally explained universe, and physical models of electricity and hydraulics. We have not understood that mana-ness represented a common *quality* of efficacy or success, retrospectively interpreted, not a universal *medium* of it.[87]

There is a kind of a priori plausibility, even attractiveness to Keesing's claim. But what if one were to suspend, for a moment, the question of what mana "really means" among the people from whom anthropologists originally learned the word?[88]

We might note, to begin with, a point already made by Durkheim: that Western metaphors of force, nowadays conventionally assigned to the lexicon of physics, themselves originate in religious usage, whence they migrated into the discourses of Western science.[89] And if Marett, Durkheim, Handy, and the rest translate mana into electricity—the dynamic medium of an emergent mass-mediated industrial life—so, during the mana moment, electricity, radio waves, and other novel forces of life and communication were often metaphorized as magical and supernatural. Mesmerism and allied theories of constitutive resonance had already opened electrical channels between inner and outer worlds, "because electricity, magnetism, and optics belonged not just to the external world but, by the later eighteenth century, reached into the psychological constitution of human beings themselves. Electricity was the stuff of nerves; magnetic and electrical flows connected individuals and their voluntary faculties through hitherto unimagined channels, as Franz Mesmer (1734–1815) and others seemed to demonstrate."[90] By the time of the mana moment, the routine invocation of the electricity/publicity simile had gone mainstream. As a new business presentation by the pioneering transnational advertising agency network J. Walter Thompson put it in 1925: "advertising is a non-moral force, like electricity, which not only illuminates but electrocutes."[91]

Durkheim might have imagined electricity coursing through the social body of the Australian corroboree. But by the same token, the crowd theorists of those years typically reached for metaphors of savagery when it came to the rampant and unpredictable energies of urban crowds.[92] If mana appeared as a kind of mystical substance to the anthropologists of the mana moment then it was because electricity and what it enabled at home was already magical. As Peters notes: "the popular reception of both the telegraph and the wireless telegraph or radio [in the late nineteenth and early twentieth centuries] shows the persistence of the dream that electricity can mingle souls. . . . Both mesmerism and telegraphy draw on a common cultural project: electrical connection between distant individuals."[93] The telegraph-spirit world connection, Peters is arguing, was quite literal: "Spiritualism, the art of communication with the dead, explicitly modeled itself on the telegraph's ability to receive remote messages."[94] One thinks here, too, of Michael Taussig's now-classic analysis of disorienting moments of techno-magical encounter in the colonial world and the infinite regress of fascinations: "we" are fascinated by "their" fascination, "they" are fascinated by "our" fascination with "their" fascination . . . and so on down the fetishistic drain.[95]

Lévy-Bruhl provides an unwittingly excellent example of this dynamic. He recounts the late nineteenth-century experience in New Guinea of Erik Gustaf Edelfelt—scientific, administrative, and spiritualist adventurer at the margins of the colonial world. When the locals decide that a portrait of Queen Victoria, hung by Edelfelt, is causing misfortunes in village, Edelfelt staunchly refuses to take it down. Lévy-Bruhl and, I presume, Edelfelt both read the refusal as an enlightened gesture of resistance to superstition.[96] But could it not just as well be taken—and not only by the villagers—as a trial of strength between one kind of magic and another?

This is why Needham's and Lukes's arguments about Durkheim

using electromagnetic metaphors in an attempt—perhaps a magical one?—to secure scientific legitimacy for the sociology of primitive life, while not in themselves wrong, are quite insufficient. The anthropologists of the empiricist settlement insisted on *verifying* mana vis-à-vis a descriptive account of local usage. Here I agree with J. Z. Smith's remark: "To remain content with how 'they' understand 'mana' may yield a proper description, but little explanatory power."[97] The point is that the accusation of ethnocentrism, while ethnographically valid in a narrowly local sense, misses the larger point: the metaphors in play are not so much more or less adequate vehicles of translation between stable cultural worlds, but rather media of constitutive resonance, of emergently elective affinity across a field that only begins to appear as a contact zone[98] in its inscription as, for example, a relation between (in the language of the mana moment) the savage and the civilized or (in the language of the empiricist settlement) bounded sociocultural worlds. The extraordinary and protean vitality of the mana concept during its heyday had to do with the way it became a medium of a doubly constitutive resonance—a wormhole term at once making and unmaking the boundaries between spirit and technology, between the magical and the modern.

Modern Savagery, Then?

At first sight, Durkheim's key image of mana making—the social energy that arises when people come together in groups, face to face, body to body—would seem to be all about proximity, not about influence across distance. For Durkheim, everything we know as society—actually, everything we know as the human—is based on the ritual mediation of this social energy under conditions of "collective effervescence." Mana in Durkheim is, one might say, a name for this sensuous potentiation of the social and, at the same time, the mode in which the social, in all its immeasurable sublimity, makes itself not only palpable but also "stimulating and invigorating"[99]—that is to say, vital.

Crucially, for Durkheim mana is not only a primitive phenomenon. It is, rather, an elementary substance that manifests in different ways in all societies: in the "hyperexcitement"[100] of the Australian

Aboriginal corroboree, but also in the enthusiasm that enables unprecedented sacrifices during revolutionary events in industrial societies and in the "phenomenal oversupply of forces that spill over and
tend to spread around" a charismatic leader. Durkheim's persistent
refrain is that mana, in all these scenarios, is a name we give to the
"passionate energies" that arise from a social collective and allow a
person or an object to take on the aura, the "dynamism" that gives
the group as such — otherwise an abstraction — incarnate and singular life.[101]

The French Revolution is Durkheim's recurrent instance of modern, democratic collective effervescence: a time not only of extraordinary collective energies but also of new gods, albeit, as it turned
out, fleeting ones. Vincent Crapanzano illuminates the connection:

> [In his book *Suicide*], Durkheim uses *effervescence*, in the English
> translation "excitement," . . . to describe the "*déchainement des désirs*"
> and the "passions" that arrive with industrialization and the undefin-
> able extension of the market — when the producer's client becomes
> the entire world. He also uses *effervescence* to describe the emotional
> intensity of the ritual crowd in [*The Elementary Forms of Religious
> Life*]. . . . The parallel between the excitement of the industrial age —
> through the market, in the crowd — and the primitive ritual experi-
> ence is noteworthy. Both are, for Durkheim, at the edge of control —
> and order.[102]

Durkheim does not actually explicitly theorize mass-mediated (non-
face-to-face) forms of collective effervescence. His examples of modern enthusiasm are, like their primitive counterparts, scenarios of
co-presence: the revolutionary assembly or crowd, the charismatic
orator's impassioned audience.[103] But the examples that Durkheim
offers certainly imply the efficacy of mana across mass-mediated
publics: the new ideals of the French Revolution — "Fatherland, Liberty, Reason" — its "dogma, symbols, altar, and feast days,"[104] and,
of course, the aura of national flags for which soldiers are prepared
to die.[105] And recall that several of Durkheim's contemporaries and
rivals, scholars whose work he knew well, were during those years
musing on mass-mediated currents of contagious enthusiasm and
the "mobile atmosphere[s]" of press publics.[106]

Mauss and Hubert's book on magic was, like Durkheim's *Elementary Forms*, ostensibly concerned with primitive practices. Like Durkheim, Mauss and Hubert assumed mana to be at the root of both religious feeling and magical efficacy, of both collective morality and personal charisma. But Mauss and Hubert's discussion is particularly suggestive regarding the relation between the possibility of the magician's work and the tides and potentials of public opinion. What happens here is a far cry from the one-way hypnotic manipulation thesis of standard mana moment crowd theory—the thesis echoed by Malinowski in his rendering of the "modern savagery" of some of our "modern pseudo-statesmen and gigantic politicanti."

To begin with, the relation between the apparently inherent personal charisma of the magician and the investments and commitments of his clientele—which Mauss and Hubert term, significantly, his public—is dialectical. On the one hand, the magician appears singularly powerful in his very person. He is what Gabriel Tarde, drawing on older mesmerist terminology, calls a *magnetizer*.[107] Mauss and Hubert write: "His words, his gestures, his glances, even his thoughts are forces in themselves. His own person emanates influences before which nature and men, spirits and gods must give way."[108] And yet this inherence of the magician's power turns out to be extimate; it relies on the public potentials that are external to the magician and yet actualized only through his mediation: "It is public opinion which makes the magician and creates the power he wields. Thanks to public opinion he knows everything and can do anything."[109]

Durkheim draws a rigid distinction between religion, which he understands to be an end in itself, expressive of the sui generis status of the social collective, and magic, which he characterizes as an entirely instrumental business, a means to a worldly end. In Mauss and Hubert, the relation between the instrumental/profane and the collective/sacred is more ambiguous. For them, crucially, magicians can only work their magic by "appropriating to themselves the collective forces of society"[110]—the resources that, in the introduction, I called the *mimetic archive*. If a magician manipulates, then he is also, as Mauss and Hubert put it, "his own dupe."[111] Not only must his magnetizing work actualize potentials that dwell in "the collective forces of society," but it also responds, whether cynically or sincerely, to an overwhelming public demand: "the magician cannot be branded as an individual working on his own for his own benefit. He is a kind of official, vested by society with authority, and it is incumbent upon the society to believe in him. . . . He is serious about it because he is taken seriously, and he is taken seriously because people have need for him."[112]

Something in Us That Is Other Than Ourselves

As we saw in the introduction, Durkheim says of mana: "So we readily conceive of it in the form of a moral power that, while immanent in us, also represents something in us that is other than ourselves."[113] At one level, Durkheim's statement can simply be read as saying "mana is the way we experience society's intimate existence in us." This would already be to acknowledge the uncanny extimacy of the social, as Durkheim understands it, its peculiarly intimate anonymity. And if this is one of the felt faces of mana, then it is also recognizable to us as the structure of mass publicity qua public communication: an intimate anonymity that only addresses us in our specificity insofar as it is also and at the same time addressing an infinitely open-ended number of others. This effect is present in the kind of advertising that elicits an intimate resonance ("Don't you just hate it when . . . ?" "You know you deserve more than . . .") even as the listener is fully aware that the same message is going out to hundreds of thousands if not millions of unknown others at the same time.[114] It's present, too, in the apparently custom-made Internet marketing prompt ("if you liked this, you'll love that") since we are at the same time quite aware that our would-be sensitively attuned recommendation has been generated by a logarithm and is only possible because of a distributed field of collective inputs.

As Michael Warner and others have argued, public sociality is stranger sociality. But this doesn't simply mean that public life requires us to know how to interact with strangers. It means, more profoundly, that insofar as our self-understandings are routed at least in part through mass publicity, we are sometimes most deeply "ourselves" in the places where we feel addressed alongside strangers ("Fellow Americans . . ."). Warner emphasizes the historical and medial specificity of how "the expansive force of these [public] cultural forms cannot be understood apart from the way they make stranger-relationality normative, reshaping the most intimate dimensions of subjectivity around co-membership with indefinite persons in a context of routine action."[115] In that regard, it is interesting to note that although Durkheim is, in *The Elementary Forms*, ostensibly dealing largely with face-to-face societies, his understanding of what it means to attain to personhood (as opposed to mere individual existence) is no less dependent on the assumption of an impersonal identification than the lineage of critical public sphere theory that stretches from Immanuel Kant through Jürgen Habermas and on to Warner. Indeed, Durkheim even provides the grounds for thinking of totems as early media of stranger sociality: a totemic clan, Durkheim notes, is united by ritual practice rather than by common residence or blood.[116]

One might say, then, that Durkheim invokes but doesn't theorize the mana of mass society; consequently, he never has to grapple with what I have elsewhere called the open edge of mass publicity.[117] As Emilio Spadola remarks: "If, in Durkheimian or Geertzian logics, ritual practices were once presumed to stage the call of a relatively closed community to itself—to 'tell themselves about themselves'... technologically reproducible rituals both expand the potential scope of 'community' and undermine any assurance of a unified 'themselves' who would respond to it."[118]

Again, mana—whether of totemism or of mass publicity—marks not just a self-relation. It's not just the feeling of the extimate presence of something constitutively anonymous deep inside the subject. It expresses the reliance of any social order on rituals that incite and contain a palpably heightened sense of circumstance. These rituals may be marked off as sacred and exceptional, and are sometimes explicitly called "religious." Or they may be subtly integrated into the routines of everyday life. For all that advertising and other kinds of commercial publicity sometimes takes grandiose forms, its ordinary, capillary operation depends on the orchestration of charismatic energies that are so low voltage (to recycle the celebrated metaphor) as to be almost imperceptible. Tracking the mana of mass society means being attentive to the play of emergent intensities that range from the spectacular to the subliminal.

The felt actualization, the palpable intensity that one might call mana involves, at the level of subjective experience, a doubling that I suspect many will recognize from decisive moments of illumination, identification, desire, and such. A sense, on the one hand, of the presence of something novel and emergent. And a sense, on the other hand, that the novelty of the situation is in some sense a fulfillment of an eternal need or the culmination of a lifelong process. That is why, whether the encounter involves an intimate partner, a social movement, a spiritual illumination, or perhaps simply the perfect pair of jeans, I can experience a situation as "just what I always wanted" (even though I didn't know I wanted it until that moment) and, by the same token, experience my new feeling of myself as "who I really was all along" (even though this is the first time I encounter myself in this light).

To recapitulate: when Durkheim says that mana is "a moral power that, while immanent in us, also represents something in us that is other than ourselves" one can see that this combination of self-immanence and self-otherness may be understood in two ways. As self-immanent beings, we encounter ourselves through the actualization of a mimetic archive that appears as a kind of extimate plenitude, a field of collectively infolded experience and potential in which we participate. As self-othered beings, the dimension of extimacy appears, at first sight, in a more "alienated" light: only by letting go of what is "merely" ourselves can we attain to the impersonal fullness of our "true" humanity.

Put this way, the idea sounds esoteric. But I am only rehearsing a standard trope of Enlightenment liberalism that makes its way from Kant's insistence that in order to participate in objective reason we must put aside all our merely personal preferences and inclinations down to Durkheim's avowedly Kantian argument that we only realize our "personhood" when we participate in the impersonal field of the social collective[119]—and that it is the force of this impersonal collective that mana expresses. One of the great virtues of Durkheim's discussion in *The Elementary Forms* is that it shows how—whether we are talking about totemism, political rhetoric, or marketing—the extimate plenitude of what I am calling the mimetic archive and the extimate impersonality of the collective are, in the end, two sides of the same coin.

So Why Mana?

A still wider project hovers. Why single out mana, after all, when one might invoke so many other now more or less discredited conceptions of all-pervasive vital energy? The idea that there are connections between vital substance and public influence is by no means new, nor does it in any sense fall under an exclusively anthropological jurisdiction.

To speak only of Western traditions, there's the ancient Greek conception of *pneuma*, a subtle substance that was supposed to link micro- and macrocosmic orders, a conception revived for magical purposes, as Couliano tells us, by Renaissance magi like Giordano Bruno. In the eighteenth and nineteenth centuries, scientists and—more interestingly for my purposes—many social and political thinkers worked with ideas of animal magnetism and mesmeric fluid.[120] Various kinds of Deleuzianism are only the most visible recent iterations of vitalistic critical theory. But one could also point to Georges Bataille's sacrificial energetics or—a particular favorite of mine—Wilhelm Reich's attempts to bring together radical psychoanalysis, control of the elements, and revolutionary Marxism through his sex-pol theory of universal orgone energy. So why mana?

This is where the empiricist settlement does us an unintentional service. Having consigned the mana moment's universalizing and speculative discourse to the intellectual dustbin, the empiricist settlement effectively preserved mana in a state of suspension between ethnographic verification and epistemological disavowal. Lévi-Strauss rapped Mauss on the knuckles for, in Lévi-Strauss's opinion, succumbing to the mystification of native concepts like mana, hau (the "spirit of the gift"), and so forth.[121] Anthropologists qua scientists could not, Lévi-Strauss argued, allow themselves to be taken in like this. Their job was to document, as objectively as possible, the operation of concepts like mana in the life worlds of their informants—to show, with the most strenuous avoidance of any prejudicial implication, how and why "they" believe in mana, while "we" do not.

Or do we?

Compare the fate of a concept like mana to those other formulations of vital substance that were once central to Western science:

pneuma, aether, mesmeric fluid, orgone energy, and so on. All of them have been subjected to what Bruno Latour calls the "purifying" separation between science and pseudoscience.[122] All of them have fallen by the wayside of the grand march of truth. Today one might be at once fascinated and slightly troubled by reminders of how much time, say, Isaac Newton spent on what is nowadays called "occult" or "superstitious" pursuits. To the extent that any of these ideas live on today, they do so among highly specialized communities of enthusiasts and cranks, or—in some suitably translated form—in the commodified discourse of the New Age. But the empiricist settlement has kept mana neither dead nor alive, neither quite theirs nor quite ours: undead. And as such, it's ready at hand for anyone interested in the vastly undertheorized common historical and intellectual roots of the anthropological imagination and mass-mediated societies. Mauss, I would argue, was not "mystified" by mana. Rather, he sensed in it an opening to questions and problems that spanned the Euro-colonial contact zone in which he was living and writing. Questions and problems having to do with constitutive resonance and, as such, with the relation between emergent energies and mediating forms, between immanence and transcendence.

So as a segue into chapter 2, I would like to remember a time toward the very end of the mana moment, when, in a Europe staggering out of an unprecedentedly brutal war that had once promised an equally unprecedented revitalization, Georg Simmel wrote:

> What we *are* is, it is true, spontaneous life, with its equally spontaneous, unanalyzable sense of being, vitality, and purposiveness, but what we *have* is only its particular form at any one time, which . . . proves from the moment of its creation to be part of a quite different order of things. Endowed with the legitimacy and stature of its own provenance, it asserts and demands an existence beyond spontaneous life.[123]

Chapter 2

Ecstatic Life
and Social Form

Collective Effervescence
and the Primitive Settlement

René Girard remarks of Émile Durkheim: "The great sociologist . . .
did what he could to gain access to the problem in sociology posed
by the juxtaposition of real immanence, a force arising within the
social order itself, and a 'transcendental' power."[1] Girard is right to
note that Durkheim zeroes in, with uncanny finesse, on what is perhaps *the* central problem in social science: the relation between real
immanence and transcendental power. Or to put it differently, between the latent resources of energy and imagination that reside in
a collective and the material and symbolic structures through which
those resources can be actualized and given form, thus also spinning
off new potentialities.

This might sound recondite. But it's at the heart of how we think
about social life and about politics. The relation between immanence
and transcendence is, for example, very much at issue in the heated
late eighteenth-century pamphlet war between Thomas Paine and
Edmund Burke over the French Revolution.[2] Whereas Paine celebrates the revolution's proclamation of transcendent rights of man
("natural rights are those which appertain to man in right of his existence"[3]), Burke deplores the imposition of such violent abstractions
on the immanent, organic lifeways—the "entailed inheritance"[4]—of
a people.

Immanence and transcendence are slippery terms. For one thing, they are politically reversible. Paine, the radical, makes a transcendental argument; Burke, the small-*c* conservative, makes an immanentist case. But equally one might find radicals on the left invoking the immanently emergent revolutionary capacities of the proletariat and conservatives on the right insisting on the transcendent authority of eternal moral values. Immanence and transcendence are also *conceptually* reversible terms. Immanence might refer to latent resources of life and imagination, something like the potentials for becoming that come embedded in a collective—in its forms of life, in its practices, in its as yet un-actualized resources. Likewise, transcendence might imply something like the hardening or actualization of those latent resources qua determinate social forms and thus a transition from becoming into being: institutional forms, linguistic forms, conceptual forms, forms that—through this transcendence—seem to take on an authority of their own. But then as soon as they're laid out like this, the terms begin to slide into each other. Transcendence can also be seen as a kind of becoming; transcending a given state of affairs is a kind of process, after all. Similarly, immanence may well appear as a state of being.

In everyday talk and in social theory, one might speak of *life* and *form*. And then it's often as if the two terms are imagined in a zero-sum relation to each other. More form means less life—isn't that pretty much the formula for the devitalizing experience of rationalization? Isn't that the underlying idea behind the assumption that conceptualizing something somehow moves it further away from its vital core, even as it enables a sense of mastery? People often talk as if form is a kind of necessary evil: we need institutions, we need structure. Yes, we do. But talking that way implies that transcendent form necessarily devitalizes, that it reduces the immanence of life by moving it away from spontaneity, from unmediated being.

By contrast, both Durkheim and his contemporary Georg Simmel suggest something more like a dialectical conception of immanence and transcendence, of life and form. The argument is not just that life and form or immanence and transcendence are only thinkable in relation to each other. The dialectical idea is that form actualizes life even as it constrains it. Equally, life lends weight and plenitude to form even as it overwhelms it. In other words, it's not that form confronts life from outside; rather, form is immanent to life, just as life is immanent to form. As Simmel noted in his extraordinary little essay "Life as Transcendence": "We are not divided into life free from limits and form made secure by them; we do not live partly in continuity, partly in individuality, the two asserting themselves against each other." And: "Insofar as life's essence goes, transcendence is immanent to it."[5]

I will be suggesting in this chapter that the implications for social theory of Durkheim's insights into the dialectic of energy and form haven't been adequately developed. This is partly, perhaps, because Durkheim disguised those insights as a theory of "primitive"[6] ritual. But it's also because, in the vicinity of vital energies, anthropology has often done what scholars tend to do: it has fallen back on epistemological problems regarding adequate ways of knowing rather than grappling with world-mattering, with questions like "what makes worlds palpably urgent rather than merely coherent"? In considering that question, this chapter doubles as an alternative anthropological genealogy for contemporary debates around the place of affect in social life and theory.

The tendency to retreat from vitality is all the more ironic (but perhaps also all the more predictable) given that the very name of our cherished anthropological method—participant observation— enshrines and enjoins the dynamic cohabitation of immanence and transcendence. This being the case, one of my tasks in this chapter is to try to keep an eye on the flickers of interference and influence between two parallel channels in anthropological thinking: the channel on which we try to make sense of how people try to establish and maintain the energy and form of the worlds in which they live, and the channel on which we try to establish and maintain the energy and form of the intellectual apparatus through which we understand our informants' world-making projects. Once again, mana provides a useful example of this uneasy doubling.

Channel one: mana as a world-mattering substance. In Durkheim's *Elementary Forms* mana is, for the societies he is describing, a palpable emanation of constituted authority only because it is *also and at the same time* the chronically unstable constituting substance that strains against all containment. Mana, as I noted in the introduction, is transcendent in that it expresses and embodies the "genuine respect" that makes us "defer to society's orders."[7] But this transcendence is only possible because mana is also an immanent and leaky vital principle. Mana will only temporarily stay still; it will only be made to express the imperative of a particular social order with great and repeated ritual effort. Its chief characteristic is contagion: "Religious forces are so imagined as to appear always on the point of escaping the places they occupy and invading all that passes within their reach."[8] Or as J. Prytz Johansen puts it, mana "expresses something participated, an active fellowship which according to its nature is never inextricably bound with any single thing or any human being."[9]

Channel two: the mana of "mana" as scholarly concept. As we saw in chapter 1, despite the empiricist settlement's best efforts to reduce mana to as plain an ethnographic datum as any other, mana, like the undead, refused to lie down. In the present chapter, before getting to a close reading of Durkheim's theory of ritual as world-making practice, I want to spend a little time on the scandalous way in which the immanence of mana seemed to many anthropologists to threaten a kind of infection of scholarly objectivity by the immanence of primitive thought. Thus, as we shall see, Claude Lévi-Strauss's denunciation of Mauss for having allowed himself to be seduced by this most Siren-like of notions. Echoes, again, of the unease that has surrounded affect theory in anthropology in more recent times.

For Durkheim, so often read as a conservative apologist for social order, social life was first and foremost in a double sense ecstatic. *Ekstasis* in the original Greek literally means to stand outside oneself. By means of the ecstasy of mana, as revealed through ritual, one begins to sense the uncanny proximity and unexpectedly tight interrelationship of Dionysian self-surrender—the famously immanent *collective effervescence* dramatized in Durkheim's affect-intensive account of the Arunta corroboree—and the transcendently Apollonian self-possession of the well-tempered, rational citizen. By means of mana, we are *beside ourselves* in two senses at once: effervescently transported and rationally self-reflexive.

Immanence and Transcendence: Toward a Dialectic

Curiously, even those anthropologists and critical theorists who acknowledge the restless traffic between immanence and transcendence seem hard put to think the relation dialectically. It is as if one side of the dialectic, immanence *or* transcendence, must be presumed as the normative orientation.

Classic sociology and anthropology have generally been invested in models of social order and its reproduction. Durkheim's theory of ritual shows, as we shall shortly see in some detail, how moral order emerges out of orgiastic disorder. Likewise, Lévi-Strauss's analysis of shamanic practice in his seminal essays "The Sorcerer and His Magic" and "The Effectiveness of Symbols," both originally published in 1949, suggest, powerfully, that whatever the "scientific" truth of the symbolic orders to which we become attached may be, *order as such* has a therapeutic and thus also a normative value.[10] For Lévi-Strauss, the shaman's mana work consists of a kind of collective version of Freud's talking cure: bringing the destitution of disorder— the matrix of suffering—into the constitutive and healing order of language.

Lévi-Strauss characterizes the nonordered material of experience not as mere absence or lack, but as an archive of palpable potentials: "hazy and unelaborated attitudes which have an experiential character for each of us"[11] and "a reservoir of recollections and images amassed in the course of a lifetime."[12] But Lévi-Strauss's "reservoir" is very much a matter of individual experience. In its literal *idiocy*, its separation from the social, lies an important dimension of the suffering it induces. For Lévi-Strauss, the therapeutic movement from virtual to actual, from destitution to constitution, is at the same time a normative movement from solipsism to sociality: "These experiences . . . remain intellectually diffuse and emotionally intolerable unless they incorporate one or another of the patterns present in the group's culture."[13]

One sees this same orientation toward order in latter-day anthropological descriptions of the Polynesian mana-tapu complex, where "mana" stands for incited, unbound potential and "tapu" expresses its bound, socially stabilized form. The presumed goal of charismatic incitement is political order: "What is called Polynesian religion might be aptly described as a kind of vitalism. . . . Implicitly, then, precontact Polynesian religion was an economy of *mana* in which generative powers were appropriated, channeled, transformed, and bound."[14] The normative aim is unquestioned: raw mana, it seems, *must* be (ritually, politically) cooked. By this analytic—which duplicates what one would have to presume to be a local ideology—only mana that has been "appropriated, channeled, transformed, and bound" has dignity and ethical force.

Bradd Shore quotes Johansen quoting Te Matahoro, a Maori elder, lamenting what looks, to the anthropological imagination, like the sad aftermath of settler-colonial cultural genocide: "The *tapus* are over; the eternal traditions are lost; the *karakias* (ritual worlds) are lost and are not understood any more today. For the *tapu* is the first; if there is no *tapu*, then all the acts of the gods become without force (*mana*), and if there are no gods, everything becomes insipid. The way of people, actions, and thoughts, is now one whirling around; they are confused and desperate in this country now."[15] One might sympathize. But is this not actually an expression of ideology at the moment of its deflation? For who other than rulers, fundamentalists, and social scientists believe that the vitality of social life is to be equated with watertight self-contained authority?

Neovitalists like Gilles Deleuze and Félix Guattari travel in the opposite direction, trying always to liberate life from order, immanence from transcendence. For them the challenge is how to recuperate from the numbing clutches of actually existing order, a virtuality and a vitality that is at once foundational and an irrepressible dimension of any constituted order: a "plane of immanence." In an avalanche of metaphors, Deleuze and Guattari hammer home the opposition between immanent virtuality (the plane) and transcendent actuality (concepts): "Concepts are the archipelago or skeletal frame, a spinal column rather than a skull, whereas the plane is the breath that suffuses the separate parts"; "concepts are concrete assemblages, like the configurations of a machine, but the plane is the abstract machine of which these assemblages are the working parts"; "concepts are events, but the plane is the horizon of events, the reservoir or reserve of purely conceptual events" and so forth.[16]

According to Deleuze and Guattari, the plane is the virtual principle of immanence that provides the prephilosophical but always shifting condition of possibility for the transcendent articulation of concepts.[17] Their first commandment—one might call it their antinormative normative obsession—is to keep plane and concept analytically distinct. That is the reason why they are avowedly and militantly antidialectical. For them, the most egregious mistake is to betray the independence of the plane of immanence to the constituting lure of concepts. We must never fall victim, Deleuze and Guattari insist, to the temptation of saying that immanence is immanent *to* something, for then "the concept becomes a transcendental universal and the plane becomes an attribute in the concept."[18]

Like iconoclasts trembling before graven images, Deleuze and Guattari's elaborate warnings against the seductive omnipotence of concepts suggest a profound terror. By contrast, a dialectical approach to the problem would preclude and refuse both the transcendence-nomos of concepts (Durkheim, Lévi-Strauss) and the purity-eros of immanence (Deleuze and Guattari). This, contrary to frequent misunderstandings, is what a negative as opposed to a traditionally positive (or, one could say, an allegedly Hegelian) dialectic implies. Dialectical thinking is often accused of reducing the world to binaries only to conjure them into transcendently synthetic unities. On the contrary: both dialectical and antidialectical thinking start with binaries. The difference is that antidialectical thinking remains attached to them, pouring all its attachment to life and multiplicity into one side of the pair while marking the other as the Bad Object that can signify only death and domination.[19] By vital contrast dialectics, as even Hegel stated quite explicitly, recognizes ceaseless becoming, life and thought in motion, constitution in destitution.[20] Again, then, I invoke my favorite monster: a dialectical vitalism that will permit thinking virtuality and actuality as mutually constitutive—and mutually destitutive—states of the mimetic archive without privileging one or the other as either ground or destination.

The crucial point to emphasize is the dialectical *ambiguity* of this excess potential. To put it simply, excess mimetic potential, qua excess, both supports and troubles power; here, again, the figure of mana is good to think with. Very often critical and cultural theorists write as if any kind of excess, undecidability or internal instability in a social formation, inherently points toward freedom. This kind of thinking is premised on the tacit assumption that authority, power, and ideology work better and more efficaciously the more seamlessly and tightly they are able to "capture" us. My own take on this un-decidability, this excess potential—one of whose names is mana—is that it is something that we observe, cultivate, *and* resist in that which fascinates us. It's an erotic relation but also an auratic relation: a "unique apparition of a distance, however near it may be."[21] A relation of more or less intense engagement that is also marked by suspension; something like what Anne Carson invokes through the ancient Greek *aidos*, which she translates as "shamefastness," "a sort of voltage of decorum."[22]

The Primitive Settlement

The empiricist settlement that founded modern ethnographic anthropology was preceded and enabled by another settlement: *the primitive settlement*. The primitive settlement constituted the primitive and the civilized as two internally coherent "worlds," thereby also establishing them as separate domains of scholarly inquiry and objects of possible comparison. The empiricist settlement did not initially undo or even much trouble the primitive settlement. As late as the 1960s and early 1970s, Evans-Pritchard and Mary Douglas were still defending the scholarly use of the term *primitive* as an intellectually useful device. On the other hand, the primitive settlement was, like all settlements, from the very beginning haunted by symptomatic returns of what it had repressed.

Peter Pels captures the predicament: "Anthropology, more than any other scholarly discourse on magic, was responsible for the interpretation of magic as an antithesis of modernity and for the production of the peculiar ambiguity and entanglement of magic and modernity," a double dynamic resulting in a "seesaw movement of denial and recognition."[23] The severe strain that this involved shows through again and again in the juxtaposition of apparently contradictory statements. So, for example, J. N. Hewitt grandly intones in a 1902 article on *orenda* (an Iroquois concept then generally understood to be equivalent to mana): "From the monody of savagery to the multitoned oratorio of enlightenment, the way is truly long" before, on the very next page, adding: "And, to a living faith and trust in the reality of this subsumed mystic potence, its reified figment of inchoate mind, human experience *in all times and in all lands* owes some of its most powerful motives and dominating activities."[24]

The denial/recognition seesaw was not simply a matter of category confusion—an inability conclusively to draw the line between magical and civilized thinking. It was also a temporal problem, a question of how to draw the line between past and present. Enlightenment was supposed to bring not only autological self-determination but also a maturely measured relation to the pull of the past.[25] As Tylor remarks: "The nobler tendency of advancing culture, and above all of scientific culture, is to honour the dead without groveling before them."[26] Tylor is well-known for his attempt to make sense of the lingering presence of apparently nonsensical or superstitious practices in terms of "survivals." But it is less often remembered that Tylor also writes of *revivals*, in an attempt to explain not only the inert persistence of superstition but also the active and enthusiastic reawakening of practices apparently belonging to a bygone age—paradigmatically magic, in the late nineteenth-century form of the spiritualist movement. Tylor is nowadays remembered for advocating a linear conception of human progress and development. Undoubtedly that was his ideal. But the facts forced him to acknowledge more meandering temporalities:[27] "For the stream of civilization winds and turns upon itself, and what seems the bright onward current of one age may in the next spin round in a whirling eddy, or spread into a dull and pestilential swamp. . . . Some well-known belief or custom has for centuries shown symptoms of decay, when we begin to see that the state of society, instead of stunting it, is favouring its new growth, and it bursts forth again with a vigor often as marvelous as it is unhealthy."[28] By pathologizing the survival and especially the revival of supposedly primitive practices in new and modern forms, mana moment scholars were able to mediate the contradiction between the othering of the primitive and its constant appearance in the midst of the civilized world.[29] As we saw in chapter 1, Tylor knew that zombies had a way of not wanting to lie down and die, even—perhaps especially—under the ethnologist's scalpel.

The really vexing thing was not the persistence of apparently magical practices in civilized countries. Such things could be explained as evidence of the unfortunate intellectual retardation of provincial folk: "The piles of 'Zadkiel's Almanack' in the booksellers' windows in country towns about Christmas are a symptom of how much yet remains to be done in popular education."[30] And among the credulous, there was always going to be a market for the services of more or less recognized entrepreneurs of the occult: provincial Protestants might on occasion call on Catholic priests and monks to "help them against witchcraft, to lay ghosts, consecrate herbs, and discover thieves."[31]

The truly disturbing phenomenon was, rather, the appearance of *new* kinds of magic, magic constitutively internal to the most modern practices. Recall from chapter 1 Malinowski's characterization of performative-hypnotic effects of mass publicity as "modern savagery." Anthropologist-philosopher Ernesto de Martino writes of the presence of "archaic realities" in our contemporary world, and one might think he is simply speaking of the persistence of magic *alongside* modern things.[32] But then he notes that "the power of archaic traditions that are still strongly active in our daily life ... *secretly support* the diversity of our cultural manifestations."[33] Even Lévy-Bruhl, supposedly the champion of an absolute distinction between primitive and civilized thinking, remarks in passing that the principle of participation—which he at first suggests is definitive of prelogical thought—"will ever be maintained," not only in institutions built on our "moral and religious customs" but in "political institutions" as well.[34]

Lévy-Bruhl's mistake, argues Evans-Pritchard, was that he overdrew his prelogical/logical binary: "he excluded the mystical in our own culture as rigorously as he excluded the empirical in savage cultures."[35] But in fact the matter is a little more complicated. Evans-Pritchard's appeal to look twice at Lévy-Bruhl is a useful reminder of the value of suspending the kneejerk "critical" gesture of bemoaning the pejoratively ethnocentric, racist assumptions of so many of the mana moment theorists' writings. Evans-Pritchard attributes a "softer" cultural relativism to Lévy-Bruhl than the hardline cognitive othering of which he is usually supposed to have been guilty—while also noting that Lévy-Bruhl consistently refused (perhaps for strategic reasons) to draw the obvious conclusions regarding the magicality of Christian theology. Evans-Pritchard is undoubtedly right about Lévy-Bruhl's deafening silence on parallels between primitive conceptions and key points of Christian doctrine. But at the same time, I would like to suggest that the salutary suspension of snap judgment that Evans-Pritchard recommends in the case of Lévy-Bruhl also discloses, once we apply it more broadly to the mana moment, the tremendous strain under which the demarcation between the primitive and the civilized invariably labored.

Consider the following passage. Lévy-Bruhl inserts a passing but crucial hint that he may after all not be talking about an exclusively primitive phenomenon into a passage that would otherwise seem to be a standard scenario of primitive muddle-and-frenzy. But then he immediately tries to reaffirm the absolute difference between the two mentalities by way of an actually-not-very-enigmatic holy trinity:

> The [primitive] ceremonies and dances . . . are intended to revive and maintain, by means of the nervous exaltation and ecstasy of movement *not wholly unlike that seen in more advanced societies*, the community of essence in which the actual individual, the ancestral being living again in him, and the animal or plant species that forms his totem, are all mingled. To our minds, there are necessarily three distinct realities here, however close the relationship may be. To the primitive minds, the three make but one, yet at the same time are three.[36]

One would think that Lévy-Bruhl's Euro-American readership, even if they missed the embedded allusion to the Father, the Son and the Holy Spirit, would not have had to reach very far for readily intelligible examples of the ritual ambiguities of participation and representation. In the Christian tradition, after all, the ambiguous status of the Eucharist—is the wine actually the blood of Christ transubstantiated (participation) or does it merely symbolize the blood of Christ (representation)?—remains a serious point of doctrinal disputation. Fast-forward: the logic of branding hovers just as ambiguously between participation and representation as any "religious" ritual. One doesn't actually have to tattoo a brand onto one's body the way, for example, some Harley-Davidson motorcycle enthusiasts do to ask what kind of act of participatory consubstantial incorporation or symbolic act of representation wearing a logo implies.

Clearly, participation needs to be released from its exile on the

Island of Outmoded Prejudicial Concepts. As it turns out, mana may just be its ticket back to the mainland of social theory.

Antipodes

At the antipode of what social psychologist William McDougall (an important influence on mana theorist R. R. Marett) called the "wide-awake, self-reliant man,"[37] mana moment primitives were, apparently, always at risk of *participating too much*, of merging indiscriminately with their surroundings. As Durkheim and Mauss write in *Primitive Classification*, in "the least evolved societies known" (which Durkheim thought were totemically organized tribes) one is apt to find "general mental confusion": "Here, the individual loses his personality. There is a complete lack of distinction between him and his exterior soul or his totem." The participation that Durkheim and Mauss at this stage imagine between humans and their totems is mimetic but, compared to the more Saussurean conception of the arbitrariness of the totemic sign that one finds in *The Elementary Forms*, it is mimetic in a crudely literal way: "He and his 'fellow-animal' together compose a single personality. The identification is such that the man assumes the characteristics of the thing or animal with which he is thus united."[38]

For Lévy-Bruhl, such participation thinking characterizes a "prelogical" mentality, as compared to the separative, analytical operations of "logical" thought.[39] The mark of primitive thinking, according to Lévy-Bruhl, is its—to Europeans—peculiarly disorienting interweaving of participatory and analytical moments: "In the mentality of primitive peoples, the logical and prelogical are not arranged in layers and separated from each other like oil and water in a glass. They permeate each other, and the result is a mixture which is a very difficult matter to differentiate."[40]

From the beginning, the alleged confusions of primitive thought are inextricable from the apparently nonstop effervescence of primitive life. Only by slowing and calming down, suggests Marett, can a more civilized reason appear: "Pause is the necessary condition of the development of all those higher processes which make up the rational being."[41] The idea of *pause* as the crucible of reason is a standard trope of Enlightenment thought. Kant and many of his contemporaries argue that humans are distinguished from other animals by their congenital helplessness.[42] Lacking much in the way of reliable instinctive orientation, and having exiled themselves from the prelapsarian (read primitive) bliss of Edenic innocence, they require the whole vast interpersonal artifice of culture to survive and to thrive. By the same token, however, the human Fall with its ensuing helplessness is also, dialectically, the starting point of freedom, since reason and morality can only develop in the gap of uncertainty between stimulus and response. In yet another twist that would be picked up and developed more fully by Freud, the unchosen pause becomes the opportunity for an ethically chosen deferral of instant gratification—and thus, again, the basis (painfully grounded in repression as it may be) of love, art, and culture.[43] The largely prejudicial figures of savage confusion and excessive exuberance serve to shore up their constant companion: the civilized citizen, judiciously deliberating at a responsible distance from the frenzy of crowds.[44]

The figure of primitive thought, cornerstone of the mana moment, has chiefly been considered from an intellectualist standpoint. In the so-called rationality debate of the 1950s and 1960s, for example, philosophers and anthropologists hash out the relation between rationality and cultural difference.[45] But it's as if the vital, affective, sensuous dimensions ascribed to primitive mentality during the mana moment seem too prejudicial, too tainted by mob frenzy—and, to many later anthropologists, too "psychological"—to be taken seriously. And so *Homo ecstaticus* is, again and again, sidelined in favor of a narrowly intellectualist conception of human sapience: *Homo explanans*.

Much ink has been spilled over the relation between magical and scientific thought since Sir James Frazer confidently declared that magic was "the bastard sister of science," "a false science as well as an abortive art."[46] Such repetitive abjections of magic and other supposed manifestations of primitive thinking were all the more necessary since, as Edward Tylor had already noted in *Primitive Culture*, the formal kinship between rationality and irrationality was more intimate than many might want to admit. Tylor points to "the Association of Ideas, a faculty which lies at the very foundation of human reason, but in no small degree of human unreason also."[47]

But as Alexander Goldenweiser would later remark, there was something misleading about the intellectualist orientation of the whole debate on primitive forms of thought and belief: "the process . . . through which religion comes to be, is conceived of as somewhat in the nature of a conscious rationalistic act, of a problem, posited and solved."[48]

The apex of the intellectualist approach to the primitive is probably Claude Lévi-Strauss's enormously influential *The Savage Mind*, in particular its first chapter, "The Science of the Concrete." Lévi-Strauss avers, with the repetitive insistence of a nervous tic, that his distinction between primitive and scientific thought is in no way prejudicial to the primitive, that magic should in no way be understood as "a timid and stuttering form of science," and that "both approaches are equally valid."[49] But the point is that, for Lévi-Strauss, the bricoleur, the practitioner of savage knowledge, is still a scientist, albeit one more reliant on "sensible intuition" and "passionate attention"[50] than is the modern engineer. Indeed, it is precisely as a (different) kind of intellectual that Lévi-Strauss can redeem the primitive.[51]

No matter how hard he works to shore up the intellectual dignity of "the science of the concrete," one still senses in Lévi-Strauss a residual suspicion of what Hegel called "picture-thinking." The bricoleur's mythical thinking attains to philosophical value despite, not because of, its sensuous attachments: "One understands then how mythical thought can be capable of generalizing and so be scientific, *even though* it is still entangled in imagery."[52] Lévi-Strauss secures both the integrity of primitive thought and a progressionist telos by imagining the work of the bricoleur not as inferior to but as *anticipatory of* "a science yet to be born."[53]

For all its sophistication, Lévi-Strauss's story in "The Science of the Concrete" comes down to the proposition that magic and myth, like science, are motivated by an underlying "demand for order."[54] Like the scientist, the savage bricoleur confronts the external world as a proto-Kantian subject who has not yet realized that he will have to trade true knowledge for existential exile from the *Ding an sich*. Maturity means putting aside the arts of mimesis—as poetically generative as they may be—and accepting, in Max Horkheimer and Theodor Adorno's mordantly ironic words, that, with the coming of enlightenment, "nature is no longer to be influenced by likeness but mastered through work."[55]

Such a bracing exhortation to put away childish things and grow up into science was also at the core of Lévi-Strauss's earlier *Introduction to the Work of Marcel Mauss*, where—in the guise of an appreciation—he reproaches Durkheim and especially Mauss for having adopted an essentially magical-mimetic relationship to the vital category of magic: mana. Durkheim and Mauss, Lévi-Strauss charges, allow themselves to be mystified by the way that mana appears in the subjective experience of primitive peoples. Thus they fail to realize that mana is really a symptom of "a universal and permanent form of thought," that it is a "floating signifier" expressing the perennial "surplus of signification" vis-à-vis the scientific rigor of understanding.[56]

Unlike, say, Bronislaw Malinowski, Lévi-Strauss never reduces either myth or science to purely instrumental motivations—to "the rumbling of . . . stomachs."[57] The pursuit of knowledge, whether primitive or civilized, is a pleasure in itself. But for Lévi-Strauss, the anthropologist qua scientist also has a special and serious duty: to push beyond and reach behind the first-order world of native discourse: "we would risk committing sociology to a dangerous path, even a path of destruction, if we . . . reduced social reality to the conception that man—savage man, even—has of it."[58] As such, the poetic invitation to participation in primitive discourse is particularly treacherous—and Durkheim and Mauss have, apparently, allowed themselves to be taken in. In a clever twist, Lévi-Strauss suggests that it is *in their writings* that mana actually turns out to be magical: "the notion of *mana* does present those characteristics of a secret power, a mysterious force, which Durkheim and Mauss attributed to it: for such is the role it plays in their own system. *Mana* really is *mana* there."[59]

The Savage Does Not Preach His Religion

In many ways, Lévy-Bruhl's version of primitive thought, the prelogical, is a precursor of Lévi-Strauss's science of the concrete. Like Lévi-Strauss's bricoleur, Lévy-Bruhl's savages are concrete thinkers; they are capable of generalization, but by participation rather than by abstraction. There is a similar concern across the two texts with problems of categorization and world ordering.[60] But unlike Lévi-Strauss, Lévy-Bruhl emphasizes the intertwining of feeling and movement, qua embodied participation, with the work of representation:

> [Primitive] mental activity is too little differentiated for it to be possible to consider ideas or images or objects by themselves apart from the emotions and passions which evoke these ideas or are evoked by them. Just because our mental activity is more differentiated, and we are more accustomed to analyzing its functions, it is difficult for us to realize by any effort of imagination, more complex states in which emotion or motor elements are *integral parts* of the representation.[61]

Perhaps Lévy-Bruhl had not read David Hume, who in the mid-eighteenth century had already remarked of human thought *in general*: "I believe it may safely be establish'd for a general maxim, that no object is presented to the senses, nor image form'd in the fancy, but what is accompany'd with some emotion or movement of spirits proportion'd to it."[62] Or perhaps Lévy-Bruhl *had* read Hume, since at a metaphilosophical level, his question is not why unitive participation leads representation astray but rather how separative analytic representation could ever have grown out of participation. Either way, the politics of the mana moment—whether the specter haunting theory is the exotic savage or the one rioting in the street outside—demanded that the more corporeal dimensions of life and thought be pushed off onto the primitive. Taking mana *too* seriously was always redolent of the anthropologist's signature pathology: going native. Or what, to Lévi-Strauss, seemed like much the same thing: playing with magic.

Alongside the dominant intellectualist take on the primitive ran an alternative, minor current that Evans-Pritchard in retrospect somewhat misleadingly dubbed the emotionalist approach. I say "misleadingly" since I take his term to be symptomatic of the strong antipsychological orientation that anthropologists inherited from Durkheim's decisive and discipline-defining demarcation between sociology and psychology. Ironically, it was Durkheim who, through his emphasis on collective effervescence, would be accused by Evans-Pritchard and others of having sinned most egregiously against his own methodological strictures: "No amount of juggling with words like 'intensity' and 'effervescence' can hide the fact that [Durkheim] derives the totemic religion of the Blackfellows from the emotional excitement of individuals brought together in a small crowd, from what is a sort of crowd hysteria.... Fundamentally Durkheim elicits a social fact from crowd psychology."[63]

Marett and Durkheim both emphasize the vital and embodied basis of religion. Durkheim, in a short essay clarifying aspects of his argument in *The Elementary Forms*, remarks that religious ideals "cannot communicate themselves to us without increasing our vitality.... This is the dynamogenic influence that religions have always exercised on men."[64] In a similar spirit a few years earlier, Marett had asserted that "under normal and healthy conditions of savage society, the religious life involves a sort of progress from strength to strength, with serious recognition of vital need as its efficient cause."[65] Marett memorably captures his practice-based approach to collective life, influenced by the pioneering work of William Robertson Smith, in the formula: "the savage does not preach his religion, but dances it instead."[66]

The rhetorical reduction of Durkheim's theory of religion to "crowd psychology" was routine. But the question of the intellectual debt that Durkheim's theory of collective effervescence owes to mana moment crowd theorists is not altogether clear cut. In an early English-language review of *The Elementary Forms*, Goldenweiser came up with the rather glib formula: "Religion, [Durkheim] says, is society, but society, we find, is but a sublimated crowd."[67] But the important points for my purposes here are (a) the tacit presumption that an association between primitive ritual and crowd behavior is inherently prejudicial, and (b) that the affective-mimetic dynamics of crowd behavior are reducible to "psychological" phenomena, which, in this discourse, tends to mean processes that happen "inside people's heads" and that are therefore not readily available to ethnographic research. Evans-Pritchard asks, much in the mode of affect skeptics many decades later: "How does one know whether a person experiences awe or thrill or whatever it may be? How does one recognize it, and how does one measure it?"[68] But as W. S. F. Pickering rightly observes: "to accept the fact of the heightening of emotions is not the same thing as to search for [or, perhaps more precisely to presume] a psychological cause."[69]

Between a Rock and a Tough Crowd

In the biblical story, Moses leads the long-suffering Israelites to the edge of the Promised Land. God assures Moses that an apparently barren rock will provide drinking water for his thirsty people if only Moses will address the rock in God's name. But, exasperated by the Israelites' restiveness, Moses turns magician in front of his people, strikes the rock twice with his staff and, when the water gushes forth, implicitly takes credit for the miracle. The Israelites drink. But because Moses has arrogated God's mana to himself, Moses and his people are refused entry into the Promised Land.[70]

Tellingly, Lévi-Strauss invokes this scene in lamenting Mauss's failure to follow through on the promise of his life's work. Ostensibly, the problem is simply the final systematizing push for which Mauss could never quite summon the discipline or the motivation: "Why," Lévi-Strauss demands, "did Mauss halt at the edge of those immense possibilities, like Moses conducting his people all the way to a promised land whose splendor he would never behold? . . . Mauss might have been expected to produce the twentieth-century social sciences' *Novum Organum*; he held all the guidelines for it, but it has only come to be revealed in fragmented form."[71]

Actually Lévi-Strauss appears to be saying that Mauss's decisive mistake (like that of his near-homonym Moses) was to have been seduced by the temptation, the sin of magic. Instead of trusting to the transcendent (quasi-divine) revelation of science, by which mana opened onto a deeper and impersonal truth, Mauss/Moses—with, Lévi-Strauss steadfastly implies, the best of intentions—stole the immanent light of mana for his own work.

It is hardly a coincidence (although Lévi-Strauss does not acknowledge any connection) that Mauss, too, invokes Moses in relation to mana-related matters, but for a very different purpose. Mauss, like Durkheim, emphasizes the energy, expectation, and efficacy generated out of collective effervescence, the ground of mana:

"the feeling of society's existence and society's prejudices."[72] Mauss invokes the "mutual exaltation," the "collective agitation," the "affective states," and the "hyperaesthesia" underpinning the workings of magic as well as of religion.[73] At root, he suggests, the mana of the magical act is a "translation" of an enormous, even desperate "social need under the pressure of which an entire series of collective psychological phenomena are let loose."[74] This is the pressure that bears down on the magician as well as on the minister, allowing him to perform his magic regardless of his own misgivings and anxieties. And this, too, is where Mauss places Moses—with the rock in front of him, God's enigmatic voice above him, and the tremendous "social need" of his exhausted people behind him: "Behind Moses, who touched the bare rock, stood the whole nation of Israel, and while Moses may have felt some doubts, Israel certainly did not. Behind the village water diviner and his wand we find the anxiety of a whole village, desperate for water."[75]

It is not much of a stretch to imagine that Lévi-Strauss fancied himself as Joshua to Mauss's Moses, the anointed one who would finally lead the next generation of his people—the wandering social scientists—into the Promised Land. (And who knows, perhaps he did? I will leave it to others to opine on whether the decline of structuralism represents a return to idolatry.) But Mauss's image of Moses in the lineage of village water diviners, the staff his wavering wand, is perhaps both rather more compassionate and rather more suggestive than is Lévi-Strauss's severe disapproval. It registers the collective basis of performative efficacy, the engagement and energy that allows mana alchemically to translate suffering into wonder. Let's just make sure to register Mauss's fundamental proposition here: that the *efficacy* and *authority* of mana rests on the affective and embodied energy of an assembly, as well as on the collective articulation of attention that Mauss—for our purposes suggestively—calls "public opinion."[76]

Lévi-Strauss sternly dismisses this whole order of phenomena as irrelevant to the anthropologist's explanatory purpose: "feelings, . . . volitions and beliefs, which, from the viewpoint of sociological explanation, are epiphenomena, or else mysteries; in any case, they are objects extrinsic to the field of investigation."[77] Where Mauss wants to consider the world-making power of mana work, Lévi-

Strauss seems eager to ward off seduction. As Martin Holbraad remarks, "Levi's Strauss' solution to the problem of *mana*'s antinomies amounts to a dissolution."[78] And yet this "dissolution" was clearly prompted by the anxious intimation of a powerful seduction, just as Adorno notes that in Kant's aesthetic theory the "'without interest' must be shadowed by the wildest interest."[79] In an aside at once prurient and condescending, Lévi-Strauss connects mana to the charismatic and the sexually alluring: "we do say of a person that he or she 'has something'; and when American slang says that a woman has got 'oomph,' it is not certain, if we call to mind the sacred and taboo-laden atmosphere which permeates sexual life, in America even more than elsewhere, that we are very far removed from the meaning of *mana*."[80] One imagines Lévi-Strauss bracing himself, like Odysseus sailing past the seductive Sirens tied to the mast, until the transcendent poise of scientific austerity has safely disenchanted this most palpably immanent floating signifier. But I will be returning to the Sirens. How could I not?

Collective Effervescence

In an earlier essay, I made a point about Durkheim's discussion of collective effervescence that I would like to repeat and elaborate here: "Emile Durkheim's *The Elementary Forms of Religious Life* is a splendidly subversive text. For starters Durkheim, quite consciously writing with and against the contemporary figure of the urban crowd, gives us something that in today's polarized theoretical landscape has become almost unimaginable: a social theory that is at once semiological and affect-based."[81] One might also say that the great advantage and advance of Durkheim's intervention is that it achieved a practice-based synthesis of what Evans-Pritchard called intellectualist and emotionalist approaches to magic, religion, and social life in general.[82] Or to put it yet another way, in a manner that will perhaps more directly point to its significance for the mana of mass publicity, Durkheim's theory of ritual helps to explain the social production of representational potency—of meaning that matters.[83]

So what happens? In the beginning is the vital assembly. Durkheim's analysis of primitive ritual draws on Spencer and Gillen's description of the Arunta corroboree in their *Northern Tribes of Central Australia* (1904), but aspires to general explanatory relevance. The "electricity" of co-presence comes first: "The very act of congregating is an exceptionally powerful stimulant. Once the individuals are gathered together, a sort of electricity is generated from their closeness and quickly launches them to an extraordinary height of exaltation."[84]

Mauss and Hubert describe a similar situation as the generative matrix of mana and thus of magic. Only the fact that they actually associate this state of mass suggestibility with the possibility of *making worlds* distinguishes their description from the largely prejudicial discourse of contemporary crowd theorists: "The collecting together of this kind of committed group provides a mental atmosphere where erroneous perceptions may flourish and illusions spread like wildfire; miracles occur in this milieu as a matter of course."[85]

Primitive people, Durkheim argues, are more easily susceptible to collective effervescence, but the principle of participation is universal.[86] Giving a positive twist to the core theme of crowd theory, Durkheim identifies the operative processes as contagion and mimetic resonance, culminating in unified rhythm and movement:

> Every emotion expressed resonates without interference in consciousnesses that are wide open to external impressions, each one echoing the others. The initial impulse is thereby amplified each time it is echoed, like an avalanche that grows as it goes along. . . . Probably because a collective emotion cannot be expressed collectively without some order that permits harmony and unison of movement, these gestures and cries tend to fall into rhythm and regularity, and from there into songs and dances.[87]

Transport becomes transgression as sexual taboos are broken with impunity. In the heat of the moment, individuals exceed themselves and become ecstatic in every sense: at once exalted and external to themselves, rising above their workaday selves. This, says Durkheim, is the root of the religious feeling. But unless that sacred ecstasy can be durably associated with an external object, it will fade as surely as "the celebrant . . . eventually falls exhausted to the ground."[88]

Nor is the sublime ecstasy readily graspable, especially to "such unformed minds," without some kind of concrete support.[89] Enter the totemic sign. "The totem is the flag of the clan"—it is at once fetish and name.[90] It absorbs and routinizes the vital energy of the collective, concretizing/arrogating its charisma. To use a term associated with the critical theory of Georg Lukács, one can say that the totemic sign reifies the mana of the group. As Durkheim notes, "the image goes on calling forth and recalling those emotions even after the assembly is over. Engraved on the cult implements, on the sides of rocks, on shields, and so forth, it lives beyond the gathering. By means of it, the emotions felt are kept perpetually alive and fresh."[91] Mana, notes Vincent Crapanzano, is extimate: "The force of ritual, of the crowd, is experienced as external to, though immanent in, the ritual participant."[92]

This is an ambivalent situation. The totemic sign becomes the affirmative monogram of a moral life in common, meaningfully articulated with other signs in a signifying system. "Because religious force is none other than the collective and anonymous force of the clan and because that force can be conceived of in the form of the totem, the totemic emblem is, so to speak, the visible body of the god."[93] As such the totemic sign is the very paradigm of representational potency, or—as Victor Turner would later characterize the twin faces of ritually supported symbolism—"communication and efficacy."[94] Subsequent discussions of the ritual management of mana-tapu (taboo) in precontact Polynesia have emphasized this efficacious symbolic "binding" of otherwise volatile vital energy: "an economy of *mana* in which generative powers were appropriated, channeled, transformed, and bound."[95]

At the same time, Durkheim effectively provides a primer in the origins of fetishism—the process by which energies and processes arising out of a human collective come not only to be mediated through an external object but also to be alienated, to be perceived as inherent properties and qualities of that object and thus separated from their social origin. In invoking Karl Marx's analysis of commodity fetishism one only needs to substitute "totemic sign" for "commodity" and be prepared to include the work of ritual and its passionate engagements under the term "labor." In both cases, the issue is the translation and displacement of the vital human energies by which new things come into the world.

Marx wrote: "the commodity reflects the social characteristics' of men's own labour as objective characteristics of the products of labour themselves, as the socio-natural properties of these things," and "it is nothing but the definite social relation between men themselves which assumes here, for them, the fantastic form of a relation between things," a "fantastic form" that Marx could only associate with "the misty realm of religion."[96] Durkheim confirms the fetish effect of the totemic sign without condemning it as an alienated reflection: "It is as though the image provoked them directly. Imputing the emotions to the image is all the more natural because, being common to the group, they can only be related to a thing that is equally common to all."[97]

Juxtaposed like this, Durkheim and Marx highlight each other's advantages as well as each other's shortcomings as fetish theorists. Although Marx is elsewhere and in general rigorously attentive to the dialectically constitutive mediation between subjects and objects, he tends to slip into a crude "reflectionist" depiction of the relation between human activity and human ideas whenever those ideas appear in the guise of religion. At that level, it's as if he thinks that the real illusion of commodity fetishism—vital relations between people misrecognized as vital relations between the things that those people themselves have made—is nothing more than a mystifyingly transcendent add-on, made to serve the interests of priests and princes, to the self-sufficiently immanent world of human labor. On this point Durkheim is emphatic and, in fact, takes what he understands as Marxist historical materialism to task for imagining that the world of representations—"the faculty of idealization . . . whether in the individual or in the group"—is an optional extra: "This faculty is not a sort of luxury, which man could do without, but a condition of his existence. If he had not acquired it, he would not be a social being, which is to say that he would not be man."[98]

If fetishism involves misrecognition, then for Durkheim it's a necessary and fundamentally constitutive misrecognition. Social life—not only morality but also reason—would be impossible without it. In Roy Wagner's memorable phrase, it is "an illusion with teeth in it."[99] Ritual mediates the raw mana arising out of collective effervescence into the cooked mana of the totemic sign, which then performatively constitutes the social orders that we recognize as such.

The totemic sign doesn't just *represent* the awareness of the social group: "It serves to create—and is a constitutive element of—that awareness."[100] Durkheim's reading of the mana work of ritual—its mediation of emergent affect and symbolic order, its (re)production of representational potency—leaves crucial clues for theorizing the making (and unmaking) of meaning, value, and charismatic authority in mass-mediated contexts as well.

Pleased to Meet Me

This is, however, also the place to acknowledge some of the reasons that Durkheim has tended to be received as a fundamentally conservative thinker. As the writings that came out of his passionate indignation over the Dreyfus affair show quite clearly, Durkheim was more than sensitive to the oppressive and reactionary force of conservative ideology in industrial societies.[101] When it came to mass democracy, Durkheim tended toward a classic liberal recipe of balancing individual self-determination with sufficient commitment to common concerns—often in rather *sérieux*, not to say po-faced, tonalities.[102] But his image of primitive solidarity unambiguously idealizes uniformity and conformity in a way that is guaranteed to raise eyebrows among those with any kind of commitment to critical theories of ideology and hegemony.

Again, it's not as if Durkheim isn't attentive to the manner in which the force of mana can come to reside not only in the happily harmonious totemic sign—"a thing that is equally common to all"—but also in the personal authority of individuals. This is what he has to say about charismatic prestige in individuals:

> When we obey someone out of respect for the moral authority that we have accorded to him, we do not follow his instructions because they seem wise but because a certain psychic energy intrinsic to the idea we have of that person bends our will and turns it in the direction indicated. . . . This is why . . . to the extent that command is command and works by its own strength, it precludes any idea of deliberation or calculation, but instead is made effective by the very intensity of

the mental state in which it is given. That intensity is what we call moral influence.[103]

It doesn't take a critical theorist to point out that such "moral influence" appears to be a core characteristic of totalitarian authority, on the left and on the right; indeed, such a diagnosis was a regular feature of the crowd theory of Durkheim's own time. Durkheim's detailed analysis in *The Elementary Forms* is of the making of meaning-that-matters in a primitive ritual scenario where, for him, a mechanical unanimity of commitment is taken for granted as the sine qua non of collective flourishing. Consequently, and especially *because*, as I have shown, Durkheim also drops hints about the applicability of his theory of collective effervescence to large-scale industrial societies, one may understandably conclude that Durkheim is, at best, celebrating authority in all its forms and, at worst, legitimating death-and-glory fascist personality cults. How, in political terms, may one reliably distinguish good mana from bad? "What allows us to differentiate," E. Tylor Graham asks, "along Durkheimian lines, a totalitarian government which sustains its power through periodic exterminations of marginal victims from a government that calls for the protection of human life on all levels?"[104]

Durkheim died in 1917, heartbroken by the death, in World War I, of his son André and so many other promising young scholars of his generation. As such, he didn't live to see the rise of fascism. Mauss did, and came to regret his own and his uncle's failure to foresee the potential political effects, in mass societies, of collective effervescence. Steven Lukes quotes from letters that Mauss wrote in the second half of the 1930s to the Danish philosopher and sociologist Svend Ranulf:[105]

One thing that, fundamentally, we never foresaw was how many large modern societies, that have more or less emerged from the Middle Ages in other respects, could be hypnotized like Australians are by their dances, and set in motion like a children's roundabout. This return to the primitive had not been the object of our thoughts. We contented ourselves with several allusions to crowd situations, while it was a question of something quite different. . . . Basically, we never allowed for the extraordinary new possibilities . . . I believe that all this is a real tragedy for us, too powerful a verification of things that we had indicated and the proof that we should have expected this verification through evil rather than a verification through goodness.[106]

These are poignant words to be sure, not least considering the times in which they were written and the sense of dashed idealism that they convey. But I want to suggest that the political extremity of those years—the real sense of an all-or-nothing choice for humanity—left theories of collective effervescence burdened with the appearance of an ethical pseudochoice between transcendent reason and immanent potentiality. I hope that I have at this point at least been able to suggest that Durkheim opens up something different and something more interesting: a starting point for a socially grounded, dialectical theory of world-making in which the mutual mediation of vital potentials and social forms occupies center stage.

Still, a crucial shortcoming in Durkheim's ritual theory is its inability to explain *addressability*—or, to put it in Althusserian language, interpellation: how is it that certain human subjects and certain nonhuman objects come to resonate with each other so as to allow a constitutive bond to form between them, a bond that allows both subject and object to *become themselves via each other*? Durkheim offers precious little to work with when, considering the ecstasy of the corroboree, one might want to ask: why *this* sign? Of course, as I noted above, one of the great advances of Durkheim's theory of totemism was that, unlike earlier theories of religion (and some later ones, for example Malinowski's), it stressed the arbitrariness of the totemic sign. The totemic animal or plant didn't represent the clan in the sense that its palpable properties were considered desirably iconic of the tribe's aspirations to, say, fierceness or majesty (of this, the humble witchetty grub totem is a perennially bathetic reminder).

Having said that, there's something unsatisfying about Durkheim's description of the moment at which the free-flowing collective energy of the clan-crowd gets laminated onto the totemic signifier: it seems at once entirely contingent and completely tautological. The totemic sign interpellates the individual participant in the ritual because it happens to be what is before his eyes at the crucial moment of ecstatic self-transcendence. But it "happens" to be before his eyes at that crucial moment because it's already the totemic sign: "Now what does he see around him? What is available to his senses, and what attracts his attention, is the multitude of totemic images surrounding him."[107] Conveniently, the circle of overdetermined representational potency (and ideological interpellation) is closed as the primitive discovers that he already bears the same marks on his body: "The decorations on various parts of his body are so many totemic marks. Repeated everywhere and in every form, how could that image not fail to stand out in the mind with exceptionally sharp relief?"[108] With a nod to The Replacements, one can only exclaim "pleased to meet me."[109]

Of course the tautological structure of interpellation is a standard trope in psychoanalytically inflected critical theory; Slavoj Žižek's work is full of jokes about it ("no wonder you look like X — you *are* X!"). But the problem with Durkheim's model of the corroboree, as with most mana moment discourses on the primitive, is its utter historylessness. It provides no sense of how one would trace a particular history of constitutive resonances in a particular place — in other words the historicity of what in the introduction I dubbed (and in chapter 4 elaborate as) a mimetic archive. And the collective uniformity of the elementary forms of religious life, as theorized by Durkheim, does little to explain what one might call our personal addressability: how, as subjects, we are interpellated by people, situations, and image objects, in more variable and situational ways.

The clan totem, as Durkheim points out, is hereditary and collective. As such, the problem of interpellation it poses is simply one of how ritual aligns people with, and invests them in, predecided generic badges of identity, which is what, in Durkheim's view, makes them social persons. But what about the relation between such collective categories and the more particularizing, even idiosyncratic dimensions of desire and identification?[110] This, too, as Michel Leiris notes, is a question of fetishism: "True fetishes are the objectivized forms of our desire — this sentimental ambivalence, a tender sphinx which one nourishes always at the center of oneself."[111] Durkheim does, briefly, address "individual totems," totems that "belong to each individual, that express his personality, and whose cult he celebrates privately."[112] But the individual totem appears in his discussion as a kind of personal supplement to the chief matter of collective experience. It's as if Durkheim leaves us only with the "forced choice" of ideology, the injunction to love that which is obligatory, to become the subjects that we always already are.[113] Indeed this is, according to Victor Turner, one of the main functions of ritual: to turn the obligatory into the desirable.[114] By the terms of the primitive settlement, this ideology-sustaining work of ritual can appear as an innocent, even joyful mechanism of solidarity in primitive societies where subjectivity is supposed to be unproblematically aligned with a shared symbolic order.

The question of a more intimate addressability is by no means reducible to a "psychological" problem. The presumption of highly intimate and individualized forms of resonance and identification—as well as all the group-based categories of identity that solicit imagination and allegiance—are, rather, anticipated and built into the generalized address of mass publicity. Indeed, this is a core aspect of the mana of mass publicity: its intimate anonymity—the way in which a *generalized* communication can feel as if it is addressing us in the depths of our *particular* personality. An obvious and rather heavy-handed example of this effect would be something like Apple's "Think Different" advertising campaign, in which our desire for non-conformist individuality is flattered by means of an invitation to conform to a standardized message. But the point is, of course, that insofar as the mana "works," it doesn't simply regiment us by channeling our attention back into a centralized, corporately owned signifier (the Apple brand). It also actually does activate quite unforeseeable associations and impulses, which then do and do not become part of the extimate structure of the Apple brand/totem.

Just as, for Durkheim, the individual totem is a kind of personal supplement to the clan totem, magic appears in his work as an individualized, entirely instrumental derivative of the morality-making end-in-itself of religious ritual. Magic, says Durkheim, is a matter of "secular utility" while religious commitments are "categorical imperatives."[115] Now, clearly this kind of distinction has profound implications for any understanding of the political dimensions of ritual. It's as if primitive religious unanimity is always already legitimate for Durkheim, rather than a contestable matter of ideological hegemony, entrepreneurially produced and reproduced in a politically contested field.

One might, for instance, read Durkheim against himself and interpret magic as a kind of subaltern mana work vis-à-vis the priestly establishment. In fact, Mauss and Hubert seem at points to encourage such a reading, arguing that practices called magical are defined by their prototransgressive marginality in relation to the hegemonic morality of religion: "A magical rite is *any rite which does not play a part in organized cults*—it is private, secret, mysterious and approaches the limit of a prohibited rite."[116] Unlike in Durkheim, for Mauss and Hubert the distinction between magic and religion is as much political and historical as it is logical: "All Jews were magicians in the eyes of the Alexandrians, for example, as well as for the mediaeval church."[117]

In fact *The Elementary Forms* is full of examples of rituals at which specialists—priests, shamans, medicine men—officiate. But the set piece mise-en-scène of the corroboree is, by comparison, notably headless. Not only does it provide no sense of charismatic agency in the activation and transmission of mana, but even if one takes the totemic sign to be the charismatic agent of the corroboree, there is no way to specify how its vital potential arises out of particular histories, out of particular mimetic archives. In fact, the usefulness of Durkheim's ambitious attempt to reconcile the affective *liveness* of participation with the semiotic durability of representation and, by extension, his immensely suggestive nods in the direction of the mana of mass publicity, are both, in the end, hamstrung by his unwillingness to extend the political analysis that he grants modern European life to the primitive—and, by implication, universally constitutive—ritual scenario.

Fascinated Presence

We have the tools, then, to think through how immanence and transcendence are mediated, and thus how worlds emerge, in a particular kind of constitutive encounter of which ritual stands as a key example. Of course not all ritual is of the spectacular, orgiastic, or even highly formalized and centralized kind that the term tends to invoke. And yet, as we will see in part II, it might be useful to keep the model of ritual encounter in mind as I pursue the problem that inevitably arises out of thinking about the making and remaking of worlds: the making and remaking of the selves that will feel resonantly addressed by those worlds and come to inhabit and uphold them. Across world-making encounters and subject-making encounters, mana persists as a symptom of order and of the excess that at once grounds and troubles order.

Plenty of anthropologists have considered the political dimensions of ritual in productive and provocative ways.[118] From Arnold van Gennep's *The Rites of Passage* to Victor Turner's *The Ritual Process* and beyond, theorists of ritual have been interested in the apparent paradox that the constitution of social order seems to require the controlled and limited destitution of established identities and hierarchies. The structural analysis of ritual in anthropology has tended, following Durkheim's and Van Gennep's early agenda-setting discussions, to explore constitution and destitution as alternating phases in a ritual sequence and has often also interpreted the annual ritual calendar itself as involving an alternation between sacred and profane seasons.

Philosopher-anthropologist Ernesto de Martino gave the theme an interesting twist in the late 1940s when, in his *Primitive Magic*, he argued that ritual—whether magical or religious does not much matter here—is a historical drama of world loss and world redemption. To imagine world loss as purely destitutive and world redemption as purely constitutive would be too reductive. Rather, on the one side, the efficacy of magical action depends on both the drama of destitutive world loss (the suspension of familiar symbolic orders and subject-object boundaries) and the constitutive potentials for participation that are triggered in states of collective excitement or agitation. On the other side, ritual depends on the corollary drama of constitutive world redemption and the inevitable destitutive potentials that any new drawing of subject-object/inside-outside boundaries introduces.

One might say that De Martino's fundamental question is the one that Durkheim's ritual theory at once tries to account for and yet still, in the end, takes for granted: how is a lived world grounded? And why *this* world rather than another? If religion, according to Durkheim, has the character of a categorical imperative, then what is it that distinguishes the imperative of *the one sacred order* from its many competitors? Malinowski touches on the problem when he observes: "A battle, a sailing regatta, one of the big tribal gatherings for trading purposes, an Australian lay-corroboree, a village brawl, are all from the social as well as from the psychological point of view essentially examples of crowd effervescence. Yet no religion is generated on any of these occasions. Thus the *collective* and the *religious*, though impinging on each other, are by no means co-extensive."[119]

Malinowski's objection, while relevant, is poorly formulated. A Durkheimian might retort, first, that collective effervescence is a necessary but not a sufficient condition for the emergence and reproduction of religion and, second, that the lively situations mentioned by Malinowski might certainly contribute in important ways to the making of moral solidarity in ways that might yet coincide with the expansive agenda of Durkheim's argument.[120] The important issue isn't so much the fact that there are forms of collective effervescence that don't produce what might be called "religion," but rather the question of why some kinds of charismatic incitements-containments-proliferations of collective effervescence become experientially compelling and authoritative and others don't.

In that regard, it is significant that De Martino uses language that strongly stresses the charismatic basis of both the constitutive and the destitutive dimensions of world making: he writes of the loss and redemption of "controlling presence."[121] One might read the notion of controlling presence as the result of a compelling mediation of immanence and transcendence, of mana mediated through symbolically stabilizing objects or representations (think totemic signs, sacred objects, charismatic images, brands, and such), but therefore also always—fascinatingly, seductively—threatening to leak out of those stabilizing objects or representations, and thus requiring constant ritual work both to reanimate and to restabilize a given world. A controlling presence is the experience of a world that *works*, that has the quality of mana-ness—of being efficacious: at once revealing an order and inviting vital, resonant engagement.[122] For De Martino, the magician, the shaman, or the priest (think also the politician, the charismatic celebrity) becomes the mediator whose action ensures the *compelling presence*—the constitutive resonance—of a world, as well as of the subjective experiences of self, identification, and desire that are possible within that world: "In this sense, the sorcerer be-

comes a kind of *magical Christ*, the mediator for the whole community, through whom the 'being-here' may be redeemed from the danger of not being here."[123]

Crucially, De Martino's model is based on a figure of *encounter* as constitutive crisis. Destabilizing encounters with threatening situations, people, or objects put pressure on the controlling presence of an existing world, such that a new controlling presence has to be achieved out of the encounter itself—what Roy Wagner calls "controlling the culture shock of daily experience."[124] De Martino presumes that this is a competitive and volatile process; a given world is compelling because of the constitutive force that it exerts against the competing worlds that threaten it.[125] What Durkheim presumes as the categorical imperative—the transcendent moral demand/guarantee of a constituted world—is, for De Martino, always and necessarily a work in progress and open to question. That is why the mana work of magic and religion exist: to manage the anxiety that attaches to the fact that all worlds must appear to be something impossible— immanently self-grounding.

> To a degree, the problem of magic powers is linked very closely to the question: "quis custodiet custodem?" or who shall supervise the supervisor? Obviously, the system of guarantees cannot conclude with some exterior guarantee that is utterly absolute and final; it must have the interior guarantee of a thought that can develop a clear, disciplined, and comprehensive point of view, one that is able to defend itself and have the courage of its convictions.[126]

The figure of encounter is important here because even as maintaining the controlling presence of a world might, from one standpoint, seem like an entirely defensive exercise—making sure that the threatening other remains other—it's actually a process of constant and risky compromise. The controlling presence of a world is sustained through setting up relations with potentially troubling external phenomena such that they become both us and not us, at once world-internal and opening up to an unfathomable outside. A double, a spirit-companion, an alter ego, a being-with, becomes necessary, De Martino suggests, when the controlling presence that guarantees a habitual life world is threatened.

The magical experience of a presence under tension, that is in danger of discharging and must be restrained . . . is expressed in the representation and experience of a "beyond" that is outside of the presence, a reflection, an echo, a shadow, a similarity, a double, etc.: the man and the stone, the man and the animal or the man and his shadow are as 'two in one' or 'one in two,' and the presence that cannot hold its ground when confronted by the world rids itself of the risk by making a compromise.[127]

De Martino is describing a phenomenon identified by Robert Codrington in the work that, as we saw in chapter 1, got the whole long debate on mana started.[128] The Melanesian *atai* is "something that is connected to a person in a particular and intimate way and which, because of this, is sacred: *something that struck the imagination from the moment it was seen,* something that the individual considered marvelous, unless it was other people who had made it appear to him as such."[129] The *atai* is an intimate companion of the primitive sort. But couldn't one just as well transpose the following description of the subject's decisive encounter into the fetish space of mass publicity, where the outcome is our companionate "participation" in political and commercial brands?

His "presence" [i.e., the subject's self-identity] is fascinated, it risks being led astray and remaining fixed upon the object, without being able to go beyond it, and so, no longer sustains itself as a presence. The redemption consists in experiencing and considering the object as an 'alter ego,' with which a regulated and lasting [and, one might add, profitable] relationship is established. . . . The process of objectification is half accomplished in the form of a compromise — the presence that is in danger of losing control masters itself by attaching its own problematic unity to that of the object.[130]

The great advantage of De Martino's approach is that it stresses the existential gap that the companion object, the *atai*, papers over so as to produce the impression of a self-grounding controlling presence, a self-grounding world. In Lacanian terms, one might perhaps interpret the *atai* as a "partial object," a stand-in that at once invokes and disavows the traumatic encounter with the inevitable remainder, the kernel of the Real that will not be symbolized and that troubles any would-be self-contained world extimately—at once from without and from within.

The critical discourse of modernity—and I include Lacanian psychoanalysis under that banner—congratulates itself on its steadfast commitment to resisting ideological closure. As Ernesto Laclau insists: "The only democratic society is one which permanently shows the contingency of its foundations."[131] But can we be so sure that we are always able to tell the difference between a steadfast "dwelling with contingency" and an uncritical absorption in ideology? Isn't there a risk that the figure of the critical modernist subject, heroically renouncing all reassurance of tradition, is itself a kind of *atai*, a "compromise" object through which "the presence that is in danger of losing control masters itself by attaching its own problematic unity to that of the object"?

We Smile

It is as if, in a general way, the discovery/invention of mana and primitive mentality during the second half of the nineteenth century allowed a deep ambiguity internal to European ideas of communion and communication—namely, the dialectical relation of participation and representation, of immanence and transcendence—to achieve at least the appearance of a therapeutic resolution: the primitive settlement that projected the division of immanence and transcendence out onto the division between primitive and civilized peoples. In Mauss's terms, one might say that the primitive settlement was a projection triggered by and responding to an overwhelming social need. In De Martino's terms, one could say that the primitive settlement answered to a crisis in the philosophical discourse of modernity triggered by the ongoing confrontation with non- or differently modern worlds. Anthropologists, as the mediating priests, were perfectly positioned to step in and redeem the controlling presence of a European self-image unsettled by the provocation of a vast new international apparatus of mass publicity and the uncanny new forms of encounter and self-displacement, not to mention the extraordinary new experiments in totalitarian authority, that it enabled.

Still, even here—perhaps especially here—there is room for comedy. As Žižek memorably observes, totalitarian command invites nothing so much as overidentification, the kind of mimetic conformity to the demands of authority that is so slavish and so painstakingly complete as to blur the line between sincerity and parody.[132] The kind of radical and indiscriminate participation that was supposedly characteristic of primitive peoples isn't just the mark of crowds regressing under the charisma of a demagogue. On occasion it has also quite deliberately been used as a wrench to be thrown into the spinning wheels of power. Among the Tungus shamans of eastern Siberia, classically studied by Sergei Shirokogoroff in the 1930s, such a state of participation was known as *olon*. De Martino reproduces a wonderful story:

> V. L. Prikonsky [by way of Shirokogoroff] reports an interesting case of collective counter-colonial olonism: during a parade of the third Transbaikalia battalion of Cossacks, one unit, composed entirely of natives, suddenly entered a state of olon. Instead of carrying out their colonel's orders—he was a Russian—the men repeated them in chorus. The colonel naturally became angry and began to abuse the men; they repeated his abuse.[133]

We smile. But the joke is only funny because it's so sad. In the world of this story, as in any totalitarian scenario, there are only two possibilities: total obedience (sincere) or total obedience (parodic). The liberal desire is for individuality to reassert itself against overwhelming command and control—if only by carving out a backstage or underground sphere in which it can thrive away from the merciless eye of Big Brother. The liberal imagination's desire is organized around the drama of freedom versus servitude, subject versus object, and—when it comes to the mana of mass publicity—the sovereign choice of the consumer-citizen.

But why is the liberal imagination so threatened by any figure of subjectivity that might involve an ambivalent compromise, along the lines of De Martino's "double," his "alter ego"? Why is Codrington's *atai* an eminently acceptable way of talking about primitive subjectivity, but suddenly, troublingly provocative as a model of civilized self-making? Why, when it comes to making sense of how people come to understand themselves as participants in mass-mediated public spheres (as opposed to primitive ritual contexts) does theory so often fall back on a crude either/or diagnostic scheme in which subjects are either autonomous (and thus critical) or heteronomous (and thus co-opted)?

As we shall see in chapter 3, the insistence on the self-determining agency of the liberal subject—and its corollary, the autonomy of the aesthetic object—stand in the way of an open-ended, ethnographically useful theory of the mana of mass society. In the next chapter, I'll be exploring the intersection of two anxieties that might at first sight appear to be unrelated but that, I will suggest, are in fact mutually constitutive. On the one hand, an anxiety about public address in which an immaculate acknowledgment as "who we really are" becomes indistinguishable from our complete erasure as self-determining subjects. On the other hand, an anxiety about the place of mana in "civilized" societies, whereby its magical effects have to be quarantined in a space marked "aesthetic": the space of art. My task in chapter 3 will be a critical working through of the interrelation between these two anxieties—one that ensures the autonomous subject, another that ensures the autonomous object—in order to clear the ground for an affirmative theory of the mana of mass society in chapter 4.

Part II

The Subject in the Social

Chapter 3

Anxious Autonomy

The Agony of Perfect Addressability
and the Aesthetic Settlement

In European mythology the most iconic representation of the anx-
iously self-determining subject is perhaps the story of Odysseus and
the Sirens in Homer's *Odyssey*. The Sirens, with their "irresistibly flattering" song; the Sirens who "with a peculiar lack of scruples, never
perform their own repertoire, only the music of those who pass by."[1]
The anxious subject is of course Odysseus, tied to the mast of his ship
as it sails past the Sirens' island, knowing that it is precisely the song
that speaks to him and him alone that he must resist.[2]

Thus far, my central concern has been how to rethink the making
and unmaking of the worlds that, more or less compellingly, invite
identification and inhabitation. Throughout, I have emphasized *encounter* as an analytical starting point: encounter as a site of crisis
and, by the same token, as a site of constitutive resonance. My discussion of how worlds come to be not only meaningful but also compellingly vital inevitably led me toward the question of interpellation. How do the worlds we encounter and inhabit *hail* us, to use
Louis Althusser's term? How do they address us such that, in our
encounter with them, we "become ourselves"? This is, crucially, not
just a question of believing or not believing, of accepting or rejecting
ideological propositions. It is just as much, perhaps even more fundamentally, a question of the sensuously resonant *object encounters*

through which one becomes—more or less consciously, more or less deliberately—a subject.

At the end of chapter 2, I moved toward the suggestion that not only inhabitable worlds but also subjective self-relations are triggered by encounters that give rise to more or less provisional settlements: the ambivalent terms of attachment, identification, and desire. These terms are ambivalent because, like all settlements, they attempt something paradoxical: to establish clear boundaries of "me" and "you," subject and object, out of relations that are premised on resonance rather than on separation, on participation rather than representation. In part I of this book, I grappled with the settlements that, in this paradoxical way, both separated and joined the "primitive" and the "civilized," following the trail left by the vital play of mana as telltale symptom. In part II, I shift my emphasis from the social to the subject (although of course the two presuppose each other). If anthropological analyses of primitive mana have tended to invoke the stable collective as both the starting point and the destination, then inquiries into civilized mana—the mana of mass politics and mass marketing—are much more preoccupied with the integrity of the autonomous (and thus supposedly critical) subject vis-à-vis the homogenizing threat of the collective (crowds, mobs, political and commercial manipulation).

This division into primitive collectives and civilized individuals is an elementary form of the primitive settlement. But as it turns out, this is not just a prejudicial subject-ethics, whereby primitives merge with their group and civilized subjects stand apart. It also involves an object-ethics, a way of thinking about, for example, the difference between encounters with the apparently treacherous seduction of consumer advertising images and the supposedly legitimate magic of encounters with those objects and images defined as art. As we shall see, the anxiety that emanates from the need to keep subjects autonomous and critical involves a parallel inquiry into the integrity of objects and the ways in which they solicit our desires. In part I, I argued that mana points to the extimacy of the social in the subject—Durkheim's "moral power that, while immanent in us, also represents something in us that is other than ourselves"—and that this is a relation of mimetic resonance. Similarly, in the present chapter, I will suggest that the *aesthetic settlement* provided a compromise that would allow the modern, autonomous subject a space of extimately mimetic resonance that wouldn't call into question his or her precious critical integrity.

The specter of Theodor Adorno hangs heavy over any discussion that invokes terms like *critical subject*, *mimesis*, and *aesthetic autonomy*. Indeed, this chapter, having set up the paradox of the autonomous subject, moves toward a detailed engagement with Adorno's thought. Here I hope to pay him the properly filial tribute of some tough dialectical love: thinking "Adorno against Adorno." The core of my argument will be that Adorno's rabid dismissal of commodified culture is problematic not because it doesn't grant consumers enough *agency* but rather because it doesn't grant them enough *patiency*. I respond, therefore, not by turning away from Adorno but rather by requiring Adorno to live up to his own dialectical standards. Can Adorno's theory of aesthetic experience as constitutively resonant encounter be pushed into the places where he would never allow it go—that is, into the places of mass culture?[3] That would allow an exploration of the mana of mass society as something more open-ended, something more ambiguous than simply the "all-powerful system of communication"[4] of a totally administered world.

In Odysseus's encounter with the Sirens, the prospect of being *perfectly addressable* by their "irresistibly flattering" song is terrifying because, in yielding, Odysseus becomes unable to tell the difference between the acknowledgment of his "true self" and the mortal danger of his complete erasure as a self-determining subject. This, I will be suggesting in the present chapter, is the myth image that haunts the vast majority of latter-day critiques of mass publicity as well, from Horkheimer and Adorno's thesis about the culture industry as an engine of mass manipulation to much more recent Internet-enabled fantasies about microtargeting and neuromarketing. It's a haunting image because it troubles any certainty about the difference between the self-realization of the subject as an autonomous actor and the total co-optation of the subject by outside forces. If the Sirens sing a song that is Odysseus's singular song, and if Odysseus for that reason must resist it, then Odysseus's survival as a subject is, paradoxically, premised on refusing that which is most deeply "himself."

We Are Not Magicians

Marketers, like ancient magicians before them, have always been
under suspicion for trafficking in what Peter Sloterdijk calls "intimacy exploitation."[5] Even before marketing assumed its modern
form toward the end of the nineteenth century, marketers have been
the targets of moralizing attacks.[6] Pimps, conmen, silver-tongued
serpents; these mana workers stand accused of exercising undue,
quasi-magical influence and of concealing corrupt motives. In response, marketers have tended to adopt a populist stance, insisting
that consumers are savvy, that they make informed and sovereign
choices, and that marketing, far from manipulating consumers, actually empowers them. Marketing exists, the argument goes, to make
sure that the consumer's wish really is the manufacturer's command.
We are not magicians, say the marketers; we are public servants who
happen to work in the realm of the imagination.

Having extended early global tendrils in the interwar period, a
rampantly revitalized marketing machine rode the post–World
War II consumer boom. Its perceived push toward a total colonization of both inner and outer spaces set off a series of moral panics
about societies tightly directed from corporate boardrooms, where
newfangled psychological techniques joined hands with the latest
subliminal media strategies to wire ordinary people's wants directly
into the production line, while at the same time turning mass con-
sumerism into the preferred technology of Cold War affect management.[7] In the 1950s Vance Packard rode the best-seller lists with *The
Hidden Persuaders*; the 1960s and 1970s saw an intellectual refine-
ment of such popular paranoiac discourses into subtle protocols of
semiotic suspicion. Ads were there to be "decoded," the better to
discover what their deceptively breezy surfaces might disclose about
would-be hegemonic ideologies of class, sex, and race in the North
Atlantic imperium.[8]

The locus classicus of the paranoid style in mass cultural analysis
is Max Horkheimer and Theodor Adorno's essay "The Culture Industry: Enlightenment as Mass Deception," written during their Califor-
nian exile in the early 1940s. We may think we're being entertained,
write Horkheimer and Adorno, but "entertainment is the prolonga-
tion of work under capitalism. It is sought by those who want to es-

cape the mechanized labour process so that they can cope with it again."[9] We may think we're getting real pleasure, but we're really just getting its semblance, a kind of perpetual striptease that always defers authentic engagement and genuine gratification. The culture industry gives us a "promissory note of pleasure" that is never cashed in. Instead "the diner must be satisfied with reading the menu."[10]

The "relentless unity of the culture industry" ensures that "the same babies grin endlessly from magazines, and endlessly the jazz machine pounds."[11] As a consumer one is only allowed to be an individual by not really being one — or, what amounts to the same thing, by conforming exactly to what the prescribed image of individuality permits: "Individuals are tolerated only as far as their wholehearted identity with the universal is beyond question."[12] Not only, say Horkheimer and Adorno, does the culture industry feed us nothing but standardized banality (including banality that is, cunningly, differentiated in a standardized way), but it also forcibly retards our ability to cultivate our human judgment by bombarding us with the inert facticity of special effects and fetishistic fragments:

> The withering of imagination and spontaneity in the consumer of culture today need not be traced back to psychological mechanisms. The products themselves, especially the most characteristic, the sound film, cripple those faculties through their objective makeup. They are so constructed that their adequate comprehension requires a quick, observant, knowledgeable cast of mind but positively debars the spectator from thinking, if he is not to miss the fleeting facts.[13]

The end result is slavish passivity: "Capitalist production hems [consumers] in so tightly, in body and soul, that they unresistingly succumb to whatever is proffered to them."[14]

One might imagine that consumers have some say by voting with their pocketbooks. But no: "Even if the masses have, as customers, an influence on the cinema, it remains as abstract as the box-office returns which have replaced discriminating applause: the mere choice between Yes and No to what is offered, an integral part of the disproportion between concentrated power and dispersed impotence."[15] Resistance has been rendered entirely anemic: "Even on those occasions when the public rebels against the pleasure industry it displays the feebleness systematically installed in it by that industry."[16] In any case, the culture industry has already co-opted the critique: "The admission that films disseminate ideologies is itself disseminated ideology."[17]

Unsurprisingly, starting in the 1970s, there was an energetic backlash to such totalizing tones. By what right, cultural studies scholars demanded, could anyone assume that audiences were being brainwashed by the mass publicity machine? Wasn't there plenty of evidence in youth subcultures and indie fanzines that consumers were doing all kinds of creative and unpredictable things? Perhaps such creative production-consumption could even be interpreted as resistance to the dominant meanings that the culture industry was trying to impose?[18]

But as anthropologist-novelist Amitav Ghosh observes, "in resisting the powers that form us, we allow them to gain control of all meaning; this is their moment of victory: it is in this way that they inflict their final and most terrible defeat."[19] Just so, the "final and most terrible" irony of the populist backlash against the audience manipulation thesis was that in celebrating popular resistance, it actually did more than the most totalizing manipulation theorists to sustain and reproduce the idea that the culture industry really *was* a grand brainwashing conspiracy, held back only by the scrappy kitchen sink heroism of ordinary people.[20] Michel Foucault teaches us that pleasure and power are inextricable, since power constitutes us as subjects in part by recruiting us through pleasure—including the pleasures of resistance: "Pleasure and power do not cancel or turn back against one another; they seek out, overlap, and reinforce one another. They are linked together by complex mechanisms and devices of excitation and incitement."[21]

Brian Moeran's and Daniel Miller's pioneering ethnographic studies of advertising production in the 1990s were useful correctives to the prevailing paranoiac presumption, because they showed that marketing is so messy and subject to so many contingencies that it becomes hard to sustain the image of the culture industry as a seamless ideological relay mechanism.[22] And yet here one is reminded of the bumper sticker: just because you're paranoid doesn't mean people aren't out to get you. Or as Adorno remarked in a letter to Horkheimer: "if one is faced with a choice between a paranoid fantasy about paranoid reality and the stupidity of healthy common sense, [then] paranoia is still more productive."[23] Just because mass publicity may not be a seamlessly functioning top-down mechanism of command and control doesn't mean that it doesn't operate by recruiting you into particular ideological complicities. Indeed, at a certain level the whole postwar debate on mass publicity as conspiracy displays an almost touching Wizard of Oz–style obsession with centralized and intentional control—the better to shore up the ever-threatened figure of the critically self-determining, autonomous (consumer) subject: the hero who will, in the end, save the world by saving himself.

But here we need to tread carefully. Judith Butler rightly notes the diminishing returns of a critical practice in which every apparently new departure turns out to be another iteration of the moment "when we think we have found a point of opposition to domination, and then realize that that very point of opposition is the instrument through which domination works, and that we have unwittingly enforced the powers of domination through our participation in its opposition."[24] Such a strategy always knows what it will find in advance. My own take is a little different. I don't read "domination" or "power" as a system that has already laid out and precontained all possible moves, especially those that might look like resistance. Instead, I'm interested in the problem of how both the supposed agencies of "domination" and those of "resistance" emerge as putatively coherent objects—for example "the culture industries" and "the critical subject," respectively. Perhaps, with a nod to chapter 2, we could call such objects *atai*s: world-redeeming partial objects that help us to make sense of and manage encounters that might otherwise be more ambiguous and unsettling.

Half the Money I Spend . . .

The nineteenth-century marketing genius John Wanamaker is supposed to have quipped: "Half the money I spend on advertising is wasted; the trouble is I don't know which half!"[25] Wanamaker's witticism is usually taken to be a wry lament about the imprecision of mass-market publicity, which, while expensive, is inevitably going to address a lot of people who do not belong to the intended target audience.

Thank God, then, for new media! Had Wanamaker lived today when, by means of the Internet, messages can be tailored and precision delivered to exactly those people who, as far as the algorithms can tell, might reasonably be expected to want to see them, he would have had no reason to wax sardonic. "One can only imagine the enthusiasm that pioneers of advertising and modern marketing like John Wanamaker would feel with the 'Pay-per-click' model," simpers one sales pitch for online advertising.[26]

Not everyone, of course, is thrilled with the new narrowcasting. Some worry that a world of customized information delivery will undermine the very foundations of liberal democracy. Cass Sunstein, for example, argues that "people should be exposed to materials that they would not have chosen in advance," and that "many or most citizens should have a range of common experiences," rather than being allowed to burrow further and further down into microniches of complacently narcissistic particularity.[27]

No doubt engaging with unexpected inputs is a Good Thing. But my concern is with a different and deeper anxiety that I take to be both ancient and especially characteristic of the present: the agony of perfect addressability, the fantasy/nightmare of being addressed as *exactly* who you are. For a long time, critical cultural theorists have insisted on some version of the autonomous subject as a bulwark against the ideological manipulations of mass publicity. But today, interactive digital media, algorithms, and the new subliminal marketing are putting new pressure on this position. For how, neuromarketers demand, can we speak of manipulation when marketing no longer necessarily addresses a self that stands apart from the marketing apparatus itself—if our desires are always already immanent in the network?[28] Critical theorists used to speak of the consciousness industry. But why worry about consciousness if we can now simply look inside people's heads to find out whether the mana is working: "brain scans show that when you put Apple 'true believers' in an fMRI machine, their brains light up in the same areas normally triggered by religion."[29]

This is of course not just an intimate drama but, at the same time, the terrifying prospect of a totally "reconciled" world in which the refuge of subjectivity-as-difference or pause, the paradoxical comfort of not being quite at home in the world, will disappear. It is "the panic which is ready to break out at any moment today: human beings expect the world, which is without issue, to be set ablaze by a universal power which they themselves are and over which they are powerless."[30] *A universal power which they themselves are and over which they are powerless*: what could be a better protodescription of the promise/panic of the Internet sublime and, for that matter, of mana?

Perfect addressability—a situation in which there is no perceptible gap between the media that address me and my innermost understandings of myself—appears at once as the perfection of marketing and as a state of psychosis. One feels a familiar kind of alarm for Caden Cotard, the antihero of Charlie Kaufman's magnificently eccentric film *Synechdoche, NY*, when he keeps encountering himself as the actual protagonist of the television ads and promotional materials that address him.[31] And John Durham Peters, reflecting on psychiatric syndromes in which viewers think newsreaders on television are actually speaking to them personally, points out that it's actually much more remarkable that most of the time most of us are able to remember that they are *not*, given the "intimate, chatty, one-on-one" tone of their address.[32]

This would seem to be an odd time still to be invoking those Patron Saints of Pessimism, Horkheimer and Adorno. Isn't their gloomy diagnosis of mass manipulation and consumer brainwashing entirely outmoded nowadays? As Timothy Malefyt and Robert Morais put it:

> The notion that advertising surreptitiously manipulates unwary shoppers into consuming unnecessary wants and needs is a carryover from a time when perceptions of shopping dynamics held consumers to be impressionable and submissive characters without agency of their own. . . . Consumer decision making is more informed than ever; with Internet search engines, Web communities, and online social networks, people have more information available to them than at any other time in history.[33]

Once upon a time, the argument goes, consumers may well have been forced passively to accept standardized product offerings, advertised to them in massified forms from on high—what advertising pros call "spray-and-pray."[34] Nowadays, however, the interactive and personalizing potentials of the Internet and social media, by way of crowdsourcing and such, have rebirthed consumer-citizens as "prosumers"—participatory and collaborative coproducers of the goods they consume.[35]

But how is the evergreen celebration of consumer agency to be reconciled with another message that marketing simultaneously disseminates: that my individuality as a consumer is no longer separate (if it ever really was) from the markets in which it finds its realization? It's not just that we now supposedly have more control over the products we buy as well as when and how we buy them. Nor is it only that data mining and real-time digital interactivity have made possible forms of surveillance that fundamentally undermine older conventions of privacy. It goes far deeper than that. One of the symptomatic tropes of the times is that, by means of digital technologies and the traces that I leave every time I hit a key or click a mouse, my subjectivity is no longer strictly internal to me as an individual but rather always already externalized in cyberspace.

Anthropologists and philosophers of language and culture will argue that in itself this is nothing new. If anything, they will suggest, it marks the long-overdue breakdown of an Enlightenment ideology of self-grounding subjectivity that was never very convincing in the first place. We have always been "in" the objects and the environments that allow us to emerge "out of" them. I don't disagree. But having registered, with Bruno Latour, that "we have never been modern,"[36] what kinds of tools can help us not only describe emergent networks of objects (some of whom, qua humans, understand themselves as subjects), but also account for our imaginative and affective investments in some of those objects rather than in others?

At a first approach, one might say that the figure of the infinitely solicitous algorithm ("it knows you better than any mortal could") is, in its intimate anonymity, at once disconcerting and reassuring. If there's something magical about it, then that is perhaps entirely appropriate. Ioan Couliano, scholar of Renaissance magic, writes this: "Like a spy wanting to procure material for future erotic blackmail, the magician must collect all the indices that permit him to file his subject under some classification or other."[37] Couliano's magician has to know his target the way only a lover can, and yet at the same time remain above the fray—utterly unsusceptible to the erotic resonance. What an extraordinary *askesis*; what superhuman discipline! "Bruno's manipulator," says Couliano, "is the man who knows all about love, *in order to learn not to love*."[38] In other words, for the true magician, the practice of magic requires a paradoxical stance: a kind of erotic impartiality—a kind of utterly committed indifference. Who or what, really, is capable of this kind of detachment? Perhaps only the algorithms that today do their impersonal work the better to reveal us to ourselves—bearing in mind that for practitioners of the occult arts, all revealing is at the same time re-veiling.

The New Subliminal

U, a digital anthropologist working in the corporate sector, is the aptly named protagonist of Tom McCarthy's satirical novel *Satin Island*. U gets tasked with producing a report for the Koob-Sassen Project, an enigmatic initiative whose only readily intelligible features are its intense prestige and its all-encompassing ambition. In the course of his increasingly disconsolate attempts to get started on the report, U moves through a series of illuminations regarding the requisite relation between participation and representation (whenever anyone asks him how the report is coming along, he replies, "oh you know—it's finding its form").

At first U wonders how to write the report. Then he decides that the report should bypass representation altogether and be a kind of experiential, participatory medium—something to be not so much read as inhabited: "What if just *coexisting* with these objects and this person, letting my own edges run among them, occupying this moment, or, more to the point allowing *it* to occupy *me*, to blot and soak me up, rather than treating it as feed-data for a later stock-taking—what if all this maybe, *was* part of the Great Report? What if the Report might somehow, in some way, be lived, be *be*-d, rather than written?"[39]

Finally U comes to the realization that nothing at all needs to be done—because the report already exists. It *is* the capillary network of data, the one-to-one map of our digitally mediated world: "a new spectre, an even more grotesque realization, presented itself to me: the truly terrifying thought wasn't that the Great Report might be un-writable, but—quite the opposite—that it had *already been written*. Not by a person, nor even by some nefarious cabal, but simply by a neutral and indifferent binary system that had given rise to itself, moved by itself and would perpetuate itself: some auto-alphaing and auto-omegating script—that that's what it *was*."[40] What price ethnography now? "Write everything down, said Malinowski. But the thing is, now, it *is* all written down."[41]

If anything (and the presence of Lévi-Strauss is explicit and strong here), U doesn't need to think the network because the network is already thinking him. Like Lévi-Strauss, U is at once cognizant of his magical forebears and blithely convinced of the superiority of his methods: "In essence it's not that much different from what sooth-sayers, ichthyomancers, did in ancient times: those wolfskin-clad men who moved from stone-age settlement to stone-age settlement, cutting fish open to tease wisdom from their entrails. The difference being, of course, that soothsayers were frauds."[42]

We are entering here onto the terrain of the "new unconscious" and the "new subliminal."[43] Compared to the affective turmoil, conflict, and suspicion that infused the old psychoanalytically inflected Marxist critiques of mass publicity, the new popular neuroscience is proudly anti-interpretive, smoothly pragmatic, and blandly optimistic. The whole long post-Platonic effort to know ourselves turns out, according to the heralds of the new unconscious, to have been a waste of time: "Evolution designed the human brain not to accurately understand itself but to help us survive."[44]

One might think that neuroscience would push marketing ideology back toward a culture-free economistic individualism. But this is not necessarily the case. The discovery of neuroplasticity—the fact that our neural networks are constantly adapting to our social environments—eats away at the old iron curtain between nature and nurture: even brains are now, to a degree, culturally mediated. But again, when it comes to publicity and the specter of manipulation, this raises no alarm bells. Quite the opposite: because our brains are now more cultural, our motivations and our desires—when not simply hard-wired and thus "natural"—are, more than ever, understood to be felicitously integrated with our cultural environments: "Neurons that fire together, wire together."[45]

Academic neuroanthropologists explore the dynamic relationship between neural networks and sociohistorical transformation, and not only at an evolutionary timescale.[46] But popular neuroscience is deliberately and radically de-historicizing. Leonard Mlodinow, for example, insists that "Freud was mainly off the mark" because "many unconscious processes can *never* be directly revealed through the kind of self-reflection encouraged by therapy, because they transpire in areas of the brain not open to the conscious mind" and, just in case this revelation should set off any new anxieties, that "the inaccessibility of the new unconscious is not considered to be a defense mechanism, or unhealthy. It is considered normal."[47]

Mlodinow seems entirely untroubled by the notion—common to psychoanalysis, market research, and the more ancient arts of eros— that "unconscious" processes are *never* "directly revealed," *not*— tautologically—because they are unconscious (by which neuroscientists mean nonconscious), but because they appear as signs that have to be interpreted. Nor does he seem to have considered the fact that such interpretation is an intersubjective process rather than a purely solipsistic loop of "self-reflection." In the realm of the new subliminal, everything that the human sciences would recognize as subjectivity, society, and history disappear completely. Conflict is never sociohistorically produced. Rather, it's a result of the adaptive difficulties modern humans encounter because, as Mlodinow puts it, we are trying to live in advanced civilizations with Stone Age brains.

Speaking of self-reflection, neuromarketing does concern itself with mimesis, but only in the most literally duplicative sense. There's no sense here that mimesis could actually be, as Elias Canetti once speculated, *the* key medium of memory, innovation, and transformation. Canetti writes: "In the enormously long period of time during which [man] lived in small groups, he, as it were, incorporated into himself, *by transformations*, all the animals he knew. It was through the development of transformation that he really became man; it was his specific gift and pleasure."[48]

By contrast, the neuromarketers advise advertisers to position models in their ads so as to *model* the forms of attention and bodily attitude that consumers will then involuntarily mimic. Mimesis is reduced here to mind-meld: "Princeton researchers . . . found that when . . . subjects communicated, neural activity in their brains became almost synchronous. A second after specific brain activity was observed in the speaker's brain, this same pattern was repeated in the listener's brain."[49] In its more sophisticated versions, neuromarketing suggests something more like the potentiating work of the magician—except that neural networks take the place of the mimetic archive. In this guise neuromarketing takes on a more populist tonality. Suddenly it looks less like it's a matter of remote-controlling hypnotized human drones, more a bottom-up activation of preexisting neural "relevance networks."

Even so it is, on the face of it, quite extraordinary that the mana moment's classic crowd theory is now so distant that these scenes of mimetic influence can appear *not* as illustrations of dystopian techniques of mass manipulation but rather as entirely democratic, even liberatory strategies of provisioning. Neuromarketing maven Tjaco Walvis, for instance, confronts the ethical question by taking his reader on a breezy detour through Kant, Mill, and Aristotle, before boiling it all down to a pragmatic appeal: "The morality of this book depends on your disposition."[50] Neuromarketing, he argues, is a neutral scientific tool that can be used for good or for evil. But the magical rub is that, unlike the bad old days of subliminal advertising panics in the 1950s and 1960s, manipulation, thanks to neuroscience, has now actually become ethically desirable: "Research . . . shows that in the case of more complex products and services, people are happier with their decisions when they have made a choice for a product without deliberation. We could say that if their subconscious is manipulated, they do not notice it and experience no negative feelings. In that case, manipulation of the subconscious could actually lead to more happiness."[51]

Slavoj Žižek gives us an entertaining analysis of a sequence in John Carpenter's film *They Live*, where the hidden or subliminal message of advertising suddenly becomes visible and explicit by means of special spectacles that function as a kind of ideology critique machine.[52] The subtly seductive Siren song of the ads is revealed in all its bluntly monochrome instrumentality: OBEY, MARRY AND RE-PRODUCE, and so on. But one would have to add that the scenario of *They Live* feels nothing short of nostalgic in the age of the neuro-digital collective. These days, the secret message is no longer secret. Or rather, these days we are told quite cheerfully that our happiness, our true self-realization, *depends* on subliminal messaging. No wonder the paranoid old panics about actually surreptitious subliminal marketing now seem almost comforting.[53]

How can the total fulfillment of the subject appear so interchangeable with its total erasure? Here's the fantasy/terror of perfect addressability at its limit: the point at which in being recognized without remainder, I cease to exist as an autonomous subject. The temptation is to cast about for residual evidence of nonsubsumed subjectivity. I might feel reassured upon receiving spam e-mails that are clearly not meant for me; it means the algorithm isn't yet perfect. Just as in the old days, culture-jammers celebrated situationist *détournements* and ad-busting exploits, so today their heirs are only too ready too lionize the latest anticorporate hacking escapade. But the point is that the algorithm wins either way. If I don't buy the mistakenly recommended product, or if I give it a low rating, the algorithm learns from its mistake. And if I try to trip it up by actually buying the product that it mistakenly recommended to me, the product that I didn't actually want, then, as far as the algorithm is concerned, the recommendation was accurate—because I bought the product.

As far as the autonomous subject goes, marketing already has it both ways. On the one hand, courtesy of the new subliminal messaging, the "wide-awake, self-reliant man" that everyone from Kant to McDougall advocates is no longer where the action is. On the other hand, as Detlev Zwick and Julien Cayla remind us, the *askesis* of self-determining subjectivity is itself now internal to marketing: "the sociocultural system of marketing," they note, aims at "producing a certain culture of self-government, in the sense Foucault used the term; that is, a culture that promotes techniques of self-care, self-improvement, and self-responsibility."[54] Needless to say, the permission pleasurably to transgress self-care, self-improvement, and self-responsibility by indulging in purchases that are clearly bad for us is *also* built into the marketing dispensation.

Contrary to received opinion, the ethics of commercial publicity are not so much about truth in advertising as they are about the ideological fiction of consumer autonomy. As Timothy Malefyt and

Robert Morais rightly remark: "The way we frame ethically question-able situations in marketing depends on where we locate the idea of individual free will, choice, and human agency."[55] The reader already knows where they stand on this question, however, since a few pages earlier they have asserted that "US consumers have free choice; they can accept or reject marketing messages based upon their evalua-tion of the promises made."[56] In other words, "individual free will, choice, and human agency" are here taken to exist unproblemati-cally and a priori. If marketing is to be indicted, the argument im-plies, it would be for standing in their way. And if that is the case, surely there can be no complaints, since today consumers have more choices, even as more and more of us are living on credit.

Indeed, many ads make it seem as if selling a product is inciden-tal to the more important task of reassuring consumers of, precisely, their "individual free will, choice, and human agency." BMO Harris Bank, for example, promises "to act on your behalf because that's the only half that matters." If the ad makes me a bit queasy, then surely it offends less by its "creative" grammar than by flattering me with the opportunistic and insincere solicitude of a corporation that I know full well will only willingly act on my behalf if that "half" turns out to boost its bottom line. Even contemporary neuroscience sug-gests that "we" (by which it generally designates middle-class Euro-Americans) are invested, above all, in not so much the idea but more profoundly the *feeling* that we have autonomous agency: "The cre-ation of a sense of agency is critically important for a variety of per-sonal and social processes, even if this perceived agent is not a cause of action. . . . Conscious will is a cognitive feeling, like confusion or the feeling of knowing. . . . [I]t shares with the basic emotions an ex-periential component—we do not just deduce that we did an action, we feel that we did it. We *resonate* with what we do."[57]

Immanuel Kant wrote that the first principle of interpersonal ethics is never to treat other people as means to an end rather than as ends in themselves. By the same token, if I feel manipulated by ads, then it is generally less because they appear to be telling me what to do than because they keep insisting that my autonomous self-determination as a consumer is (a) absolutely sacrosanct and (b) en-tirely and necessarily congruent with their corporate self-interest. What kind of autonomy is that? Clearly something has to give.

We, the Barbarians

As I showed in chapter 2, intellectualist approaches to religion tend to focus on the question of belief rather than on vital practice. In the same way, critics of mass publicity hang on to these questions—do consumers believe in advertising, or don't they?—so as not to have to confront the more complex and ambivalent problem of our resonant entanglements with mass-mediated images. Here, too, it's as if the question of belief helps to salvage the figure of the autonomously self-legislating subject, even as salvaging that autonomy is precisely what allows one to *choose* to be seduced by advertising.

At the level of belief, I might adopt a skeptical, adult stance the better to be a child at the level of resonance. I want to have it both ways, to sustain my sense of autonomous self-determination just enough so that I can choose to be seduced. The agony of perfect addressability is averted by making sure that I stand to one side of myself—this too is a kind of *ekstasis*, only this time in the name of an ambivalent compromise between self-preservation and self-yielding. As Žižek suggests: "such a self-probing attitude, far from effectively threatening the predominant ideological regime, is what ultimately makes it 'livable.'"[58]

In a 1962 essay significantly titled "Advertising, the Magic System," the highly regarded literary critic Raymond Williams accuses consumers not of being too materialistic but rather of not being materialistic *enough*. A sensible relation to an ad, Williams suggests, would be to accept that a beer, for example, is really just a refreshing drink that might make you a bit tipsy, not a virility enhancer. A car is a means of transport, not an emblem of sophistication. And so on. Williams is not wrong to call advertising a magic system. The anthropologist Roy Wagner echoes the point: "Success depends on the ability to objectify convincingly, to talk about the product in terms of other things in such a way that those other things seem to be qualities of the product. In this way advertising is like the 'magic' of tribal peoples."[59] But like so many strenuously sober critics in the orbit of its mana, Williams is apparently too impressed by its enchantment to credit its magic to anything other than naive belief.[60] For Wagner, too, belief is decisive for advertising to work: "Its effectiveness . . . depends upon the user's belief in the spell and the significance of the transformation. . . . All the consumer has to do is believe in the magic and buy the product."[61]

Of course no one affirms the power of advertising more than the ad buster, just as the iconoclast is the one who really brings graven images to life. The iconoclast participates in—reactivates—the mana of the icon.[62] Just so, the greatest threat to the auratic object is not sacrilege but rather indifference. Most of us, perhaps, come to arrangements with ourselves and with the mana of mass publicity that hover somewhere between the full drama of defacement and the ennui of total detachment.

The Norwegian novelist Karl-Ove Knausgård suggests that, paradoxically, it is precisely our disenchanted insistence that an ad is "not real" that allows us both to be enchanted by it and, in another paradox, thereby boost our sense of ourselves as self-determining agents: "we know very well that it is trying to manipulate us into buying a particular product, but that doesn't stop us from looking at it; . . . We know someone wills it, and we know that the connection between the product and the ad for it is incidental, so that whether we buy it or don't buy it is our own decision. No one has deceived us. The peculiarity of advertising is that it works and doesn't work at the same time."[63] Of course advertising itself also often collaborates in this suspension by adopting an ironic tone: "we're not really selling you anything, so you don't really have to take us too seriously." One might add that in the age of the new subliminal, when advertising messages are stealth-embedded in all kinds of communications, this whole question of believing or not believing has become quaint, even nostalgic. For doesn't it depend on being able to tell the difference between advertising and nonadvertising? And who can confidently draw that line today?

At the same time, the question isn't just what isolated individuals believe or don't believe; it is also a matter of what each of us believes about the belief of those around us. An iconoclastic critic of, say, consumerist ideology—just like a standard anthropological analysis of religion—presumes the belief of others.[64] As Jean Baudrillard once remarked: "Not believing in [advertising] still means believing sufficiently in other people's belief in it to adopt a skeptical stance."[65] Such well-meaning pedagogical paternalism is widespread and familiar. Against Williams one might declare, with Lévi-Strauss: "The bar-

barian is, first and foremost, the man who believes in barbarism."[66] The theorists of the primitive settlement projected the naïveté and terror of total belief onto the savage because they could not confront it in their own thought—and yet their writings are full of it, from the anxious investment in the transcendent authority of science to dystopian scenarios of mass-mediated brainwashing. By contrast, there is plenty of ethnographic evidence that those "primitives" onto whom moderns projected their own superstitious natures were in fact quite comfortable with an ambiguous world. E. E. Evans-Pritchard said it best: "Faith and skepticism are alike traditional."[67]

I might say, with Žižek, that my belief in the belief of others sustains ideological fantasy while at the same time allowing me to disavow any direct belief on my own part.[68] If this sounds needlessly convoluted, consider the sociologist Michael Schudson's insight regarding the motivations of corporate advertisers.[69] It's not that corporations necessarily believe in the efficacy of advertising, Schudson explains. Rather, they advertise because their competitors advertise. In the same way, as a consumer of advertising I don't need to believe in it as long as I believe that someone else believes in it. As such, and like magic, advertising works by itself; it doesn't require anyone to believe in it directly. Indeed, the condition of its efficacy is my self-determining and autonomous skepticism toward its claims. My supposedly immunizing critical skepticism allows me to resonate in good conscience.

The Aesthetic Settlement

The defense of the enlightenment subject turns out to be inextricable from the ideological legitimation of mass publicity: in both cases, autonomous self-determination (whether of critical reason or of its supposedly pragmatic expression, consumer choice) must be defended. And the first step toward that defense is the containment of the worldly source of all manipulation: magic. As we saw in chapter 2, the mana moment theorists tried to contain the play of magic—the play of participation over representation—by means of the primitive settlement. If magic popped up in the modern world then, by the terms of that settlement, it could only be as a kind of atavism, an untimely throwback to primitive instincts. This is the logic behind Malinowski's decision to call advertising modern savagery. The trouble was, however, that magical effects also made themselves felt elsewhere, in ways and in places that were not only inextricable from the aims of civilization but actually considered indispensable to its progress. This, in turn, becomes the basis for yet another settlement: the aesthetic settlement. By the terms of the aesthetic settlement, magic is given a special dispensation to appear as a vital principle of civilization as long as it can be demarcated as "art." As James Siegel notes of the containment that the modern notion of "literature" attempts: "The institution of literature keeps magical language in a bounded place, at least under ordinary circumstances."[70]

In Europe, this structure goes back at least to the late eighteenth century. By the mid-nineteenth century, E. B. Tylor was arguing that the world-historical transition from a "tropical" to a "temperate" age meant giving up myth in favor of science and submitting to the hardwon distinction between fiction and fact. But art stands outside this logic, carving out a wormhole shortcut between past and present: "A poet of our day still has much in common with the minds of uncultured tribes in the mythological state of thought."[71] The intimation that there is a close affinity between magic and art crops up with clockwork regularity. Alexander Goldenweiser locates the "threshold of Art" in the neighborhood of ritual effervescence, since they share a pleasure in intemperate poiesis, the "overproduction of thought, emotion, and activity."[72] In *Totem and Taboo*, Sigmund Freud draws a direct line not only from the delusions of primitive magic—the "omnipotence of thoughts"—to modern neurotics, but also, in its modern, nonpathological form, to artists.[73] And Durkheim, in *The Elementary Forms*, suggests that surplus effervescence can take the form of artworks.[74]

The point is not just that an association between primitive magic and modern art was a commonplace of the mana moment and beyond—indeed, as James Clifford and many others have discussed, the association became an important and conscious identification for many modernist artists during the mana years.[75] The point is also that magic-art appears, in this light, as a kind of *pharmakon* within civilization: a substance that marks its vital progress as much as it threatens its certainties. As the "bastard sister of science," magic, according to its early intellectualist critics, involves indiscriminately imagined, mistaken associations and affinities—in short, participations: the linkages that Frazer categorizes as "sympathetic" and "contagious" magic. Its promiscuous participations create a fog of fantasy from which the certainties of mature science can only extricate themselves with the greatest difficulty and patience. Lévi-Strauss calls the syndrome of magic—of mana—"that *floating signifier* which is the disability of all finite thought . . . even though scientific knowledge is capable, if not of staunching it, at least of controlling it partially." Note, however, what that ellipse in the quotation contains: the aesthetic exception, symptomatically erupting as a parenthesis, acknowledging that this *self-same* floating signifier is "also the surety of all art, all poetry, every mythic and aesthetic invention."[76]

If the "surety" of art is also the "disability" of science, and yet the flourishing of art is an indispensable sign of the vitality of a civilization, then the only solution must be to create a space apart for (to draw a magic circle around?) art. Under the aesthetic settlement, mana work was encouraged, but only insofar as it confined itself to the autonomous/sequestered domain of the aesthetic and did not explicitly presume any regulatory authority in the zones of, for example, politics, economics, and religion: "As long as art does not insist on being treated as knowledge, and thus excludes itself from praxis, it is tolerated by social praxis in the same way as pleasure."[77] On the one hand, this sequestering of art domesticates it: "Neutralization is the social price of aesthetic autonomy."[78] On the other hand, the autonomy is *real*; it provides a refuge in which a noncoercive relation to the object-world can be cultivated as a palpable indictment of a thoroughly instrumentalized society: "by its aversion to praxis [art] simultaneously denounces the narrow untruth of the practical world."[79]

As Horkheimer and Adorno observe just a few years before Lévi-Strauss would wrestle with his floating signifiers, the autonomy of art, its being set apart in this way, only emphasizes its genealogical kinship with magic, that is, the extimacy that both art and magic suffer/enjoy vis-à-vis the social order: "Art has in common with magic the postulation of a special, self-contained sphere removed from the context of profane existence. Within it special laws prevail. Just as the sorcerer begins the ceremony by marking out from all its surroundings the place in which the sacred forces are to come into play, each work of art is closed off from reality by its own circumference."[80] Horkheimer and Adorno (and, in a more ambivalent way, their close friend and interlocutor Walter Benjamin) share with the mana moment anthropologists an investment in the aesthetic settlement. Like the anthropologists, they identify the kinship between magic and art with mana (having borrowed the concept from Mauss and Hubert): "It is in the nature of the work of art, of aesthetic illusion, to be what was experienced as a new and terrible event in the magic of primitives: the appearance of the whole in the particular. The work of art constantly reenacts the duplication by which the thing appeared as something spiritual, a manifestation of *mana*. That constitutes its aura."[81]

The conventional enlightenment narrative of scientific progress imagines the advancement of science in terms of a progressive improvement of referential "fit," whereby concepts move closer and closer to a one-to-one correspondence between signifier and signified, or, to put it a different way, to a successful subsumption of the world by thought. Like the early mana moment anthropologists, Horkheimer and Adorno also believe—more stridently than Lévi-Strauss ever did—that enlightenment has in fact liberated human beings from a superstitious immersion in myth. But unlike the mana moment anthropologists—and unlike Lévi-Strauss—they are also convinced that enlightenment has, by this "diremption" (violent tearing apart) of reason and magic, put itself on a course to self-destruction, as science turns into an entirely instrumental project of world mastery that gradually alienates human beings from external as well internal nature. As such, aesthetic experience in the form of autonomous art—the enlightened descendant of magic—promises a kind of return that is not a regression: a conscious and deliberate dialectical mediation of reason (representation, transcendence) and the senses (participation, immanence). This is the mutual mana of magic and autonomous art (and, perhaps, of anthropology as well?): the scandalous, apparently unreasonable "appearance of the whole in the particular" rather than the scientific subsumption of the particular by the whole.

But precisely *autonomous* art. Under the aesthetic settlement, as far as Horkheimer and Adorno are concerned, the mana of mass publicity—advertising, commercial entertainment, mass-mediated oratory, and such—can only be a kind of cruel and reprehensible joke, a regressive deployment of quasi-magical powers in the interests of an ever-more tightly "administered society." The implacable, alienating discipline of bureaucratic reason joins hands with the organized erotics of the commodity form. Add to this that Horkheimer, Adorno, and Benjamin are developing their arguments in the Europe of the 1920s and 1930s, under the advancing shadow of fascism, and it's certainly no surprise that the mana of mass publicity should appear in their work as the collective effervescence of eroticized death. Modern savagery to say the least. And yet the remarkable thing is that their response to this unbearable situation is precisely *not* to throw the baby of mana out with the bathwater of the fascist mob.

The Primacy of the Object

If the Enlightenment insisted on the autonomy of the critical subject, then the aesthetic settlement, as the therapeutic complement to enlightenment, insisted on a parallel autonomy of the object. Adorno's and Benjamin's aesthetics are also object ethics; they extend Kant's human ethics to our human relations to objects. Of course both Adorno and Benjamin have plenty to say about particular works of art. But if art, especially for Adorno, has to remain autonomous, then it is not so that it might be an end in itself (although a refusal of the instrumentalities of politically committed art, of what to Adorno was simply propaganda, is crucial). Rather, its autonomy creates a sanctuary in a relentlessly rationalizing world for the constitutive and creative resonance of mimetic response. As such, aesthetics is always, in this tradition, about much more than "art"; it's about preserving a register of sensuous experience, a mode of resonating with the world, that refuses to be evaluated or guided by questions like, "Is this useful?" or "Will this sell?"

Against one-way mastery of passive objects by active subjects, Adorno and Benjamin are both convinced that the only hope for real human progress is to recultivate our archaic mimetic faculty, whereby human subjects will once again become sensuously receptive to the "aura" of objects—the ability of objects to *look back*, to assert their priority vis-à-vis human subjects.[82] Both Benjamin and Adorno insist that the mimetic faculty, like the magic that flourishes in the midst of modernity, is not extinct in modern humans; indeed, Benjamin remarks that the mimetic faculty continues to play a "decisive role" in all our "higher functions" today.[83]

For Horkheimer and Adorno, mana marks what Adorno elsewhere calls the *primacy* (or, depending on the translation, the *preponderance* or *precedence*) of objects—the excess of objects in relation to the subjects who would presume to know them. This excess of objects is at one level a logical principle: "An object can be conceived only by a subject but always remains something other than the subject, whereas a subject by its very nature is from the outset an object as well."[84] But in an age of techno-bureaucratic hubris, the primacy of objects is also an ethical principle. One could even call it, following Sloterdijk, an erotic principle: "Artists and eroticists live under the impression that the things want something from them rather than that they want something from the things, and that it is the things that entangle them in the adventure of experience."[85]

Adorno's point regarding the primacy of the object is thus not only the well-known epistemological one made by Kant, that is, that we must remain rigorously modest in the face of our ability to know the world not as it is in itself but only as it presents itself to us through our faculties of perception and conception. The Kantian principle also informs the sociocultural relativism of the empiricist settlement in anthropology: our duty as anthropologists, it prescribes, is always to resist the idea that we could ever have access to the world-in-itself, as opposed to the variety of worlds that the symbolic orders of the many cultures of the world create.

Adorno is saying something more than this. For him, the primacy of objects serves as an ethical reminder not only of the Kantian point that our categories will always be inadequate to the world, but also as a reparation for the violence that we moderns have done to *ourselves*. In our hunger for mastery—of both nonhumans and other humans—we have alienated ourselves from the world to such an extent that, except for under certain very particular circumstances, we now imagine ourselves as self-contained subjects confronting an equally self-contained external world: "The distance of subject from object, the presupposition of abstraction, is founded on the distance from things which the ruler attains by means of the ruled."[86] And this is where mana could appear both as the charisma of human mastery and as the slippery medium of its undoing. What René Girard once said of sexuality might usefully be adapted to describe mana here: "one of those primary forces whose sovereignty over man is assured by man's firm belief in his sovereignty over it."[87]

Adorno is no conventional Romantic; he is in no way advocating an organic return to some primeval communion with nature. Rather, the central line of the argument that he develops with Horkheimer in *Dialectic of Enlightenment* is that the project of enlightenment can only be redeemed and brought back on track by a dialectical reconciliation of our conceptual representation of objects with an aesthetic—or mimetic—participation in them. It is no coincidence that Adorno understood an ethical approach to knowing as a kind of *yielding* to objects: "Knowledge of an object is brought closer by the act of the subject rending the veil that it weaves about the object. It can do this only when, passive, without anxiety, it entrusts itself to its own experience. In the places where subjective reason senses subjective contingency, the primacy of the object shimmers through: that in the object which is not a subjective addition. Subject is the agent, not the constituent, of object."[88] For Adorno, what differentiates "good" from "bad" object primacy is that in the good version, the subject's act of "rending the veil," the act that allows the primacy of the object to "shimmer through," is a conscious, deliberate, and critical commitment to an opening.

An opening to what? *To that in the object which is not a subjective addition.* Here we are in the neighborhood of what I have described as the mimetic archive: that layering—in our senses, in the objects and images we live with—of *another history*, a history, mimetically available to us, that can flash up at a moment of resonant encounter. Many of Adorno's key examples are modernist musical works in which the labor of composition involves a dialectical movement between the intentional rigor of the composer and the immanent historical requirements of the musical materials with which the composer is working. The composer's poised attunement to these immanent requirements allows the object primacy of the materials, historically conditioned as they are, to "shimmer through" and thus mimetically condition the work of composition as well as the act of listening.

In "primitive" times, Adorno suggests, no "rending [of] the veil" was necessary because representation and participation had not yet been "dirempted." Primitive society is, for Horkheimer and Adorno, marked by a *bad* object primacy insofar as undirempted consciousness is entirely unreflexive. Under such conditions, human beings are in the first instance entirely dominated by a mythicized nature and, later, by the priests and princes who set themselves up as the technicians and embodiments of natural-divine powers: "*mana*, the moving spirit, is not a projection but the echo of the real preponderance of nature in the weak psyches of primitive people."[89] In industrialized society, by contrast, a conscious and critical orientation toward object primacy becomes *the* liberatory hope for a world in which instrumental reason—with its advanced subject-object diremption—has become so hegemonic as to have reversed itself into a kind of myth.

No Mana of Mass Publicity?

Art, magic, and marketing sit uneasily alongside each other here. Or should that read "irreconcilably"? For as much as Adorno and Benjamin both insist on the aesthetic autonomy of the object as a redemptive source of modern mana, neither of them are prepared to concede that such redemptive mana might arise in the space of commercial mass publicity. Why not?

Many others have detailed the formidable debate between Adorno and Benjamin on the politics of aesthetic experience.[90] For my purposes here, I only want to emphasize one point: that for both Benjamin and Adorno, the meeting of mana and mass publicity, the massification of magical power—whether commercial or political—is inherently dangerous. For Adorno it leads to the quasi-ritual solemnity, the "bestial seriousness" of bourgeois recreation and, from there, on to the fascistic integration of dream, nation, and death.[91] Benjamin, too, waxes ironic about the risible reversibility of magic and marketing: commodity as arcanum and arcanum as commodity,[92] and warns of the production of a controlled concentration of mana in charismatic mass leaders: "This results in a new form of selection — selection before an apparatus — from which the champion, the star, and the dictator emerge."[93] The "irresistibly flattering" address of the Sirens' song appears here in a calamitous guise: the seduction of a totalitarian fusion of self and group, subjectivity and myth.

Faced with the tyranny of mass publicity, both Benjamin and Adorno sequester mana/aura in the space of the autonomous artwork. From there, however, they promote very different agendas. In the name of mass liberation — for the sake of "the new, historically unique collective which has its organs in the new technology [of photography and cinema]"[94] — Benjamin consigns the autonomous artwork, with all its priest-mediated mana, to the dustbin of history.[95] Adorno, conversely, clings to it as the only refuge of freedom in the age of administered mass culture. Above all, Adorno insists, art must remain autonomous — even if the very category of autonomy, because it necessarily depends on certain social and historical conditions, is paradoxical. For Adorno, art betrays itself when it slips into advocacy: "Artworks that want to divest themselves of fetishism by real and extremely dubious political commitment regularly enmesh themselves in false consciousness as the result of inevitably and vainly praised simplification."[96] He accuses Benjamin of the same lacuna with which Mauss is, around the same time, indicting his own earlier work with Durkheim: an inability clearly to distinguish the grounds that produce liberatory/autonomous and murderous/propagandistic forms of mass affect. And yet both Adorno and Benjamin hold the auratic experience of mana to be irreducible and precious away from the space of mass publicity.

Adorno, as we have seen, links mana to the irreducible ethical principle of the subject's yielding to the primacy of the object. Benjamin, when he is not directly discussing mass media, similarly treasures an auratic mode of experience in which an object's full presence to the senses is at the same time the guarantee of its integral self-containment: "What, then is aura? A strange tissue of space and time: the unique apparition of a distance, however near it may be."[97] With Horkheimer, as we have seen, Adorno closes the loop by explicitly acknowledging the connection between mana and what Benjamin meant by aura—a sense of a "spiritual" capacity in objects that is at once secular and sacred: "The work of art constantly re-enacts the duplication by which the thing appeared as something spiritual, a manifestation of *mana*. That constitutes its aura."[98]

But here too—in the debate between Benjamin and Adorno— mana erupts as a symptom marking an uneasy settlement. By what logic can the mana of autonomous artworks be clearly distinguished from that of, say, advertising? Why does the mana/aura that ema-nates from the autonomous artwork automatically turn authori-tarian when it is commodified? Is there any *inherent* reason why the kind of subject-object resonance that Adorno admits for autono-mous aesthetic experience cannot also occur with commercial pub-licity? The aesthetic settlement sought to make magic safe for civili-zation by granting it the protected preserve of art. But did it also hobble attempts to track the ambiguous resonance of mana—its world-supporting and its world-exceeding power—in political and commercial publicity? What is the source of the extraordinary, ma-levolent power that such publicity would seem to emanate, such that only the magical talisman of autonomous (art) objects can guarantee the continued autonomy of the subject?

Objects Talking under the Lingering Eye

Contrary to the charge that generations of populist media scholars have by now leveled at Adorno's culture industry thesis, his mistake is not that he doesn't grant ordinary people enough agency, enough subjective self-determination. His mistake, as I suggested at the be-ginning of this chapter, is that he doesn't grant them enough patiency, enough constitutive resonance. Adorno has decided, on pure prin-ciple, that the commodity form of mass publicity cannot involve any moments of object primacy that are not always already utterly regi-mented by a totalitarian project of political and ideological domina-tion. By the same token he proceeds to deny us denizens of the mass public sphere any real critical-aesthetic (mimetic) capacity to open ourselves to such moments of object primacy that would not simply take the form of a slavishly regressive obedience to the marketer-as-

Führer. And yet when it comes to loosening Adorno's vice-like grip, the way out turns out to be the way in.

Adorno wrote a fat and fabulous book—*Negative Dialectics*—whose core motif is that Hegel, the great dialectician, was not, in the end, dialectical enough. My argument here will be that Adorno falls victim, in the gap between the ideals of his aesthetic theory and the actuality of his culture industry screed, to the same problem. Hegel, Adorno argues, insisted that dialectical thought had to contain a moment of yielding to the irreducible immanence of the world, and thus an opening to becoming other in the very act of conceptualizing the other: "To comprehend a thing itself, not just to fit and register it in its system of reference, is nothing but to perceive the individual moment in its immanent connection with others."[99] This is the real promise of dialectical thinking: that it reaches for the "possibility"—the as-yet un-actualized potential—in every "hardened" object.[100] And this, says Adorno, is what Hegel held out as a necessary moment in any authentic philosophy: that "thought should not proceed from above but rather relinquish itself to the phenomena."[101] As Hegel put it in his *Phenomenology of Spirit*: "Scientific cognition [as opposed to merely formal understanding] demands surrender to the life of the object, or, what amounts to the same thing, confronting and expressing its inner necessity."[102]

But in practice, Adorno points out, Hegelian dialectics betrayed its own dialectical principle: "implicitly, each single definition in it was already preconceived."[103] The structure of Hegel's deductive system in practice "prevents that dedication to objects that is systematically postulated."[104] The particularity of the world that Hegelian dialectics engages remains, for all its ambition, mute (and anthropologists might recognize here something of the discomfort that our more "scientific" sister social sciences tends to inspire in us): "Despite the program of self-yielding, the Hegelian thought finds satisfaction in itself; it goes rolling along, however often it may urge the contrary. If the thought really yielded to the object, if its attention were on the object, not on its category, the very objects would start talking under the lingering eye."[105] As such, Adorno charges, "Hegel left the subject's primacy over the object unchallenged."[106] Consequently, "Hegelian logic has advance assurance of what it offers to prove: that the concept is absolute."[107] In the end, Hegel's thought reliably produces the world that it claims to discover: "reality is so arranged by philosophy that it will yield to the repressive identification with philosophy."[108]

Others, especially thinkers in the neovitalist tradition stretching from Bergson to Deleuze, have argued that such repressively self-fulfilling prophecy is inherent to dialectical thinking and evidence of why it must be abandoned. Adorno, however, pushes in the opposite direction, insisting on the primacy of the object as the ethical ground of a truly dialectical orientation to the world that will remain critical and conceptual by insisting on a moment of sensuous-mimetic yielding. And because the aesthetic settlement enshrines this openness to the mana of the object encounter, aesthetic experience becomes, for Adorno, the paradigm of a noncoercive way of thinking-relating, the intimation of a world that might, literally, re-member itself: "The primacy of the object is affirmed aesthetically only in the character of art as the unconscious writing of history, as anamnesis of the vanquished, of the repressed, and perhaps of what is possible. The primacy of the object, as the potential freedom from domination of what is, manifests itself in art as its freedom from objects."[109]

But this is where Adorno short-circuits. This is where Adorno's own thought does what he accuses Hegel's of doing—allowing itself "advance assurance of what it offers to prove." In Adorno, unlike in Hegel, it is not that the "subject's primacy over the object [remains] unchallenged" or that "the concept is absolute." Rather, Adorno's absolutely implacable and unshakably a priori diagnosis of the all-but-total reification of the administered society guarantees that aesthetic experience will, until some indeterminate future when the commodity form and repressive thought no longer swallow ordinary experience, remain confined/protected in the autonomous space imposed on/granted to it by the aesthetic settlement. As a consequence, just as Hegel doesn't live up to his own dialectical standard, so Adorno never has to follow to the end the dialectical implication of his own insistence on object primacy. That would require of Adorno the one thing that he absolutely refuses: to confront the mobility (and not just the regimentation) of mana in the space of mass publicity.

That Adorno feels that he has to keep warning his readers against seduction; that he has to keep uncovering and exposing the treacherously instrumental logic of ostensibly genuine social forms; that he has, despite his own dialectical commitments, to keep insisting on the empirical reality of "total administration"[110] — all this suggests that even (or perhaps especially) Adorno must be palpably aware that even (or perhaps especially) the lure of the culture industry is not as completely rationalized as he keeps saying it is. And yet it is precisely Adorno's own dialectical insistence on the primacy of the object that allows me to make this point. To be faithful to his own commitments, Adorno should have granted the culture industries the same dialectical attention that he recognized in his paradoxical formulation of aesthetic autonomy.

The autonomy of art, Adorno argued, was necessarily and constitutively dependent on certain social and historical conditions of possibility, most particularly the commodification of art that began by liberating aesthetic practice from the patronage of priests and princes but later threatened to subordinate it to the entirely heteronomous standard of exchange value. I would maintain that Adorno's position on aesthetic autonomy is still a crucial corrective to the kind of sociological reductionism that one finds in Pierre Bourdieu's work on taste and social distinction.[111] For Bourdieu, aesthetic experience *cannot* be autonomous *because* it is socially mediated; consequently, aesthetic discourse is, for Bourdieu, always an ideological cover for class prejudice.

Adorno makes quite a different argument. For him, it is only because of its dependence on given social and historical conditions of possibility that aesthetic autonomy is real. As he puts it: "Art is autonomous and it is not; without what is heterogeneous to it, its autonomy eludes it," and "art is the social antithesis of society."[112] Adorno is fully aware that the discourse of aesthetic autonomy can easily collapse into ideology: "The principle of autonomy is itself suspect of giving consolation."[113] But insofar as it upholds the real primacy of the object, it provides a kind of ideologically enabled bulwark against ideology. As such, it resonates profoundly with the dialectic of mana — its constitutive and destitutive play.

But Adorno is almost totally unwilling to grant any of this dialectical movement to the products of the culture industry. I say "almost totally" because Adorno does allow a fleeting moment's grudging approval to those elements in mass-marketed culture in which he senses

survivals of the physical integrity of the circus—"the stubbornly purposeless expertise of riders, acrobats, and clowns."[114] Here the key is
both the stress on the integrity of the physical as against the prostitution of "higher values" to the market, and the stubborn purposelessness that he attributes to this physical expertise—in other words,
its kernel of refusal, as he sees it, of commercial instrumentalization.
But apart from that, the thorough subordination of mass cultural
production to an external law—the law of the market—means that
the sensuous objectness of its constituent materials is given no room
to speak in the creative process. And as such, the material potentials
of the culture industry's products are entirely subordinated to the
regimentation of the commodity form.

Surely, however, this is an unsupportable argument? Marshall
Sahlins influentially suggested in the mid-1970s that Marx was only
able to sustain the coherence of his totalizing world history of capital because he kept deferring the problem of the culturally variable
conditioning of use value. For all of Marx's ruminations on the mysteries of exchange value whereby singular substances like wheat and
iron could be measured according to a single standard, Sahlins notes,
he "does not tell us why wheat and why iron."[115] In order to keep
his unified global history of capital together, Marx, Sahlins argues,
acknowledges but cannot develop the particular and plural cultural
conditioning of use values.

Although for reasons that I develop in chapter 4, I prefer not to
follow the culturalist path of Sahlins's intervention, I would nevertheless make a similar claim regarding Adorno's culture industry
argument. Here, too, the claustrophobic coherence that Adorno attributes to the culture industry's "total administration" is only possible because he forecloses any consideration of the ambivalent
ways in which the commodity images it produces may resonate—
and, crucially, that the ambivalence of these resonances may actually
be the basis of whatever power and influence commercial culture is
able to exert (rather than only serving as wiggle room for resisting
that power and influence). By foreclosing this possibility, Adorno
safeguards a vision in which there are only two possible relations to
mass publicity: submission or resistance. And as such, I want to suggest, he actually hampers our ability to understand the ways in which
ideological attachments emerge from constitutive encounters that

are sometimes traumatic, sometimes joyful, sometimes exasperating, and sometimes indifferent.

To be quite clear: I do think that aesthetic autonomy is a real and important issue. And one may grant that a creative practice that is guided by the sensuously immanent potentials of its materials—immanent potentials that are themselves, as Adorno insists, socially and historically mediated—is quite different from a creative practice in which those immanent potentials come second to a prior calculation about what will sell. The principle applies even within commercially oriented genres like popular music: *Graceland* will always be a different artistic beast than *Grease* (which is not at all to deny the real and resonant pleasures of the latter!). But to suppose that the mana of the materials out of which mass cultural products are made will be completely regimented once it enters into public circulation simply because it has been subordinated to an instrumental logic during the production process grants an entirely implausible degree of totalizing power—I would like to say magical power—to the commodity form.

Adorno did see in Benjamin's work on the Paris arcades a conceptual program for "the dialectical salvation of the commodity" in which, because of the temporal gap between the time of Benjamin's writing in the 1930s and the historical actuality of the arcades in the nineteenth century, the sensuous elements that had gone into their commodity forms could be redeemed and refunctioned.[116] But for Adorno, it seems, only this kind of temporal distance to the commodity form allowed him to dare to imagine that it might yet submit to the love of what I would have to call the authentic fetishist, a love that had the power to restore the autonomy of sensuous objects, thus retroactively negating commodity fetishism: "Things congeal in fragments of that which was subjugated; to rescue it means to love things."[117]

But couldn't one imagine a kind of generalized aesthetic autonomy that, having broken out of Adorno's magic circle, the magic circle of the aesthetic settlement, would permit an ethnographic exploration of the mana of mass society? The stakes would no longer be all-or-nothing redemption-or-damnation—whether of Adorno's autonomous object or of Benjamin's "new, historically unique collective." The gain would be an ability to track, here and now, the dialectical work of the mana of mass society at any number of scales: from the highly coordinated and regimented forms of large-scale public rituals down to the most contingent and quotidian encounters with mass-mediated forms. The question, then, wouldn't be the presence or absence of aesthetic autonomy—as if that were ever an all-or-nothing matter—but rather its differential availability to attempts, at every level of the social process, to conjure, if only for a moment, the controlling presence of a "world" out of the mana of mass publicity. These "worlds" may lay claim to political and cultural authority— what I have elsewhere called "performative dispensations."[118] But they may also last only for a few days, hours, or even minutes—long enough to create a space of possibility in which something or someone can be affirmed or transformed.

The Sirens, Again

I started this chapter with the anxiety of perfect addressability: the fantasy/nightmare of a world in which subjects and objects finally find their exquisite realization in each other, thereby effectively ceasing to exist as separate entities at the very moment of their fulfillment. Something of this terror hangs over everyday intimations of both the excessive rationalization of the marketing machine and the magically seductive character of mass publicity. For Horkheimer and Adorno, if the Siren song of mass publicity is in fact seductive, then it's only because it activates a deep human yearning for resonance that the long progress toward enlightenment has long since repressed. For them, Homer's story is an allegory of the struggle of a rational consciousness with the traces of an almost-forgotten mimetic faculty. The new Siren song of the culture industry offers, they claim, only bogus intimacy, an embrace whose tenderness is entirely calculated: "It contrives to make that appear near and familiar to its audience that has been estranged from them and brought close again only by having been heteronomously manipulated."[119]

Consequently, the prospect of yielding to the Sirens can, in Horkheimer and Adorno's view, only be regressive: "If the Sirens know everything that has happened, they demand the future as its price, and their promise of a happy homecoming is the deception by which the past entraps a humanity filled with longing."[120] The Sirens, old and new, are for Horkheimer and Adorno a fatally infantile short-cut back to the pure reconciliation, the "avaricious" and "immediate desire" of mimetic participation—the "bad" version of the "good" mimetic resonance that the artist undergoes by yielding (critically, judiciously) to the primacy of the object.[121] The only way forward, in a society as damaged as ours, is to stand firm—lashed to the mast—so as to ensure the "strong ego that is requisite to the experience of the nonstereotypical."[122] In a society premised on immediate but false gratification, an austere commitment to keeping a better future in view becomes imperative: "For the sake of happiness, happiness is renounced."[123]

But what if the world doesn't have to be divided between the tyranny of regimented banality and endangered aesthetic autonomy, between "total management" and "what does not allow itself to be managed"?[124] What if the dialectical provocation of aesthetic au-tonomy—the mana of the primacy of the object—is as much a per-petual potentiality in the Siren song of the culture industry as in the ostensibly authentic artwork, albeit differently so? What if an en-gagement with mass publicity doesn't have to mean either a totaliz-ing ideology critique or a celebration of popular pleasures? Perhaps this is the truly difficult thought, attached as social and critical theory has tended to be to one-way narratives of either disenchantment and rationalization or emergence and vital becoming? Perhaps "the sys-tem of total functional rationality"[125] functions here as a zombie tar-get whose constant undead returns guarantee the reassurance of knowing which way to shoot?[126]

My purpose in the present chapter has been to approach some familiar problems in the critical study of mass publicity from a dif-ferent angle. Instead of getting caught up in the hegemony-resistance clinch that has suffused so much of what has been written on the politics of the media, I wanted to show that most of these debates are in fact based on the same normative ideal of the self-determining, autonomous subject as the very agencies and genres of publicity that they're critiquing. By bringing mana back into the mix, I hoped to reopen the question of the "magic" of mass publicity—not now from the standpoint of manipulative persuasion, but instead from the per-spective of the aesthetic autonomy of the object. My hope has been to suggest that there are at least plausible grounds for thinking that the mana of the autonomous art object, so jealously guarded by Adorno and so ambivalently dismissed by Benjamin, might yet reappear, uncannily, as the mana of mass society, thus violating the terms of the aesthetic settlement that the critical theorists shared with the mana moment anthropologists.

In chapter 4 I offer an opening on the basis of the journey we have taken so far: an outline for a positive anthropological theory of the mana of mass publicity, organized around the interplay of *eros* (resonance, immanence) and *nomos* (order, transcendence). If in chapter 3 I have circled around the autonomous subject as an obsessive bulwark against the seductions of mass mana, chapter 4 speaks directly to the problem of constitutive resonance. How is it that I am ever able to feel resonantly and comprehensively addressed, such that I experience a moment of encounter—with a person, a movement, an object, an image—as the fulfillment (at least for a moment) of a long journey, even though I might not have known I was on that journey until the moment of encounter? What is it that is activated, that comes alive, in that resonant encounter? Should this activated substance be called "culture," as anthropologists and marketers alike have tended to call it, or is a different concept necessary? And how to begin to think about the *intimate anonymity* of such resonances—the way a decisive encounter is at once personal and generic?

Chapter 4

Are You Talking to Me?

Eros and Nomos in the Mimetic Archive

Here's the odd thing about Odysseus and the Sirens. If the song the Sirens are going to sing really *is* the song that addresses Odysseus and Odysseus alone, if it really is custom composed to both fulfill and undo him in all his singularity, then why does he need to stop up the ears of his crew?[1] If the oarsmen are susceptible as well, then clearly the song can't be so acutely aimed. It's as if, by stopping up their ears and lashing himself to the mast, Odysseus wants to sustain his own fantasy/nightmare of a message that is meant only for him. *I alone was to hear their voices*, Homer has him saying.[2] But the words are ambiguous. Does Odysseus mean that the song is actually resonant for him alone, or that he wants to do everything in his power to make sure that only he (and not an indefinite general public) will be available to feel exquisitely addressed by its call? Suddenly, the story begins to look like an allegory of the work someone might do to convince themselves that public communication really *does* single them out, unique and integral in their addressability (in their responseability) as well as in their determination to resist.

And yet something resonates, something is activated. If Odysseus thinks he has to tie himself to the mast, then the encounter is already working. But what is the substance, the material that is activated in the resonant encounter? And how to think about the movement

between resonance and form, such that an activated resonance becomes recognizable as a certain kind of relation: love, commitment,
duty, subjection, resistance, boredom, indifference, revulsion, and
so on? These are questions of pragmatic interest for all those mana
workers, political and commercial, who want to activate attention
and harness commitment. But they are also questions with a certain intimate resonance for each of us. They have to do not only with
whether we find a politician charismatic or a fancy brand desirable
but also with how we narrate, to ourselves or to others, the idiosyncratic rhythms and pathways of our personal attachments.

As for the substance that resonates, my task in this chapter is to
make a case for what I am calling the mimetic archive. In order to
make that case, I first need to show why a conventional conception of culture—which is generally what anthropologists lean on
when they want to explain why people behave and respond in certain ways—will not suffice for the task at hand. I offer the notion
of a mimetic archive as a way to think more clearly about how we
are sociohistorically conditioned creatures and yet at the same time
only become "who we always were" in an emergent, resonant way.
In each of the earlier chapters, I've explored ways in which anthropology and critical theory has at once acknowledged and disavowed
this fact, constantly pointing to constitutive resonance (mana always
marks the spot) while at the same time pushing it into a safe(-ish)
zone of otherness: magic, the primitive, art. Thinking with the mimetic archive is, I hope, a way of reducing the anxiety that seems to
surround the idea that we are constitutively resonant beings. And
perhaps it even offers a way to begin thinking through the discomfort that flashes up around the notion of charisma: a mana term that
points to the proximity of the powers that can heal and illuminate to
those that can drive people to kill.

Eros and Nomos

Throughout this book, I've used conceptual pairs: energy/form,
immanence/transcendence, participation/representation. In each
case, I've tried to put them into dialectical motion, arguing that this
is in fact both how social life "works" and how—in a critical mode—

one may best interpret its workings. In each case, I've also tried to show how anthropology and social theory have both recognized and obscured this dialectical dynamic, containing its play through the deployment of settlements. I've had occasion to discuss the empiricist settlement, the primitive settlement, and the aesthetic settlement, but one could invoke and explore many others.

In this chapter, I want to suggest a final conceptual pair: *eros* and *nomos*. Eros, of course, means *love* or *desire*, but I want to use it here in an expanded way to invoke the activating force and sensation of constitutive resonance. Nomos is often translated as *law*, but can also mean something more like conventional order or distribution. My proposition is that a dialectical dynamic of eros and nomos may be a useful way to think about mana—its resonant force, and in particular the way this resonant force appears at the same time as something *both* emergent/open-ended *and* established/law affirming.

Eros and nomos are profoundly and ambivalently interrelated. The legitimacy of law may be idealized as a kind of love; indeed, every polity built on something more than force alone pursues, in some form, an eros of nomos. And yet eros also habitually rebels against nomos. The constitutive shock of what Elizabeth Povinelli calls "the intimate event" is what liberal thought recognizes as a radical self-grounding of the subject through the love of another.[3] As such it is an event of intimately relational self-determination ("through you, I have become more than ever myself") that appears as radically immanent, suspending all external law. And yet all intimate events have their conditions of possibility, a kind of virtual or potential nomos that, in retrospect, gives them the appearance of inevitability, necessity, even fate ("we were made for each other"). The "we" in this construction may be an intimate couple. Or it may be you and the political or commercial image/objects that you encounter. Or it may be you and the more amorphous, wider contexts that you imagine as the world in which you live. In every case, the *intimacy* of the intimate event marks, as Lauren Berlant puts it, "the conditions under which a historical moment appears as a visceral moment."[4] By the same token, it is also, at least potentially, how a visceral moment appears as an intelligible moment—the place where we can *make sense*, in every sense.

Eros and nomos are at play in marketing—the advertiser's ambition is, after all, to awaken a desire that can be experienced both as deeply personal—"the ad speaks to *me*"—and that can at the same time be harnessed to the nomos of the brand qua project and intellectual property. They are at play in politics—whether the erotic object is a single, charismatic leader or the distributed enthusiasm of a social movement, the enthusiast's commitment should feel like both the fulfillment of a personal destiny and the working out of a collective task. And of course eros and nomos are at play in personal relationships. Whether the decisive encounter is with someone who becomes "my person among all others" or whether it's with someone who activates a less exclusive relation, the resonant activation of eros is rendered intelligible in terms of a nomos that articulates it as a certain kind of situation that is at once palpably unique and recognizably equivalent to others of its sort.

Such encounters are moments in the making and remaking of selves and of the worlds that address them, which is to say that they invoke horizons of imagination as well as prospects of power. And as my reinvocation of Odysseus and the Sirens suggests, this is an ambivalent matter. Odysseus wants to be singled out, he wants the song to be *his* song and his song alone. That way, he can both affirm himself by resonating with its singular address and save himself by resisting its call. In relation to the Sirens' call, Odysseus appears, in a curious way, at once completely *full* (the subject flawlessly hailed) and completely *empty* (the subject as minimal difference—"the gap which separates the One from itself"[5]).

Odysseus's ambivalence, I want to suggest, illustrates the discomfort that we still feel around the mana of mass publicity—in the enchanted realm of political and commercial eros. Enchantment is fine, even valorized as romance, when it comes to personal relationships; indeed, one of the functions of the modern conceptual division between the personal and the political has been, as Jürgen Habermas shows, to provide a safe haven for eros away from the instrumentalities of the market and public life.[6] That such an erotically evacuated conception of public life should have been articulated in a Germany only just beginning to recover from its murderous mass infatuation with Nazism is hardly surprising. But the problem is that political analysis continues, by and large, to equate the mana of mass publicity with irrational, reactionary, even fascist tendencies—the dark side of political theology. Journalistic accounts of crowd enthusiasm seldom hesitate to reach for primitivist metaphors. Likewise, many academic accounts read the more charismatic aspects of present-day public life as "modern kinds of political mysticism"[7] much as Bronislaw Malinowski derogated mass publicity as modern savagery.

Confronted as we are today with appallingly routinized spectacles of mass violence in the names of piety and patriotism, the question of how to theorize the mana of mass publicity is as urgent as it has ever been. For starters, I think it's crucial not to reproduce the common mistake—grounded in the primitive settlement—of opposing irrational enchantment to disenchantment as the condition of progressive reason. I've had occasion to remark before that any relationship—personal and/or political—has to be affective in order to be effective.[8] Likewise, there is no vital nomos without resonant eros. So how best to theorize the world-and-self-making force of constitutive resonance critically without reaching for the autonomous subject as the perennial backstop?

In the present chapter, my discussion of the mimetic archive draws heavily on Theodor Adorno and Walter Benjamin. In that connection, we might do well to remember that precisely Adorno and Benjamin are two of our most delicate theorists of the confrontation between the powers of eros and the experience of fascism. A notebook entry from 1960 has Adorno lamenting:

> It is a wholly irreparable disaster that in Germany everything connected in any way at all with a nearby happiness, with home, has been taken over by the reactionary camp: by philistinism, by cliquishness, by the self-righteousness of the narrow-minded, by the heartwarmingly sentimental, by nationalism and, ultimately, fascism. One cannot enjoy so much as an old nook or cranny without feeling shame or a sense of guilt. This means the loss of something that should have been preserved for the progressive cause.[9]

We might consider Adorno's elegiac acerbity as the other half of Benjamin's insistence on taking the liberatory potentials of political eros seriously, even at the height of the Third Reich. In a 1938 reflection on Herbert Marcuse's "Philosophy and Critical Theory," Benjamin urged:

Critical theory cannot fail to recognize how deeply certain powers of intoxication [*Rausch*] are bound to reason and to its struggle for liberation. What I mean is, all the explanations that humans have ever obtained by devious means through the use of narcotics can also be obtained *through the human*: some through the individual—through man or through woman; others through groups; and some, which we dare not even dream of yet, perhaps only through the community of the living. Aren't these explanations, in light of the human solidarity from which they arise, truly political in the end? At any rate, they have lent power to those freedom fighters who were as unconquerable as "inner peace," but at the same time as ready to rise as fire. I don't believe that critical theory will view these powers as "neutral."[10]

Yes. But how *might* critical theory view these powers, if they are, indeed, at the root of both the most "irreparable disaster[s]" and of freedom "*through the human*"?

Perhaps we need to begin by shifting the terms of the debate.

Beyond the Culturalist Détente

It may seem curious to begin with the complicities of the anthropologist's t/rusty old friend: the culture concept. And yet so much has been obscured by its commercial and political appropriation.

Take, for example, the strategic agreement that marketing and anthropology reached, sometime in the 1970s, regarding the explanatory value of the culture concept. It's not that many anthropologists or even all that many market researchers put much faith in the concept nowadays. Like the magic of advertising, the magic of culture is these days largely something that other people are supposed to believe in. But its great ideological advantage, when it comes to the relation between marketing and anthropology, is that it permits a fusion, without apparent contradiction, between irreducible difference and the alleged universality of *Homo consumens*.

Starting in the 1970s, a wave of North American anthropologists, largely trained in the structuralist-tending symbolic anthropology of the period, made their way into advertising and marketing. The question is how and why this kind of culturalist anthropology resonated so comfortably with the marketing imagination. As Timothy Malefyt and Brian Moeran remark: "The compelling notion that 'culture' is the invisible glue that holds together the unexplainable behaviour of consumers, or that it taps into underlying motivations and needs, or that it can even, at times, stand for the value of the brand, is simply too alluring an ideal for marketers to pass up."[11] In the mid-1980s, anthropologically trained market researchers absorbed the critique of representation that hit anthropology courtesy of James Clifford, George Marcus, Michael Fischer, and others. So, for instance, Rita Denny and Patricia Sunderland acknowledge, as an earlier generation of marketing anthropologists did not, that the work of mass publicity is a powerful force in the *making* of culture.[12]

Just as Marshall Sahlins has for many years forcefully polemicized against the would-be universal *Homo economicus* of *la pensée bourgeoise*,[13] Denny and Sunderland make the crucial point that reminding marketing folk about culture is valuable in itself, given the long-standing tendency for marketing theory—in both its academic and folk variants—to list toward psychological individualism. The reminder is perhaps more urgent than ever today, when "these hucksters of the symbol"[14] are, as we saw in chapter 3, jumping on the vulgar neuroscience bandwagon in order to lend reductive and ethnocentric presumptions about human behavior the spurious authority of biological "hard-wiring."

And yet the culturalist reflex in marketing has itself become a trap, in that it presents only two analytic alternatives: either the universalizing individualistic psychology of *Homo economicus* or the integrally pluralized culturalist song that anthropologists have been trying to teach the world to sing for the last century or so. That this is a false choice already becomes evident as soon as one notices that marketing discourse often operates not with *either Homo economicus or* the culturalist quilt but rather with a particular *kind* of culturalism that permits an underlying assumption of autonomous, rationally economizing subjects to survive fully intact.

So, for example, marketing discourse will assert, simultaneously and without contradiction, that subjectivity and desire are culturally mediated *and* that today's consumers have more choice and are better informed than ever before. *Homo economicus* simply puts on differently colored clothes as he travels from one country or "culture area" to another.[15] While this reconciliation of rational choice and cultural specificity may seem like a kind of sublation, this too is an optical illusion. On both sides of the equation, the individual is really just a secondary product of a structure that is presumed to be primary. The only difference is that the anthropologists call this structure "culture" and stress its historical contingency, while the marketers and the economists understand the underlying structure to be universal and invariant, simply a function of human nature.[16]

The culturalist détente between marketing and anthropology thus turns out to be based on a critical dead end: marketing keeps faith with the figure of rationally choosing consumers, and anthropology chips in to affirm that their choices will always be conditioned by culturally specific regimes of value. The consumer remains sovereign and everyone else gets paid. But here the conventional anthropological critique—showing that *Homo economicus*, far from being a universal index of human nature, is itself a socioculturally conditioned understanding of the human—doesn't go far enough. While the critique is valid in itself, it doesn't help to explain the persistence of our attachment to the figure of the autonomously choosing individual beyond its status as a cultural formation like any other. Why does this figure have such mana? What is the source of the fascination it exerts? On what substance does it thrive?

Mimetic Archive

In order to understand both the mana of mass publicity and the mana of the concepts that we use to interpret and analyze the mana of mass publicity, it may be useful to address the question of resonance directly. Why do some things resonate and not others?

Anthropologists have typically answered such questions by reaching for the culture concept: culture conditions how we resonate. Consider, for example, Claude Lévi-Strauss, who argues that "signs allow and even require the interposing and incorporation of a certain amount of human culture into reality. Signs, in Peirce's vigorous phrase," observes Lévi-Strauss, "'address somebody.'"[17] But to say that signs address us because they mobilize culture is little more than a tautology since "culture" is only a name for the routinized patterns of our addressability. The question to be asked, rather, is how this activation of resonance—which, having been articulated, then can take on the durable and predictable appearance of "culture"— happens in the first place?

Adorno's and Benjamin's writings, partly developed in dialogue with each other, contain important clues as to how what Marcel Mauss and Henri Hubert called "the collective forces of society" might be translated into a context of mass publicity. Mauss and Hubert were keen to stress that, in writing of such collective forces, they were not replacing psychological mysticism with a sociological variant. The collective forces of society were the reservoir, the resource that fed both delusion and reason. "The whole society," Mauss and Hubert noted, "suffers from the false images of its dream."[18] At the same time, "those collective forces which we are trying to uncover produce manifestations which are always, at least in part, rational and intellectual in nature."[19]

By likening these collective forces to an *archive*, I want to invoke the sense of resources deposited and variably available for excavation and citation—for activation. By calling it a *mimetic* archive, I am picking up on the suggestion, crucial to both Adorno and Benjamin, that the mana potential that resides in our collective experience-environment is something that we activate and apprehend as much by sensuous, mimetic tactics as by discursively citational means. It is at least as much unconscious as it is conscious. And insofar as we activate it sensuously and mimetically, we operate by way of what Benjamin, in a famously enigmatic passage, identified as the medium of the mimetic faculty: "nonsensuous similarity."[20]

What might this mean? Mimesis by way of *sensuous* similarity is easy to grasp: the play of likeness. Benjamin accords sensuous similarity an important place in the early experience of both the human race and in each individual childhood: onomatopoeia in language, children playing not only at being shopkeepers or teachers but also windmills and trains. And it is this literal, duplicative notion of mimesis and sensuous similarity that James Frazer enshrines as the operative principle of "sympathetic" magic: sticking a pin in an effigy of the person you want to harm, making the sound of thunder when you want it to rain, and so forth.[21]

But *non*sensuous similarity in Benjamin works, as Miriam Hansen explains, on the order of "affinity [*Verwandschaft*], rather than *sameness*, identity, copy, or reproduction" and its skilled actualization "crucially depends on a third element, the . . . mimetically gifted reader."[22] Nonsensuous similarity is what comes alive when Adorno's aesthetic subject yields to the primacy of the object (see chapter 3). Again, the point is not just one of attending to objects differently; the idea is that through such a transformed practice of attention, other historical potentialities start pressing on the present, other resonances become available for actualization.

Benjamin's primary example of a system based on nonsensuous similarity is language — a proposition that will be puzzling to anyone starting from the Saussurean presumption that a linguistic sign comprises a conventional and arbitrary relationship between a signifier and a signified (Benjamin: "language, as is evident to the insightful, is not an agreed-upon system of signs"[23]). Benjamin is working with a more esoteric conception of language in which our lexicon, spoken and written, is an archive of long-forgotten but potentially powerful correspondences through which, if the conditions of attention are right, "like a flash, similarity appears,"[24] connecting not only ostensibly dissimilar things, but also, like mana, leaking out across space and time to create sudden — and powerfully constitutive — resonances between objects, between subjects and objects and between the present and the deep past.[25] Pushing beyond the simplistically literal like-affects-like logic of Frazer's sympathetic magic, Christopher Bracken draws an explicit connection between "participation" (as one might find it in theories of "primitive" mentality like that of Lucien Lévy-Bruhl) and Benjamin's nonsensuous similarities: "The notion of participation is 'incomprehensible' because it endows perceptible objects with imperceptible properties, yet only a theory of participation can explain how things that are sensuously different can be nonsensuously similar."[26]

The mimetic archive is socially and historically conditioned — which is not to say that it is reducible to existing historical narratives. As with Adorno's notion of a "world of images," Benjamin's mimetic archive, Hansen explains, "has a collective substratum and a material grounding in unconscious and preconscious states, in dreams and daydreams," which, unlike the collective unconscious or archetypes of Jung, is by no means imagined as an "invariant, archaic reality." Rather, these participations "have their reality in the historical processes sedimented in them, refracted at the experiential level."[27] The mimetic archive is irreducible to individual psychology, since it is "stored" as much in the material world and in our innervated, embodied interface with it as it is "in our heads."[28] As Adorno makes clear, the mimetic impulse erupts spontaneously, but its forms of expression are just as historical as the explicitly articulated social structures to which it responds. Again, to speak of mimesis here—especially with stereotypes of the primitive and the mob never far away—by no means implies mere repetition or duplication. In Benjamin and Adorno's hands, the mimetic faculty activates latent yet historically embedded—let's say immanent—resonances that open the way for transformation.

If I may repeat a quotation from chapter 3, Elias Canetti posits the transformative power—and, not to forget, the pleasing play— of mimetic innervation as the origin of humanity as such: "In the enormously long period of time during which [man] lived in small groups, he, as it were, incorporated into himself, *by transformations*, all the animals he knew. It was through the development of transformation that he really became man; it was his specific gift and pleasure."[29] Ages later, at the other end of a long historical process, Benjamin surmised that it was the long inheritance of this archive, infinitely layered, *"virtual yet immanent,"*[30] out of which, by means of more transformations, "the new historically unique collective"[31] might arise.

I find the idea of mimetic archives useful for making sense of the social dialectic between historically layered, sensuously resonant potentials and their renewed—Benjamin might have said "redeemed"—actualization in discourse, built form, and social practice. The archive comprises both sides of the dialectic: the virtualities and the actualities. By comparison, conventional conceptions of culture, with their heavy stress on representation and structures of meaning, capture only one side of the process. The problem with such analytics of culture is their tendency toward stasis and reification. For all our sophisticated models of historical process and structural transformation, culture theory's stated challenge has always been how to explain change, as if transformation was somehow an additional and subsequent feature of fundamentally static states of social being. In the mimetic archive, by contrast, there is no priority of being over becoming or vice versa. Immanence and transcendence are twinned concepts that freeze-frame moments in an ongoing dialectical process. Mana indicates the palpable dynamic power of this dialectical process: an actualized social order bursting with immanent potentials and, conversely and at the same time, immanent potentials pushing toward ordered actualization.

Eros: Floodabilities

Adrian, the scrappily entrepreneurial hero of Iain M. Banks's novel *Transition*, counsels: "Course, any fuckwit can just tell somebody else what they already know they want to hear. The creative bit, the real value-added bit, is knowing what they want to hear before they know it themselves. They really appreciate that. That pays dividends."[32]

One might say that mana workers—whether professional or not, whether profane like Adrian or draped in sacred vestments—pursue esoteric knowledge for pragmatic ends. At one level, magic is an art of eros, a science of susceptibilities. What makes one thing or person resonate with another? What can such resonances bring into—or keep out of—the world? What are the representations that, deployed at the right time, will facilitate participation? From practitioners of the ancient arts of eros to contemporary neuromarketers, all of them mana workers, these are the decisive questions. Ioan Couliano makes explicit the connection between the magic of yore and the mana of mass publicity:

> The magic that concerns us here is theoretically a science of the imaginary, which it explores through its own methods and seeks to manipulate at will. At its greatest degree of development, reached in the work of [sixteenth century friar, philosopher, and magus] Giordano Bruno, magic is a means of control over the individual and the masses based on deep knowledge of personal and collective erotic impulses. Insofar as science and the manipulation of phantasms are concerned, magic is primarily directed at the human imagination, in

which it attempts to create lasting impressions. The magician of the Renaissance is both psychoanalyst and prophet as well as the precursor of modern professions such as director of public relations, propagandist, spy, politician, censor, director of mass communication media, and publicity agent.[33]

To say that such magicians "know the culture" is only a clumsy approximation. A mana worker, more precisely, is one who knows how to read the nonsensuous similarities of the mimetic archive, and to activate them by way of the imagination.[34] For ancient and Renaissance magicians, eros was the principle of constitutive resonance across the archive: "Eros, presiding over all spiritual activities, is what ensures the collaboration of the sectors of the universe, from the stars to the humblest blade of grass. Love is the name given to the power that ensures the continuity of the uninterrupted chain of beings; pneuma is the name given to the common and unique substance that places these beings in mutual relationship."[35]

Modern consumerist ideology puts autonomously acting subjects first, their choices modulated by "their" cultural preferences. From the Platonic theory of eros onward, by contrast, the capacity to affect and to be affected—and thus the experience of desire—expresses not a motive that originates in the individual, but rather the activation of the individual's latent belonging to another. (The locus classicus of this idea is Aristophanes's fable about the origin of eros in Plato's *Symposium*. Human beings appear here as once-spherical self-contained creatures bisected by Zeus as punishment for their arrogance and, ever after, driven by an erotic search for their lost other half.[36]) The capacity to *become who one always was* through a constitutive resonance with another is, in Sloterdijk's wonderful term, a question of mutual "floodabilities":[37] "Long before the axioms of individualistic abstraction established themselves, the psychologist-philosophers of the early Modern Age had made it clear that the interpersonal space was overcrowded with symbiotic, erotic and mimetic-competitive energies that fundamentally deny the illusion of subject autonomy."[38]

Eros here has a temporal dimension; through its mana work I remember myself in the other. Thus the deep basis of the romantic cliché "we were made for each other." "We do not love *another* object, a stranger to ourselves, [fifteenth century humanist scholar and magus Marsilio] Ficino thinks. . . . We are enamored of an unconscious image."[39] For Ficino, a person's addressability is astrologically and prenatally determined, making him or her receptive, through life, to certain images. "Through Neoplatonist doctrine, Ficino means to provide a transcendental basis for the empirical psychology of Eros. This field is bound by the completely unconscious choice made by the soul from among the phantasms capable of becoming the object of love."[40] This notion of an immanent, intimate matrix, transcendentally constituted, also appears as the kabbalistic *tselem*, literally an "image" but also a kind of companion astral body, which, according to Gershom Scholem, configures "the unique, individual spiritual shape of each human being," the individual's *principium individuationis*.[41] The *tselem* was, as Miriam Hansen points out, a primary early influence on Benjamin's conception of our susceptibility to aura.

In the Platonic scheme, as revived in the Renaissance, memory—one's personal mimetic archive—is central to eros because it is the immanent basis of the desire to be (re)united with one's special object: "If the organ of the vulgar drive for union is the attraction and bonding system comprising the eyes, blood and heart, followed by its genital supplement, the organ of the longing for union with the sublime subject-object is the memory."[42] In the late eighteenth and early nineteenth centuries, mesmerists offered therapies based on the recollection of the earliest and deepest bonds: "the patients of magnetism 'remembered' a state of their selves, as it were, in which they were animated and coordinated from the center of the mother in the mode of ecstatic vegetability."[43] And from here it is but a short step to the "lost object" of Freud's oceanic state and the whole psychoanalytic pathos of a subject who can only achieve normative autonomy by knowing how and when to transmute the earliest bonds of constitutive resonance into "healthy" adult object choices among people and commodities.

In the Lacanian tradition on which subsequent theorists of subjectivity and ideology like Althusser and Žižek draw, the trigger for our joyously constitutive (but also perpetually frustrated) encounters with the imaginary and symbolic orders through which we come to experience ourselves as subjects with identities and desires is our distinctively human *lack*. Like Kant and Hegel before him, Jacques Lacan understood the congenital incompleteness of human beings to be both the origin of our bondage and the gateway to our freedom, as compared to the comprehensive instinctive programming of non-human animals: "we find in man a veritable *specific prematurity of birth*," Lacan remarks, leaving us with "a certain dehiscence [splitting open] at the heart of every organism."[44]

In place of Lacanian lack, Sloterdijk suggests a kind of constitutive plenitude: a prenatally grounded synesthetic experience of "biunity"—a two-in-one *being-with* that is prior to the subject-object diremption, the gap in which a lifetime of desires will flourish. Rather than the indiscriminate participation of Freud's oceanic state or of Lévy-Bruhl's prelogical mentality, Sloterdijk's biunity proposes the human universality of an early experience of relationality (*not* merger) that is presubjective and nonobjectifying. If the Lacanian figure of identity-as-lack suggests a paradoxical bridge across a central absence ("I am my image insofar as it is not me"), then Sloterdijk's figure of the biune reimagines constitutive extimacy but with all the immanent plenitude of the mimetic archive.

The Lacanian lack-story has us spending our lives chasing the impossible realization of a lost plenitude that never existed. Sloterdijk's primary biunity, by contrast, suggests something rather less tragic. On the one hand, he lays out the origin of all the narcissistic delusions of consumer-citizens who come to self-consciousness believing, way before they are ever explicitly told, that the customer is always right:

> The incipient subject [the fetus and the neonate] claims the unconditional right to settle as an absolute consumer in the milieu it finds—
> a milieu that has obviously existed since primeval times and seemingly knows no other purpose than to fulfill the needs of the intruder at all costs. . . . Thus the original oral truth function, the elemental consistency of the child's consumptive participation in the mother, is reinforced by the consumed party. The mother-eater is always right, and is right to be right: its drive to absorb is based on an immemorial biological truth relationship, in the sense that its claim to nour-

ishment through the mother generally encounters the accommoda-
tion of the mother's breasts; where there is an unmistakable appetite,
there is also the unmistakable dose.[45]

On the other hand, and bearing in mind that the "incipient subject"
has to let go of its early alter egos, from the placenta to the breast to
the mother as such, Sloterdijk also provides a rehabilitated theory of
transference. Transference, Sloterdijk proposes, is not merely a compensatory lamination of identification and desire onto present-day
substitutes for irretrievably lost original objects. Rather, moments of
erotic resonance with new people, places, and things are, in effect,
rememberings, reactivations of the deep matrix of biunity. Such
resonances may take regressive and damaging forms. But they may
also open onto future transformations: "transference is the formal
source of the creative processes that inspire the exodus of humans
into the open. We do not so much transfer incorrigible affects onto
unknown persons as early spatial experiences to new places, and primary movements onto remote locations."[46] Sloterdijk playfully re-
phrases Wittgenstein: "The limits of my capacity for transference are
the limits of my world."[47]

Just as one can read Lacan's mirror stage essay as a story about
the scopic self-stabilizations that we all seek out in daily life, rather
than taking it literally as a description of constitutive self-encounter
through mirrored reflection in early childhood, so Sloterdijk's biunity argument does not have to be grounded in prenatal experience
to be analytically useful. As it happens, it resonates suggestively—
constitutively?—with Ernesto de Martino's argument (see chapter 2)
about magic as the drama of the loss and redemption of the "controlling presence" through which we experience not only the self-
grounding of our life worlds but also our coherence as subjects in
relation to the objects that surround us. De Martino's discussion of
the *atai*, the companion object, the double, the familiar, seems to be
describing something virtually identical to Sloterdijk's biune transference relation.

As Sloterdijk says, biunity must be imagined multisensorially, not
least in order to challenge the primacy given to the scopically alienated moment of self-recognition dramatized in Lacan's well-known

story of the mirror stage. Sloterdijk, then, provides an opening to thinking the various modalities of public affect that prevail in mass-mediated societies as something other than Malinowski's "modern savagery" or, alternatively, as more or less desperate compensatory attempts to paper over the abyssal gap of subjectivity. And by stressing the element of *potentiation* (as opposed to only regression) in the resonantly constitutive encounter, he enables an exploration of how the innervated, multisensorial potentials of the mimetic archive can be actualized in unexpectedly "binding"—erotic—ways.

Made for Each Other

Mana workers think they know what they're doing—or at least they try to distract the rest of us by making us argue about whether their magic is "real" or not, whether we "believe" in it or not and so on. As I've had occasion to observe before, the truly uncanny thing is never the success or failure of mana work as such, but rather resonance events that lack a plausible narrative to explain, contain, and claim them: eros without nomos.

All of us participate in many ways in boosting the power of magic—if only, as I suggested in chapter 3, by making such a song and dance about not believing in it. More generally, though, the experience of eros—of constitutive resonance—triggers a need for a nomos that will make it intelligible and perhaps tractable. Encounter is, as I argued in the introduction, primary. In the absence of a grand manipulator, the resonators themselves will come up with a magical system. As Bradley Pearson, Iris Murdoch's protagonist in *The Black Prince*, reflects: "Surely it was lovers who discovered astrology. Nothing less than the great chamber of the stars could be large and steady enough to be context, origin, and guarantee of something so eternal."[48] Eternal—but also, every time, unprecedented. Anne Carson notes: "All lovers believe they are inventing love."[49]

The encounter with a situation, person, or object that makes me exclaim "this speaks to me!" is not the moment in which my pre-existing desire finally meets an object that promises to satisfy it, although that is how I will almost immediately experience it and that is how marketing would prefer to portray its service to humanity. Rather, it is in this moment of encounter that a potential in the mimetic archive—what Gabriel Tarde called a "potential force of belief and desire which is anchored in all kinds of sleeping but unforgotten memories"[50]—finds, in the object, the organizing occasion of its actualization *as* a desire that I can experience as *mine* (and which, for that reason, I can also take personal pride in resisting).

Two things are worth noting about this encounter. The first is its relative contingency: under slightly different conditions—a different place, a different mood, a different object—"my" desire would have actualized in a different form, thus producing not only a different object of desire but also, crucially, a slightly different *subject* of desire, a different desiring me. The relation is not random; given my particular social and historical relation to the mimetic archive, some forms and subject-object relations are more likely than others (and these are the resonance probabilities that any good mana worker will seek to discover). But the point is that the effect travels both ways at the moment of encounter, constituting simultaneously an object and a subject of desire. This, I take it, is the meaning of Wilhelm von Humboldt's words: "What man necessarily needs is simply an object that will make possible the interaction between his receptivity and his autonomous activity."[51]

The second thing to note about the encounter that prompts me to exclaim "this speaks to me!" is its retroactive effect: once the contingent actualization of *this* desire by means of *this* object has taken place, it will feel as if it was, in retrospect, inevitable. And of course in a sense it was—just not necessarily *this* desire as the vital form of *this* subject-object relation. This retroactive sense of inevitability is what Žižek describes as "the dialectical reversal of contingency into necessity, that is, the way the outcome of a contingent process takes on the appearance of necessity: things retroactively 'will have been' necessary. . . . The process of becoming is not in itself necessary, but is the *becoming* (the gradual contingent emergence) *of necessity itself.*"[52]

Mladen Dolar usefully illustrates this curious combination of contingency and necessity—or, more precisely, this contingent production of necessity—through the classic encounter narrative of romantic love:

A young hero quite by coincidence and through no endeavour of his own meets a young girl in some more or less extraordinary circumstances. What happened unintentionally and by pure chance is [then] in the second stage recognized as the realization of his innermost and immemorial wishes and desires. . . . The moment of subjectivation is precisely that moment of suspension of subjectivity to the Other (Fate, Providence, Eternal Plan, Destiny, or whatever one might call it). . . . The situation is contradictory since it presupposes the freedom of an autonomous choice and demands its suppression. This contradiction is reconciled in a strange logic of *post festum*: the young man has chosen only by recognizing that the choice has already been made, regardless of his freedom of choice. . . . In other words, choice is a retroactive category; it is always in the past tense, but in a special kind of past that was never present. The moment of choice can never be pinpointed; it passes directly and immediately from a "not yet" to an "always already."[53]

Adman Brian Barton once remarked: "If you want to find out about people, try selling them something."[54] There is a deep truth to his observation as long as one understands the manifestation of the consumer self—"who the consumer really is"—in the contingent and retroactive sense suggested by Žižek and Dolar. The unpredictable contingencies of actual encounter implied in Barton's phrase—"try selling them something"—is crucial, since a product/consumer pairing, just like an online date match, can look, as the saying goes, "perfect on paper" and yet in practice activate no resonance.

The sacred and particular "fatedness" that one may attribute to one's most intimate human relationships as well as to one's most passionate attachments to objects—"we were made for each other"—is haunted by a double intimation: that the relationship is generic and that it is contingent. Georg Simmel captures this unease poignantly in his classic essay on the stranger: "A skepticism regarding the intrinsic value of the relationship and its value for us adheres to the very thought that in this relation, after all, one is only fulfilling a general human destiny, that one has had an experience that has occurred a thousand times before, and that, if one had not accidentally met this precise person, someone else would have acquired the same meaning for us."[55] I would modify Simmel's statement only insofar as it seems to presume, uncharacteristically, the indifferent stability of the subject vis-à-vis the object — "someone else would have acquired the same meaning for us." But the relation is surely doubly contingent: someone (or something) else would have actualized, in the place of this meaning, a somewhat different meaning and, by extension, I would have become someone else as well.

Again the crucial point is that the resonant relation is contingent but not arbitrary. Žižek remarks that the retroactive positing of causal inevitability — "it had to happen" — undermines the principle of sufficient reason: "this principle only holds in the condition of linear causality where the sum of past causes determines a future event — retroactivity means that the set of (past, given) reasons is never complete and 'sufficient,' since the past reasons are retroactively activated by what is, within the linear order, their effect."[56] But again one would have to add that the relation between potential causes and actualized effects is conditioned or "colored" by the historicity of the mimetic archive. Within its matrix, some "destinies" are more likely to come to pass than others. The mana of mass publicity activates destinies and attachments that subsequently exude the charisma of fate. Mana, as Roger Keesing points out, is "a quality of efficacy manifest in visible results," a "retrospective pragmatism."[57]

Nomos: Charisma

The eros of the intimate event, the resonance in which I encounter, with a thrilling sense of illumination, "who I always was," is at one level a paradigmatically private experience, unique and untranslatable. And yet at the same time, it invariably links me — explicitly or implicitly — to the revelation, stabilization, and inhabitation of a *world* in which my intimate self-encounter *finds a place*, where it is linked to expectations of reciprocity and hierarchy. This, then, is the intersection of eros and nomos: intimate resonance and external social order, love and law. One name for the appearance of this revelatory intersection of eros and nomos is *charisma*.[58]

Charisma is the "odd one in" among Max Weber's triad of legitimate forms of authority. It's no accident that Weber explicitly links charisma to mana[59] and to the "collective excitement produced by extraordinary events."[60] Unlike traditional and legal-bureaucratic legitimation, both oriented toward stability and impersonal reproduction, charisma is a transformative, often revolutionary potentiating capacity understood, by those who fall under its influence, to be singularly concentrated in exceptional individuals. Given that Weber's concept of charisma hovers ambiguously—but vitally— between primitive and civilized images of authority, it's also no surprise that it should have been revived as an analytical category precisely at the moment of decolonization, when the peoples that colonial authority had classified as primitive were now suddenly claiming to be modern.

Charisma took on new life as a problem in political theory, in other words, as a result of the breakdown of the geopolitical order that had undergirded both the mana moment and the empiricist settlement in anthropology. For the sociologist Edward Shils, the special charisma of the leaders of the new nations had to do with their ability constitutively to mediate between the primitive charisma of their people's traditions and the modern charisma of the secular state: "They are themselves almost always charismatic men in the conventional sociological sense—strikingly vivid personalities and extremely sensitive. They arouse the charismatic sensibilities of others and they do so largely because they pulsate in response to the symbols in which charisma is latent."[61]

While a familiar fetish effect makes charisma look and feel like an inherent power emanating from particular individuals, it may perhaps better be understood, as S. N. Eisenstadt suggests, as the ability to actualize potentials present, in a diffuse and distributed way, in the social environment or, in my terminology, in the mimetic archive: "a crucial aspect of the charismatic personality or group is not only the possession of some extraordinary, exhilarating qualities, but also the ability, through these qualities, to reorder and reorganize both the symbolic and the cognitive order *which is potentially inherent in such orientations and goals* and the institutional order in which these orientations become embodied."[62] Or, as Stephan Feuchtwang has more recently elaborated: "the power of the charismatic leader stems from his or her ability to create an immediately psychological reality in person, in gestures, words, and deeds from a previously dispersed set of expectations."[63]

Tarde, writing during the mana moment, was still using the mesmerist terminology of magnetism to describe this effect. Having noted, as we saw a little while ago, the existence of "a certain *potential* force of belief and desire which is anchored in all kinds of sleeping but unforgotten memories," Tarde credits the actualization of this potential to "the magnetizer," who, like any good mana worker, "is able through a chain of singular circumstances to open the necessary outlet to this force." The magnetizer, Tarde says, does not even have to speak. "He need only act; an almost imperceptible gesture is sufficient."[64]

The truth of charisma, like that of mana, lies in its capacity and in its efficacy. And its efficacy depends on its ability to actualize potentials by means of discriminatingly activated participation: "The formula 'participatory reason' implies the thesis that there are appropriate and inappropriate participations whose difference is akin to that between true and false."[65] In a similar vein, A. M. Hocart suggested that, in Fiji, mana implied the opposite of being wrong, where, he claimed, the local language had no word for a falsehood or a lie. Hocart quoted a "Fijian authority" on this point as follows: "A thing is *mana* if it operates; it is not *mana* if it does not."[66] Charismatic efficacy—mana work—depends not only on expert esoteric knowledge but also, as the sine qua non of the nimble deployment of such knowledge, on the kind of "passionate attention" to the infolded potentials of the concrete world that Lévi-Strauss attributed to the bricoleur.[67] As Michael Taussig notes of the shaman's craft: "All these tricks require inordinate skill, inordinate technique, inordinate empathy with reality."[68]

Depending on the magic, such empathy with reality may involve more or less elaborated schemes of cosmic correspondences by which nonsensuous similarities can be activated. Again, this is not so much a matter of the simplistically literal "sympathetic" and "contagious" participations of primitive magic à la Frazer, but rather of the kinds of esoteric symbologies, as in astrology or in marketing, that mediate chains of secret resonance between entities. The roots of charisma lie, one might argue, in the skills of the "mimetically gifted reader"[69] whose "passionate attention" was, in the European sixteenth century, the mark of the magus: "the encyclopedically sensitive, polyvalently cosmopolitan human who learned how to co-operate attentively and artfully with the discrete interdependencies between the things populating a highly communicative universe."[70]

Shils suggests a usefully inclusive characterization of the charismatic individual as an embodiment of "the connection with vital things":[71] "The person who through sensitivity, cultivated or disciplined by practice and experience, by rationally controlled observation and analysis, by intuitive penetration, or by artistic disclosure, reaches or is believed to have attained contact with that 'vital layer' of reality [what Shils has slightly earlier termed "the vital force which underlies man's existence"] is, by virtue of that contact, a charismatic person."[72] Shils observes that this "vital layer" or, as he also puts it, "vital center" of a social order is what we tend to give names like "God." Indeed, for Shils, the social "centrality" of such notions, notions of which divinity is one subset, has to do with the way that they bring order to vitality—or, in the terminology I'm using here, nomos to eros: "The centrality is constituted by its formative power in initiating, creating, governing, transforming, maintaining, or destroying what is vital in man's life."[73]

Mana Fractalized

Most sociological discussions of charisma presume its dramatically concentrated embodiment in human individuals: paradigmatically, the charismatic leader. Likewise, the classic Durkheimian ritual scenario imagines a concentration of mana in clearly demarcated sacred persons, objects, places, and times of year, ritually separated from ordinary or "profane" everyday life. To be sure, the mana of mass publicity also brings major political, religious, and commercial foci of collective identification into sharp and often spectacular relief. Our age certainly has its share of mass rituals—rallies, megaconcerts, sports events, election spectacles, and sacred as well as secular days of effervescence—and that effervescence gets pumped up to the point of exhaustion in the echo chamber of the multimedial twenty-four-hour news cycle.

It's not, as a hasty reading of Michel Foucault's *Discipline and Punish* might suggest, that we have moved from an era of spectacular yet intermittent occasions of effervescence to an era in which we are engaged and incorporated by means of impersonal and affectless micrologies of power for which no detail of our everyday life is too trivial to serve the telos of administrative integration. Nor is it only that megaspectacles persist alongside otherwise stealthy modes of governmentality, as noisy distractions from the "real" mechanisms of rule. For the mass-mediated worlds we inhabit now, the characteristic challenge is the integration of eros and nomos in modes that are adequate to the peculiar address of mass publicity. This means, as Michael Warner has so eloquently shown, a distinctive juxtaposition of intimacy and anonymity.

This isn't a zero-sum game. It's not just, as the standard critique of the mass society would have it, that we are simply struggling to defend the integrity of the last little patches of "personal life" that an increasingly intrusive system of publicity grants us. The puzzle, rather, is the delicate and dynamic interplay of eros and nomos in a situation where we are most deeply "ourselves" in the places where we feel addressed alongside strangers. Looking back at Durkheim's *Elementary Forms* from this perspective produces a disorienting sense of recognition, since — once our own increasingly baroque medial apparatus is subtracted — isn't this exactly what Durkheim says about collective effervescence: that mana, primitive and modern alike, is the feeling of the intimacy of the impersonal? What's going on here?

Durkheim already gives us a clue. Totemic societies, he claims, divide their annual cycle into two clearly distinguished seasons: a sacred season, a time of gathering, ritual, and collective effervescence; and a profane season, a time of dispersal, subsistence, and mundane concerns. The distinction between sacred and profane is fundamental and absolute. By contrast, Durkheim remarks, "in the more advanced societies, there is virtually no day on which some prayer or offering is not offered to the gods or on which some ritual obligation is not fulfilled."[74] In fact, so dispersed has the ritual calendar of modern societies become that, aside from the major marked events that one finds in all societies, the very distinction between the sacred and the profane starts blurring: "Among the people called civilized," Durkheim remarks without further developing the implications of the point, "the relative continuity between [sacred and profane dimensions of life] partially masks their interrelations."[75]

Extrapolating from these brief comments, one might speculate that compared to the seasonal seesaw that Durkheim attributes to totemic societies, in mass-mediated societies the sacred/profane relation becomes fractal. By this I mean that the field of constitutive tension—the field of mana—established by the polarity of sacred and profane is clearly discernable at a large scale in the form of major collective events, but then also replicated at finer and finer levels of resolution all the way down into the most capillary dimensions of everyday life.[76] As Durkheim himself suggests, the sacred/profane tension is not exclusively a feature of rituals and social practices that would necessarily qualify as "religious." Rather, it marks the dynamic relation between transcendence and immanence that makes the dialectic of eros and nomos possible.

What Bodies?

The charismatic activation of this fractal field of mana involves a constant oscillation between two figures: on the one hand, the transcendence of the auratic object or leader and, on the other, the immanence of the distributed substance of the community or the field of circulation. Charisma was originally a theological concept and expressed, from the very first, this constitutive tension between transcendence and immanence. "From inception (or invention), then," Raphael Falco notes of the Pauline early Christian community, "the charisms were components in a hierarchical order designed to promulgate a centralized and personal authority."[77] At the same time, "the Pauline congregation is both egalitarian and hierarchical, led from below and governed from above."[78] A problem that is at once theological and political soon develops: how to balance the tension between "the leader's body as flesh and the leader's body as a symbol of charismatic unity"[79]—the doubling so influentially explored in the context of medieval royal authority by Ernst Kantorowicz under the rubric of the king's two bodies.[80]

It is hardly surprising, then, that this immanence/transcendence tension accompanies the concept of charisma as it travels from the face-to-face religious community to the intimate anonymity of mass publicity where, like Durkheim's sacred/profane relation, it fractalizes. The "charismatic unity" of the devotional community is now also the charismatic unity of the mass-mediated political polity and of globalized consumer brand identification. As to the *source* of charisma, the main difference in the contemporary world is that—and the preoccupations of the mana moment were in significant part symptomatic of this transition—sovereignty is, as Eric Santner puts it, *excorporated*: it is now normatively supposed to reside not so much in the singular bodies of kings as in the distributed flesh of the people.[81]

Shils is already on to something along these lines when he argues that modern democracies have not so much witnessed a comprehensive withering of the sacred, what Weber (following Friedrich Schiller) called disenchantment, as a simultaneous attenuation and generalization of charisma. Putting his finger on something a bit different than the comprehensive routinization of charisma that Weber had discussed (the difficulty of durably institutionalizing the charismatic force first manifested in a singular individual/event), Shils proposes something like an ordinary, everyday low-voltage mana: "It seems to me that an attenuated, mediated, institutionalized charismatic propensity is present in the routine functioning of society."[82]

Weber had already paved the way for such an idea; alongside the big picture melodrama of the charismatic leader, he had proposed categories like the charisma of office, the charisma of kinship, and hereditary charisma.[83] But Shils makes the point quite directly: in democratic societies, authoritative institutions like the state and the courts—and therefore also their key incumbents—*participate* (the word should be understood here in the full Lévy-Bruhlian sense) in the charisma of the sovereign people. As such, just like Durkheim's totemic signs—and, for that matter, corporate brands—these authoritative institutions come to do that double mana work (at once vampiric and form giving) that might—without prejudice—be called fetishism. Indeed, one doesn't have to take the political trajectory presumed in Euro-American histories of sovereignty too literally. After all, the fractalization of mana is not—as Durkheim suggests—necessarily historically subsequent to its centralization in a singular body, whether imagined as a god or as a human sovereign. At the same time, one should perhaps take seriously the proposition that there is something historically unique about mass democratic sovereignty, especially insofar as it claims a form of self-determination that is at once corporate and anonymous, collective and distributed over vast distances.

The political challenge, as Shils observes in a significant footnote, is what kind of charismatic embodiments are adequate to popular sovereignty. In political terms, it is not so much a matter of popular eros rebelling against nomos as such (although it may well be represented as such). The question, rather, might be what kind of nomoi are most adequate to the energetic potentials of mass eros: "In modern societies where belief in both the charisma of the populace and the charisma of the highest authority is a common phenomenon, the tensions of populism and constitutionalism are not uncommon"—not to mention the juxtaposition of distributed and centralized charismatic authority that one finds in so many populist movements.[84] But, following Santner, the point can be pushed further. From a pragmatic point of view, the problem becomes: what sorts of entities or institutions might adequately—which is to say charismatically, efficaciously—mediate the dispersed mana of the people with the singular purpose of the state? The twentieth century saw many attempts to solve that problem, ranging from the secular-sacral indexes of nationalism, via polities juxtaposing some form of quasi-divine kingship with mass democracy, to the "charismatic impersonality" of the Leninist party form, which, as Ken Jowitt observes, combines heroic charisma with impersonal bureaucracy.[85]

Similarly, the legitimation of consumer marketing rests, in no small measure, on its claim to address this tension: to provide a truly populist—an immanently resonant—mediation of "the collective forces of society" with prestigious-erotic foci of attention. Such a system relies on a constant attempt to balance centralization with dispersal, broadcasting with point casting. On the one hand, as Emilio Spadola notes: "The ongoing constitution of a technologically interconnected space promotes the fantasy of a unified and uniform—which is to say, transparent—sphere, and uniform subjects of communication in which rituals take place. Mass mediation accompanies an ethics of transparent, self-present subjectivity as a condition of modern belonging. In doing so, it highlights difference *as* communication: precisely those communicative rites, both secretive and mystifying, which can now be said to 'resist' integration and total oversight."[86] On the other hand, as Bjørn Schiermer points out, the very media apparatus that, at one level, dreams of capture and closure can nevertheless only work by proliferating difference: "Mediation makes room for a multitude of dislocated, asynchronous and decentralized but connected 'micro-gatherings' around shopping windows, televisions, fashion magazines, internet blogs or through word of mouth."[87]

We may, for example, understand consumer branding as a mode of profitably managing the mana of mass society. On the one hand, branded commodities circulate as widely as possible, entering into the smallest crevices of our everyday lives. On the other hand, their circulation is driven by their participation in the singular and centralized mana of the brand, an auratic source that must remain a kind of inviolable and untouchable *arcanum* (a sacred effect that is legally secured by exclusive corporate ownership of the brand). The open secret of this fetish-effect is that this arcane mana is extimate: it is at once "in us" as consumer-citizens (our labor of attention, desire, and resonance produces it) and "outside us" (it is coordinated and controlled by agencies beyond our control). It is at once immanent and transcendent, at once a medium of participation and a regal representation.

Perhaps the most characteristic and at the same time the most preposterous feature of commercial publicity is that it contrives to convince each one of us—individually—that this vast, impersonal system exists only to serve our personal autonomy. Every advertisement contains the same implicit and extremely seductive proposition: that the whole world is organized so as to serve my personal self-realization. The proposition is all the more appealing because it *is* so implausible—because we are always already disappointed. As Lauren Berlant observes: "There is no place sufficiently under the radar to avoid the insult that the world is not organized around your sovereignty."[88]

Underlying both the mechanisms of mass publicity and the consumer-citizen's thwarted-yet-always-celebrated sovereignty is a fantasy of perfect reconciliation: an image of eros and nomos aligned, all the way from the grandest structures of the social to the most intimate textures of our dreams. The charismatic "bodies" of mass publicity—whether auratic brands, national flags, mass assemblies, or the embalmed bodies of long-deceased heads of state—are not to be understood as pathological remnants of a sacral age which, on the "civilized" side of the primitive settlement, we are now supposed to have transcended.[89] They are not objects that have forgotten that they were supposed to be transitional. Rather, like mass-mediated versions of Durkheim's totemic signs, they are the indispensable and always unstable mediators of eros and nomos, the vital vessels of the mana of mass society.

The Chocolate Side of Power

This has been a book about constitutive resonance. If resonance is to be understood as the secret of how we come to recognize ourselves as well as how we come to inhabit the worlds that may or may not recognize us, then what does this imply for an understanding of power? Is resonance a tool of power? Is it what seduces us into conformity, into identification with dominant ideologies? Or does resonance trouble power, resisting, in its open-endedness, any authoritative inscription?

Perhaps these aren't our only alternatives. For isn't it precisely the fact that any ideological order can only stabilize authoritative nomos by inciting resonant eros that enables what Sloterdijk superbly calls "the chocolate side of power": "Politics is not only the art of the possible, as has been said, but just as much the art of seduction. It is the chocolate side of power that assumes first, that order must prevail and, second, that the world wants to be deceived."[90] To be sure, "deception" might seem a loaded term here, insofar as it implies the possibility of another, healthier world, that of the undeceived. But the deeper problem is the normative presumption that one is *deceived into order* and the corollary presumption that liberation takes the form of *breaking with order.*

Could it be that just as Odysseus needed the Sirens' song to be *his* song without remainder so that he could feel affirmed in refusing it, so the desire to be able to know how to resist continues to need power to be *trying to administer us without remainder*, so that, against power, spaces and practices that exceed such administrative co-optation can be cultivated? As Steven Klein notes, democratic theory, in its pursuit of modes and methods of radical resistance, unwittingly reproduces "Weber's underlying assumption that everyday or normal politics is a domain of calculation [and] that in order to be stable, political institutions must render concrete phenomena orderly and predictable" precisely so that theory can oppose it with the "ruptural anti-institutional agency of the people."[91] In this way, the otherwise inadequate idea that institutions engage and rule us primarily by means of calculation and normalization gains plausibility and inflicts, to invoke Amitav Ghosh once again, its "final and most terrible defeat" on precisely the energies that would wish things to be otherwise.

The important point about "the chocolate side of power" is surely the reminder that a social order needs to be affective to be effective. In other words, because power must be grounded in a mimetic archive that necessarily exceeds its aims and ambitions, one can acknowledge, with Terry Eagleton, that "there is something in the body which can revolt against the power which inscribes it; and that impulse could only be eradicated by extirpating along with it the capacity to authenticate power itself."[92] Michel Callon makes the same point about marketing. Here, too, the assertion of control relies on something that comes from beyond the apparatus and that always overflows the instrumental concerns of brand managers and bean counters: "In the economy of qualities consumers are . . . a constant source of overflowing. And it would be counter-productive to simply suppress those overflowings, because in order to function, markets of the economy of qualities need them."[93] Robert Foster elaborates: "Consumer overflowings, then, are sources of innovation and competitive advantage for a firm as well as sources of uncertainty and challenges to expertise and authority."[94]

There's something disturbing about the way brands charismatically appropriate and then sell back to consumers "the meanings, social relations, and affect that consumers themselves have produced."[95] But there's also something reassuring about this dependency of the charismatic brand (or leader) on a substrate that belongs to all of us, since we can in principle choose to withdraw our collaboration and our identification and even work to destabilize the brand's charisma. "On the one hand," Foster observes, "consumer agency—in the form, for example, of unique product experiences (cocreated or not)—is a source of the surplus value that firms extract as rent by charging premium prices for the use of their brands. On the other hand, consumer agency is a source of disruption, of unruly overflowings that escape capture and can even destroy value—notably, the value of brands, favourite targets of no logo-style corporate anti-globalization activists."[96]

But should we really feel so reassured? Or to put it differently: doesn't this whole way of thinking about power—how worlds and the subjects who inhabit them are made, sustained, and unmade—remain misleadingly attached to an opposition between capture (power) and escape (resistance)? Perhaps the problem is that too many analyses of power and ideology are set up as a zero-sum game between agents of domination that are bent on co-opting us completely and heroically resistant subjects whose complex interiorities and intentions will always elude full capture. As Berlant notes, critics of the totalizing mechanism du jour—capitalism, the state, neoliberalism, whatever—often tend to posit, on the one hand, "a world-homogenizing sovereign with coherent intensions that produces subjects who serve its interests," and, on the other hand, the side of resistant subjects, "a singularity so radical that, if persons are not fully sovereign, they are nonetheless caught up in navigating and reconstructing the world that cannot fully saturate them."[97]

Berlant goes on to remind us that "sovereignty, after all, is a fantasy misrecognized as an objective state: an aspirational position of personal and institutional self-legitimating performativity and an affective sense of control in relation to the fantasy of that position's offer of security and efficacy."[98] But the sovereignty at issue here, of course, is not only that of the subject—the ordinary person, the consumer-citizen, the one who is both desiring and coping. It is also the sovereignty that person projects onto the agencies that address them in modes of command, reprimand, seduction, and so on. So, for example, insofar as I am invested in resisting mass publicity—in asserting my sovereignty against its call—I am also invested in the coherent intentionality of its agencies. Above all, I am invested in *its* supposed investment in addressing *me*. Alenka Zupančič suggests that there is, in the psychoanalytic sense, something hysterical about repetitive, apparently critical unmaskings of the perfidies of power. Precisely in the apparent act of unmasking the inconsistencies and perfidies of power, "the hysteric is much more revolted by the weakness of power than by power itself, and the truth of her or his basic complaint about the master is usually that the master is not master enough."⁹⁹

And like all magicians, like all would-be masters, the mana workers of the mass publicity machine are, in turn, deeply invested in convincing their clients as well as their consumers that they know what they're doing, that they have a plan, and that the plan will work. Foster notes that marketing theory acknowledges and grapples with the indeterminacies introduced into marketing practice by "consumer overflowings." Of course marketing professionals will only get paid if they devise ever-new ways to make it look as if all indeterminacies can be made to serve the bottom line. Hence crowdsourcing, prosumption, and other such quasi-democratic reinventions of mass marketing.

Here I think it's crucial to make two points. First, the one that Horkheimer and Adorno made long ago—namely, that it's not that marketers actually *are* in control, but rather that they must convince themselves, each other, and the rest of us that they are.¹⁰⁰ This, for example, is the reason why the prospect of a presidential candidate succeeding without the now-usual micromanaged messaging machine is terrifying to publicity professionals—just as consumer marketing executives dread inexplicable success more than they fear failure (which can always be explained away).¹⁰¹

Second, the very fact that marketing is *not* a watertight machine is in fact—and half behind the backs of its practitioners—not necessarily a cause for relief but rather also and at the same time the most important source of whatever resonant influence the commercial media are able to activate. The surplus element, that which is not fully integrated, the extimate obtrusion—this is the lure that seduces. Dolar: "This little bit of surplus is finally the motor of any ideological edifice, its fuel, the award elusively offered to the subject for entering into ideological turmoil. The structural problem of ideology is ultimately that this fuel cannot be integrated into the edifice, so it turns out to be at the same time its explosive force."¹⁰²

Why should social theory, thinking all the while that it's engaging in ideology critique, collaborate with the self-representation of publicity experts? But too often it does. Ironically, self-styled critics lend the powers that be the kind of totalizing and all-subsuming appearance they could otherwise only aspire to in dreams. And this totalizing appearance then operates as a foil for the tireless search for other spaces, "heterotopias,"[103] from which to challenge the grasp of states and markets. But mana has no outside. Its difference as well as its identity is immanent. Its immanent *in*coherence is at once the principle of its seduction and the secret of its instability. And here again Eagleton puts it splendidly: "Ideology must not so thoroughly center the subject as to castrate its desire; instead we must be both cajoled and chastised, made to feel both homeless and at home, folded upon the world yet reminded that our true resting place is infinity."[104] If one wants to occupy a position of hope—and why wouldn't one?—then one could say that power doesn't understand its own queerness. As critical theorists, we should be careful not to make the same mistake. The question is not so much "how can we make a space for difference against power?" The question is, rather, "what can we gain from the effacement of difference within power's self-understanding (but not within its operation)?"

Franz Kafka's (very) short story "The Silence of the Sirens" adds an enigmatic twist to the story of Odysseus's near miss. In Kafka's version of the encounter, Odysseus sticks wax in his *own* ears as well as lashing himself to the ship's mast. Within the story, Kafka's narrator gives us two interpretations of this. Perhaps, by sticking wax in his ears, Odysseus fails to realize that the Sirens are only *pretending* to sing: "For a fleeting moment he saw their throats rising and falling, their breasts lifting, their eyes filled with tears, their lips half-parted, but believed that these were accompaniments to the airs which died unheard around him."[105] Or perhaps, the narrator muses right at the end, Odysseus really *is* "so full of guile, . . . such a fox"[106] that he only pretends not to know that the Sirens are only pretending to sing?

In the first variation, Odysseus is so naively preoccupied with his own cleverness that he doesn't notice that the Sirens own him without even *having* to sing—although Kafka's narrator expresses uncertainty as to whether the Sirens "thought that this enemy could be vanquished only by their silence, or because the look of bliss on the face of Ulysses [Odysseus], who was thinking of nothing but his wax and his chains, made them forget their silence."[107] This suggestion haunts Kafka's story: that it is actually the *Sirens* who end up seduced by the blissful self-absorption of Odysseus's commitment to autonomy. Or perhaps, as in the second variation, Odysseus is actually the one who keeps the whole deception going by pretending not to know that there is nothing to hear. Kafka's narrator speculates that Odysseus "held up to [the Sirens] and to the gods the aforementioned pretense merely as a sort of shield."[108]

But whom is Odysseus really protecting with his shield? Himself or the Sirens? Or perhaps the gods that oversee their encounter? Odysseus could just be pulling a fast one on the Sirens. But maybe he's doing their pride as much of a favor as his own. The Sirens sense an unusual self-possession in Odysseus—whether it comes from naïveté or cunning doesn't much matter. In Kafka's story, Odysseus *undoes* the Sirens: as he sails by, lashed and plugged, the Sirens "no longer had any desire to allure; all that they wanted was to hold as long as they could the radiance that fell from Ulysses' great eyes."[109] The only reason the Sirens aren't "annihilated" by the encounter with this idiot savant/sly fox, Kafka's narrator says, is that they possess no consciousness. One might speculate that this is because they're like the algorithms that can know us so intimately because they aren't distracted by their own desires. Or perhaps the Sirens have no consciousness because, as with Horkheimer and Adorno's culture industries, they rely on us to believe that some kind of coherent intentionality is really in control behind "their eyes filled with tears."

The pretense that Odysseus holds up to the Sirens and the gods like a shield may be intended to protect his own resistant agency by protecting the appearance of a coherent counteragency to be resisted—because the alternative is more difficult to bear. As Dolar observes in the course of his own interpretation of Kafka's story: "We cannot resist silence, for the simple reason that there is nothing to resist."[110] Kafka's narrator introduces the story with the line: "Proof that inadequate, even childish measures may serve to rescue one from peril."[111] But what peril? The peril of being sucked in by an overwhelmingly coherent seduction machine that might just address you perfectly? Or the more terrifying prospect of the reorientation that becomes necessary once we acknowledge the *in*coherence of the agencies that address us, the resonant contingency of our encounters?[112]

Slipping T/ropes, Ticking Clock

We have traveled a great distance since the mana moment a century ago, and yet in many ways our present is full of echoes. Like the mana moment anthropologists, we too live in a time in which the conditions of communication are undergoing rapid and radical transformation. During the mana moment, the transition from telegraph through cinema and on to radio seemed to proliferate uneasy spirits and insinuate unseemly participations. Today we are living through a digital revolution in which the universal fungibility of binary code translates all previously separated representations into a single, immanent substance that migrates between devices and interfaces with all the virtuality and virality once ascribed to mana. The mana moment saw the end of the great imperial formations in Europe and the rise of the nation-state as universal political form, although colonial ambitions hung on for a few more decades. We too are living through the end of empire, as the receding American Century opens the way for other pretenders. We too sense the gap between enormous energies and exhausted institutions.

These are the times when generative re-membering becomes possible, when the t/ropes of our long-standing settlements start slipping and concepts apparently long dormant reveal their slow and patient subterranean crossings. At the end of the introduction, I adapted a line of Benjamin's to suggest that mana now "has something to say to us only because it is contained in the ticking of a clock whose striking of the hour has only just reached *our* ears."[113] Having traversed, now, the intervening chapters, I can only hope that some of these clock chimes, previously buried in the settlements that have kept them muted, have become audible and re-cognizable.

I've tried in these pages to stage a series of resonant encounters — between past and present, between anthropology and critical theory, between assertion and speculation. If I have in some sense been able to "redeem" mana, then, by the same token, I should now be ready to let go of it. Because mana was only ever a symptom, a key, a sign of potentialities to be uncovered in a shared mimetic archive. And my work, as a critic rather than a commentator, has been to remain attentive to what *lives* in this symptom.

Another passage from Benjamin comes to mind, by way of a closing thought. It seems only appropriate that I found it in Benjamin's essay on Goethe's *Elective Affinities*:

> The history of works prepares for their critique, and thus historical distance increases their power. If, to use a simile, one views the growing work as a burning funeral pyre, then the commentator stands before it like a chemist, the critic like an alchemist. Whereas, for the former, wood and ash remain the sole objects of his analysis, for the latter only the flame itself preserves an enigma: that of what is alive. Thus, the critic inquires into the truth, whose living flame continues to burn over the heavy logs of what is past and the light ashes of what has been experienced.[114]

Notes

1   Durkheim 1995 [1912], 213. Schiermer 2016 reminded me of this passage during the final stages of writing.

2   Durkheim 1995 [1912], 192.

3   Ibid., 209.

4   Ibid., 322.

5   Mauss 2001 [1902–3], 111.

6   Taussig n.d.

7   Saunders 2016, 50.

8   See Santner 2011 and 2015 for discussions of this problem of the "excorporation" of the collective democratic flesh.

9   See my discussion of branding as a practice of "keeping-while-giving" (a term I adapted from the anthropologist Annette Weiner) in Mazzarella 2003b, chapter 6. See also Foster 2013 and Nakassis 2012, 2013.

10 As Slavoj Žižek glosses it, the extimate is "the irreducible trace of externality in the very midst of 'internality,' its condition of impossibility (a foreign body preventing the subject's full constitution) which is simultaneously its condition of possibility" (Žižek 1999a, 117).

11   Handy 1927, 27.

12   By "mass publicity" I mean not only those techniques of persuasion that we know as advertising, marketing, and public relations, but also all the practices of address, circulation, and reception that amount to what we might, more inelegantly, call "mass publicness"—i.e., the modern condition of finding oneself interpellated as part of a polity in which one is expected to "find oneself" among millions of people one will never meet. This is at once a question of "imagined communities" (Anderson 1992), of "the public sphere" (Habermas 1989 [1962]; Warner 2002), and of "public culture" (Breckenridge 1995; Mazzarella 2005; Pinney 2001).

13   Sloterdijk 2011 [1998], 559.

14   Carson 2014 [1986], 39.

15   Hirschkind 2006; Mahmood 2004; Spadola 2014.

16   Similarly, "ex-citation."

17   Hirschkind 2006, 78.

18   Berlant 2011, 84.

19   Benjamin 1999a, 392.

20   Ibid., 462, 463.

21   Bhabha 1984.

22   Berlant 2008, 2011; Gregg and Seigworth 2010; Leys 2011; Massumi 2002, 2015; Mazzarella 2009; Stewart 2007.

23   Stewart 2007, 87.

24   Eagleton 1990; Haug 1986, 1987.

25   Berlant 2011, 67.

26   Clifford and Marcus 1986. See also Marcus and Fisher 1986. For a set of retrospective views, see Starn 2015. David Norbrook makes a parallel point about historiography: "In what has become a standard narrative, an old, unthinkingly positivist and apolitical historicism has been superseded by a new historicism that has become aware for the first time that historical writing is not unproblematically and apolitically objective" (1996, 330).

27   Da Col and Graeber 2011, x.

28   Ibid.

29 Ibid.

30 Ibid.

31 Ibid., vii–viii, original emphasis.

32 Ibid., xiv.

33 Ibid., viii.

34 Da Col and Graeber invoke Umberto Eco here: "one should not only be preoccupied by the ontological constraints but also with the licenses of *dire quasi la stessa cosa*—of 'almost-saying' the same thing when translating—and accepting that linguistic incommensurability does not entail incomparability but a *comparability in becoming*" (ibid.).

35 Žižek 1999a, 128n2. For some of my critical reflections on these tendencies, see Mazzarella 2009, 2010, 2013b.

36 Mazzarella 2013a, 26.

37 Viveiros de Castro 2013, 477.

38 Meillassoux 2008.

39 See Shaviro 2014 for a lucid and sympathetic exposition of some of these currents.

40 Viveiros de Castro 2013, 477.

41 Lukács 1971 [1923], 99.

42 Ibid., 118.

43 Viveiros de Castro 2013, 475.

44 On immunology as a figure for world-making, see Duclos forthcoming, Esposito 2011, Santner 2011, and Sloterdijk 2013 [2009].

45 Adorno 1973 [1966], 62.

46 Kohn 2015, 314.

47 Ibid.

48 Ibid., 315.

49 Ibid., 320.

50 Durkheim, 1995 [1912], 209.

51 Ibid., 213.

52   Horkheimer and Adorno 2002 [1944].

53   Althusser 2008 [1970].

54   Sloterdijk 2011 [1998], 479.

55   Hume 2000 [1739-40]; Smith 1984 [1759].

56   Kant 2009 [1790]. Tellingly, Shaviro's (2014) exploration of present-day "speculative realism"—a philosophical variant on the ontological turn—ends with a reading of Kant's third critique. To my mind, Shaviro's attempt to give the third critique an exceptional status in Kant's oeuvre—the better to preserve the "Kantian catastrophe" that motivates the ontological turn—misses the constitutive relation that Kant imagined for aesthetic judgment vis-à-vis speculative judgment.

57   See, for example, Kant's discussion of opulence in the second book of his *Anthropology from a Pragmatic Point of View* (Kant 1996 [1798]).

58   Sloterdijk 1987 [1983], 110.

59   Hegel 1998 [1835], 442.

60   Derrida 1981 [1972], 71.

61   Peters 2015, 354.

62   Benjamin 1994, 509.

Chapter One

1   Quotation attributed to Pliny, printed on the inside of the first pouch of rolling tobacco that I purchased as I set out for India to conduct my dissertation fieldwork.

2   Durkheim 1995 [1912].

3   Mauss 2001 [1902-3], 111. The form of the citation marks the erasure of Hubert's name from subsequent editions of the work that he wrote with Mauss.

4   Ibid., 50.

5   Malinowski 1935, 237.

6   Ibid.

7   Ibid.

8   Ibid., 238.

9 Thus runs Malinowski's speculative linguistic history: "having started using language in a manner which is both magical and pragmatic, and passed gradually through stages in which the magical and pragmatic aspects intermingle and oscillate, the individual will find within his culture certain crystallized, traditionally standardized types of speech, with the language of technology and science at one end, and the language of sacrament, prayer, magical formula, advertisement, and political oratory at the other" (Malinowski 1935, 236).

10 Couliano 1987 [1984], 104.

11 Couliano draws centrally on Giordano Bruno's sixteenth-century treatise, *De Vinculis in Genere* (Of Bonds in General). The idea of magical-erotic binding provocatively resonates with the etymological roots of the word *religion* in the Latin *religare*, again denoting binding.

12 Sloterdijk 2011 [1998], 559.

13 See Howe 1978 and McKinnon 2010 for illuminating discussions of elective affinity as a category.

14 Howe (1978, 375) notes that some chemists of the late eighteenth century objected to the principle of elective affinities because the element of contingency seemed to thwart reliably predictive laws of cause and effect. As we shall see in chapters 3 and 4, contingency haunts the would-be science of marketing in much the same way.

15 Couliano 1987 [1984], 104.

16 Couliano does, however, grant a special place among modern magicians to psychiatrists and psychoanalysts, inheritors of the great tradition of face-to-face magic.

17 Marett 1914a [1908], 106.

18 Peters 2001.

19 Mauss 2001 [1902–3], 132.

20 Morgan, quoted in Immergut and Kosut 2014, 281.

21 Malinowski 1948 [1925], 24, 78.

22 Holbraad 2006, 189.

23 King 1892, 140.

24 Durkheim 1995 [1912], 192.

25 Handy 1927, 28.

26 Keesing 1984, 138.

27 Ibid., 148, italics added.

28 Codrington notes with satisfaction that he had, as early as 1878, by means of a letter prompted the great philologist and Orientalist Max Müller to insert a mention of mana into a lecture. See also Tomlinson 2006, 174, for some pre-Codrington references to mana.

29 Codrington 1891, 118–19.

30 Ibid., 191.

31 Mauss 2001 [1902–3], 137.

32 Durkheim 1995 [1912], 195.

33 Malinowski 1948 [1925], 24, 78.

34 Webster 1913, 846.

35 Jonsson 2013 offers a fine discussion of how the deeply ambivalent figure of "the masses" in interwar Europe marked a crisis of representation: how to give palpable and intelligible form to democratic passions.

36 Musil 1995 [1952], 3–4. See Jonsson 2000 for a fine and, for our purposes, extremely apt analysis.

37 Nye 1995. As Leela Gandhi (2014, 36) shows, the New Imperialism also triggered a boom in ostentatious consumption in England, further stoking anxieties about the effect that such material excess might have on the moral fiber of the rich and, by way of pedagogical example, the ethical energies of the poor.

38 Benjamin 2003 [1940], 328.

39 Stocking 1995, 147.

40 See, for example, Blom 2008.

41 Simmel 1997 [1918].

42 Ibid., 77.

43 Lévy-Bruhl 1966 [1910], 345.

44 Pels 2003.

45 Mann 1996 [1924].

46 Freud 1990 [1913].

47 Quoted in and translated by Crapanzano 1995, 103.

48 Firth 1940, 483.

49 Ibid., 497.

50 Evans-Pritchard 1965, 33.

51 Firth 1940, 502. Valerio Valeri would later be sharply critical of Firth's exclusive reliance on explicit verbal references: "Indeed, if there is a criticism that can be raised against Firth's treatment of mana in Tikopia it is that he uses as sources of information only verbal statements about mana. Presumably a ritual that involves mana can tell us a lot about this notion even if the corresponding word is never pronounced during the performance" (Valeri 1985, 98).

52 A recurrent tendency in the mana debates has been to try to explain "impersonal" versus "personal" conceptions of mana by situating them sociologically. Paul Radin (1937) argued, for example, that it depended on what kind of informant you were asking in any given society. The more "theological" aspect of impersonal mana, he suggested, would be the way that native intellectuals would put the matter, whereas ordinary laypersons would tend to perceive it in more concretized and personalized forms. Decades later, Roger Keesing (1984) noted that a substantivized conception of mana as a "force" tended to go hand in hand with the development of more hierarchical social relations in the eastern sections of the Polynesian region.

53 Leach 1985, 252.

54 Sahlins 2012, ix. In addition to Firth 1940, see, for example, Blust 2007, Evans-Pritchard 1929, Hogbin 1936, Keesing 1984, MacClancy 1986, Mondragón 2004, Needham 1976, Shore 1989, and Valeri 1985. Claude Lévi-Strauss's critique of Mauss's reading of mana was an important and influential exception to this trend—one to which I will return in chapter 2.

55 Evans-Pritchard 1965, 9. As Evans-Pritchard fairly notes, the analytical method of Tylor, Frazer, and the other "progressionists" (a term he submits as a more accurate designation than the more widely accepted "evolutionists") consisted largely of alternating between narcissistic psychological projection ("If I were a horse . . .") and entirely imaginary just-so stories along the lines of "how the leopard got his spots."

Incidentally, Jane Harrison, writing in 1921, reminds us that Frazer himself clearly felt that he, unlike even more purely speculative thinkers, was rigorously responsible to the factual record. Harrison critiques a certain fanciful theory about the origins of kingship by remarking: "It is the answer of what Dr Frazer calls the 'armchair philosopher with his feet on the fender,' and not of the man who seeks his facts among the savages of to-day in Uganda, in Malay [*sic*], in Central Australia, in Japan" (Harrison 1921, 19).

56 "It is one of the aims of social anthropology to interpret all differences in the form of a typical social institution by reference to difference in social structure" (Evans-Pritchard 1929, 641).

57 Marett 1914a [1908], 101. See Meyer 2015 for a defense of the continuing usefulness of Marett's social-psychological approach to religion.

58 Ibid., 104.

59 Goldenweiser 1915b, 636n5.

60 Codrington's seminal 1891 presentation, for instance, prefaces his discussion of mana with a level of methodological reflexivity that can only strike the present-day reader as ahead of its time: "every one, missionary and visitor, carries with him some preconceived ideas; he expects to see idols, and he sees them; images are labeled idols in museums whose makers carved them for amusement; a Solomon islander fashions the head of his lime-box stick into a grotesque figure, and it becomes the subject of a woodcut as 'a Solomon island god'" (Codrington 1891, 118). He then proceeds to ignore his own warning almost entirely.

61 "Thus, the force of magic is not a universal force residing everywhere, flowing where it will or it is willed to. Magic is the one and only specific power, a force unique of its kind, residing exclusively in man, let loose only by his magical art, gushing out with his voice, conveyed by the casting forth of the rite" (Malinowski 1948 [1925], 76).

62 Boyer and Howe 2015, 16.

63 "It is a collection of absurd reconstructions, unsupportable hypotheses and conjectures, wild speculations, suppositions and assumptions, inappropriate analogies, misunderstandings and misinterpretations, and, especially in what [Jevons] wrote about totemism, just plain nonsense" (Evans-Pritchard 1965, 5).

64 Leach 1985, 235.

65 Ibid., 248. By comparison it is interesting to note that the study of comparative religion, in the tradition so influentially consolidated by Mircea Eliade (a tradition to which Ioan Couliano intimately but

ambivalently belonged) went in exactly the opposite direction to the empiricist settlement in anthropology. Its practitioners pursued an anti-empiricist reconstruction of Frazerian arguments by way of phenomenology and existentialism (I owe this point to a personal communication from Jeremy Walton).

66 As Leach notes, Evans-Pritchard was himself a convert to Catholicism and evidently troubled by what he felt to be the arrogantly superficial rationalism of much of what had passed for an anthropology of religion. Indeed, the closest Evans-Pritchard gets to an empathetic gesture vis-à-vis the Victorians is to suggest that they were preoccupied with primitive religions "largely, I suppose, because they faced a crisis in their own" (Evans-Pritchard, 1965, 4).

67 Ibid., 33.

68 Ibid., 110.

69 Ibid., 100.

70 Tylor 1874 [1871], 157.

71 Ibid., 159.

72 Evans-Pritchard 1965, 112.

73 Comaroff and Comaroff 2012, 6; see also Dussel 1995 [1992], Trouillot 1991, and Wilder 2015.

74 See Miller 2008; Žižek 1999d.

75 Lévi-Strauss 1987 [1950].

76 Marett 1914b [1910], 193.

77 Marett 1914a [1908], 119.

78 Marett 1914b [1910], 200–201.

79 Durkheim 1995 [1912], 192.

80 Ibid., 217.

81 Handy 1927, 28–29.

82 Hannerz 1992, 264.

83 Significantly, it was Handy—the purveyor of the most extended metaphorization of mana as electricity—who also qualified the metaphor most explicitly as a purely pragmatic heuristic device, referring to his own "description of the theory of mana in terms of electricity, which

has been pursued only for the sake of illustration and not because I believe mana to have anything to do with electricity" (Handy 1927, 29).

84 Lukes 1972; Needham 1967 [1963].

85 Needham 1976, 82. The reactionary minority view, articulated as late as 1938 by J. H. Hutton, was that mana came out sounding like a substance not because anthropologists translated it that way, but because primitive peoples thought in concrete rather than in abstract terms: "Primitive language is very rich in concrete terms, exceedingly poor in abstract, and no doubt the lack of any terms other than concrete ones, representing a similarly restricted mental imagery, has been largely responsible for the idea of soul-substance" (Hutton 1938, 23).

86 Keesing 1984, 148.

87 Ibid., 149–50.

88 Matt Tomlinson (2006) revisits Keesing's intervention and notes, from the standpoint of his fieldwork in Fiji, that the substantialization of mana may in part be an effect of "foreign" translation, but if so, it is a translation that has been taking place for many years as a result of Methodist Christian missionary work in the area. In any case Fijians themselves, Tomlinson points out, nowadays commonly use "mana" in precisely such a substantialized way. Like Tomlinson, Mac-Clancy (1986) notes that the meanings of mana have, unsurprisingly, not remained static in Pacific usage since Codrington and the others launched it onto the Euro-American stage: "It is *because mana*-notions are floating signifiers that they have retained their function" (Mac-Clancy 1986, 149). For example, Banks Islanders, who in Codrington's day held *mana* and Christianity to be incompatible, have more recently come to speak of *mana* as a "bad" form of power associated with "traditional" lifeways.

89 Pickering 1984, 210. In writing his novel *The Elective Affinities*, Goethe quite clearly understood himself as probing the metaphorical interchange between the natural and the cultural sciences. As he put it in an advertisement for the work: "It appears that the author's continued studies in the physical sciences have occasioned this strange title. He would like to remark that in the study of nature one very often makes use of moral imagery in order to bring closer something far removed from the circle of human knowledge, and so he wished in a moral case to trace a chemical metaphor back to its spiritual origins" (quoted in Howe 1978, 372–73).

90 During 2002, 21.

91 Quoted in Lears 1994, 217.

92 Borch 2013; Jonsson 2013; Mazzarella 2010; Schnapp and Tiews 2006.

93 Peters 2001, 94.

94 Ibid.

95 Taussig 1993; see also Jones 2010.

96 Lévy-Bruhl, 1966 [1910], 57.

97 Smith 2004, 134.

98 Pratt 1992.

99 Durkheim 1995 [1912], 211.

100 Ibid., 218.

101 Ibid., 212-15.

102 Crapanzano 1995, 391n2.

103 See Schiermer 2013 on this point.

104 Durkheim 1995 [1912], 216.

105 Ibid., 222. Bjørn Schiermer usefully collates Durkheim's key examples of modern media of effervescence: "Durkheim speaks of collectively articulated and intensified sentiments of 'devotedness,' 'attraction,' 'desire' and even 'love' for certain objects . . . and he mentions a multitude of modern 'fetishes': besides 'Fatherland, Liberty, Reason' (1995: 216), modern humanism (1994), Kantian morals (1974: 35-79) and the national 'flag' (1995: 228-9), we find cultural personalities or 'leaders' (1995: 215), but also objects for collectors' mania, such as 'stamps' (1974: 87, 1995: 228-9), or of consumerist desire, such as 'pearls,' 'diamonds,' 'fur coats' and 'laces,' 'attire' and the 'whims of fashion' (1974: 86)" (Schiermer 2016, 132; the 1994 reference is the same text—Durkheim's essay "Individualism and the Intellectuals"—that appears as Durkheim 1973c [1898] in my list of references).

106 Tarde 1969 [1901], 284; see also Le Bon 2002 [1895].

107 Tarde 1903 [1890], 78 ff.

108 Mauss 2001 [1902-3], 41.

109 Ibid., 50.

110 Ibid., 111.

111 Ibid., 118.

112 Mauss and Hubert are exceptionally interesting on the vexed question of belief. Generations have argued back and forth about whether magicians cynically exploit the naive credulity of their clientele (but see Taussig 2006a for an exceptionally suggestive reading of this problem). Again, Mauss and Hubert's take is dialectical. They begin by suggesting that the elaborate seriousness of magical rites suggest, on the part of the magician, at least "a genuine will to believe in it" (Mauss 2001 [1902-3], 116). In the heat of the ritual, moreover, the magician may be transported into "nervous and cataleptic states" in which "he may truly fall prey to all kinds of illusions" (117). At the same time, in subjecting themselves to such states, magicians are, in a sense, deliberately and consciously creating the conditions of deception, even if—note the twist here—this is done with the greatest sincerity: "we are forced to conclude that there has always been a certain degree of simulation among these people. We are in no doubt that magical facts need constant encouragement and that even the sincerest delusions of the magician have always been self-imposed to some degree" (118). If suggestion is at work here, then it works both ways. The suggestibility of the crowd depends on—indeed *demands*—the voluntary suggestibility of the magician: "The magician then becomes his own dupe. . . . The magician pretends because pretense is demanded of him, because people seek him out and beseech him to act. . . . in most cases he is irresistibly tempted by public credulity" (118).

113 Durkheim, 1995 [1912], 213.

114 This is what Paddy Scannell (2000) calls "for-anyone-as-someone structures" of communication.

115 Warner 2002, 57. It is significant, perhaps, that the "counterpublics" part of Warner's argument seems to have been more influential than his insistence, with the Kantian-Habermasian tradition, on the intimate anonymity of publics as such. It is only by acknowledging the intimate anonymity characteristic of publics that we can acknowledge not only the standard normative project of becoming-citizen (the askesis of public subjectivity) but also the mana of mass publicity (see, e.g., Wedeen 2007).

116 "Their unity arises solely from having the same name and the same emblem, from believing they have the same relations with the same categories of things, and from practicing the same rites—in other words, from the fact that they commune in the same totemic cult" (Durkheim 1995 [1912], 169).

117 Mazzarella 2013a.

118 Spadola 2014, 27.

119 "[Reason] is the power of the mind to rise above the particular, the contingent, and the individual and to think in universal terms. From this point of view, one can say that what makes a man a person is that by which he indistinguishable from other men; it is that which makes him man, rather than such and such a man. The senses, the body, in short everything that individualizes, is, to the contrary, regarded by Kant as antagonistic to personhood" (Durkheim 1995 [1912], 273).

120 Darnton 1968; Sloterdijk 2011 [1998].

121 Lévi-Strauss 1987 [1950].

122 Latour 1993.

123 Simmel 1997 [1918], 89.

Chapter Two

1   Quoted in Graham 2007, 37–38.

2   Burke 2006 [1789–90]; Paine 1998 [1791].

3   Paine, 1998 [1791], 119.

4   Burke, 2006 [1789–90], 31.

5   Simmel 2010 [1918], 13, 9.

6   From this point on, I will ask readers to fill in their own scare quotes around this word.

7   Durkheim 1995 [1912], 209.

8   Ibid., 322.

9   Johansen 1954, quoted in Sahlins 2012, x.

10 Or is it that order as such is staged as having a normative and thus a therapeutic value? Thanks to Shannon Dawdy for the provocation.

11 Lévi-Strauss 1963a [1949a], 171.

12 Lévi-Strauss 1963b [1949b], 203.

13 Lévi-Strauss 1963a [1949a], 171–72.

14 Shore 1989, 143.

15 Quoted in ibid., 148.

16 Deleuze and Guattari 1994 [1991], 36.

17 Deleuze and Guattari suggest that planes of immanence should be imagined archaeologically, stratigraphically, rather than genealogically. Sometimes elements of one burst through into another (can we think this along with Benjamin's notion of historical redemption—the "now of recognizability"?) Planes of immanence "succeed and contest each other in history" (Deleuze and Guattari 1994 [1991], 39).

18 Ibid., 44–45. In his final essay, "Immanence: A Life," Deleuze wrote: "We will say of pure immanence that it is A LIFE and nothing else. It is not immanence to life, but the immanent that is nothing is itself a life. A life is the immanence of immanence, absolute immanence: it is complete power, complete bliss" (Deleuze 2001 [1995], 27). Deleuze proposes that such absolute immanence accompanies all actualized forms of subjects and objects, but is also transcendent in the sense of not being reducible to historical or biographical time.

> A life is everywhere, in all the moments that a given living subject goes through and that are measured by given lived objects: an immanent life carrying with it the events or singularities that are merely actualized in subjects and objects. This indefinite life does not itself have moments, close as they may be to one another, but only between-times, between-moments; it doesn't just come about or come after but offers the immensity of an empty time where one sees the event yet to come and already happened, in the absolute of an immediate consciousness. (29)

In some respects, then, the relation between virtual immanence and actual subject-object relations might seem to resemble the dynamic I am proposing for the mimetic archive. And in some ways I would be happy for this to be the case. My worry is that Deleuze has bequeathed to his many followers a lopsided investment in the purity of becoming that, when brought to bear in empirical social science research, tends to become complicit with a too-hasty corollary presumption that any actually existing social institutions or forms are simply mechanisms for constraining and disciplining vitality. The parallel with my argument about the populist backlash against Adorno's critique of the culture industry in chapter 3 will be clear.

19 Some readers will know that this is a pet peeve of mine, a point
    repeatedly made against the tide. Versions of the argument appear in
    Mazzarella 2009 and 2010, and in Mazzarella 2013b, 191, I had occa-
    sion to remark: "the list of reified oppositions marches on two by two:
    politics against police (Rancière), molecular against molar (Deleuze
    and Guattari), intuitive against conceptual knowing (Bergson). In
    every case, the narcissistically 'critical' valorization of the first term
    brings the second back in the mode of the undead. A zombie concept,
    leached of the complexities of life but reliably indestructible. The Bad
    Guy in the melodrama of Critical Theory." Do I repeat myself? Very
    well, then I repeat myself (I am fixated, I inhabit obsessions).

20 As Hegel puts it in his Encyclopaedia Logic, the dialectics is "in gen-
    eral the principle of all motion, of all life, and of all activation in the
    actual world" (Hegel 1998a [1817], 171).

21 Benjamin 2002b [1936], 104-5.

22 Carson 2014 [1986], 20.

23 Pels 2003, 5, 17; see also Jones 2010.

24 Hewitt 1902, 35, 36, italics added.

25 I'm adapting the term "autological" from Povinelli 2006.

26 Tylor 1874 [1871], 157.

27 Like Frazer, Tylor—whatever the accusations of ungrounded specula-
    tion that were later thrown at him—believed himself to be an empiri-
    cal scientist, prefacing *Primitive Culture* with the sanguine diagno-
    sis: "It is not too much to say that a perceptible movement of public
    opinion has here justified the belief that the English mind, not readily
    swayed by rhetoric, moves freely under the pressure of facts" (Tylor
    1874 [1871], viii).

28 Ibid., 136-37.

29 In certain respects, the "diffusionist" position of W. H. R. Rivers and
    his associates at Cambridge was a bridge between the hardcore pro-
    gressionism of a Tylor or a Frazer and the bounded sociocultural
    relativism that came to dominate anthropology after the empiri-
    cist settlement. In a lecture on the relation between primitive magic
    and dreams, Rivers emphasized that it was necessary to distinguish
    between primitive mentality, whose associated practices might travel
    and intermix with more advanced institutions, and primitive society.
    In this way, Rivers was able to hang on to the concept of the primitive

while at the same time acknowledging the historical complexity of any actually existing society: "Though existing cultures may not be primitive in the sense that they represent simple and uncontaminated stages of social development, we can safely accept the primitive character of their mentality and take them as our guides to the history of *mental* development, though they are of very questionable value as guides to the order of *social* development" (Rivers 1918, 24).

30 Tylor 1874 [1871], 132.

31 Ibid., 115.

32 De Martino 1988 [1948], 118n79.

33 Ibid., 152, italics added.

34 Lévy-Bruhl 1966 [1910], 344, 347.

35 Evans-Pritchard 1965, 91.

36 Lévy-Bruhl 1966 [1910], 76, italics added.

37 McDougall 1908, 97.

38 Durkheim and Mauss 1963 [1903], 6.

39 Simon During (2002, 17) notes that Lévy-Bruhl adapted his notion of "participation" from Neoplatonist philosophy.

40 Lévy-Bruhl 1966 [1910], 89.

41 Marett 1914b [1910], 197. The pioneering classicist Jane Ellen Harrison attempted to clarify myth and ritual in the ancient world by way of Durkheim and Freud. On the constitutive gap, she wrote:

> In animals who act from what we call instinct action follows immediately or at least swiftly on perception, but in man where the nervous system is more complex perception is not immediately transformed into action, there is an interval for choice between several possible courses. Perception is pent up and, helped by emotion, becomes conscious representation. In this momentary halt between perception and reaction all our images, ideas, in fact our whole mental life, is built up. If we were a mass of well combined instincts, that is if the cycle of perception and action were instantly fulfilled, we should have no representation and hence no art and no theology. (Harrison 1921, 27-28)

42 Kant 2001 [1786], 1996 [1798].

43 Freud 1959 [1921].

44 Mazzarella 2010.

45 Wilson 1991 [1970]; Stambach 2000; Tambiah 1990.

46 Frazer 1922 [1890], 57, 13.

47 Tylor 1874 [1871], 116.

48 Goldenweiser 1917, 113–14.

49 Lévi-Strauss 1966 [1962], 13, 22.

50 Ibid., 15, 5.

51 By emphasizing the differences between concrete and scientific think-ing, Lévi-Strauss was, despite his suspicion of the affective, closer to Lévy-Bruhl's *problematique* than to a project like Paul Radin's *Primitive Man as Philosopher* (1957 [1927]), which tried to show that primitive societies contained classes of people who, in a formally significant way, could be likened to Western intellectuals.

52 Lévi-Strauss, 1966 [1962], 20, italics added.

53 Ibid., 11.

54 Ibid., 10.

55 Horkheimer and Adorno 2002 [1944], 13.

56 Lévi-Strauss 1987 [1950], 53, 63, 62.

57 Lévi-Strauss 1966 [1962], 3.

58 Lévi-Strauss 1987 [1950], 57.

59 Ibid.

60 Lévy-Bruhl 1966 [1910], 98 ff.

61 Ibid., 23.

62 Hume 2000 [1739–40], 240.

63 Evans-Pritchard 1965, 68.

64 Durkheim 1973d [1914], 160.

65 Marett 1914b [1910], 191.

66 Ibid., 175.

67 Goldenweiser 1915a, 728. And Ruth Benedict, in a survey article on the anthropology of religion, boiled Durkheim's contribution down to "religion as the outcome of crowd excitement" (Benedict 1938, 627).

Nevertheless, as W. S. F. Pickering (1984) observes, Durkheim does not use the word *foule*, and the only vaguely crowd-psychological work that he actually cites is Otto Stöll's *Suggestion und Hypnotismus in der Völkerpsychologie* (1894). If anything, Pickering suggests, we might do well to look for Durkheim's inspiration in Henri Bergson's concept of *élan vital*. Still, Pickering also appends a chart demonstrating the close resonance between Durkheim's understanding of the corroboree and core crowd psychological concerns. See also Mellor 1998.

68   Evans-Pritchard 1965, 44.

69   Pickering 1984, 401.

70   As Simon During points out, Moses has always already been under suspicion of being a magician (2002, 3–4).

71   Lévi-Strauss 1987 [1950], 45.

72   Mauss 2001 [1902–3], 155.

73   Ibid., 159, 160.

74   Ibid., 154.

75   Ibid., 161.

76   Ibid., 50.

77   Lévi-Strauss 1987 [1950], 56.

78   Holbraad 2006, 194.

79   Adorno 1997 [1970], 11.

80   Ibid., 55.

81   Mazzarella 2009, 296.

82   I should add that this was not quite Evans-Pritchard's own opinion of Durkheim's achievement. Acknowledging its greatness, Evans-Pritchard nevertheless had little time for Durkheim's theory of ritual, which he called "the central and most obscure part of Durkheim's thesis, and also the most unconvincing part of it" (Evans-Pritchard 1965, 61).

83   Pinney 2004.

84   Durkheim 1995 [1912], 217.

85   Mauss 2001, 162.

86 In an extemporaneous commentary, Durkheim exemplified the unusually positive spin that he gave to crowd energy *in general*: "We indeed know from experience that when men are all gathered together, when they live a communal life, the very fact of their coming together causes exceptionally intense forces to arise which dominate them, exalt them, give them a quality of life to a degree unknown to them as individuals" (quoted in Pickering 1984, 387).

87 Durkheim 1995 [1912], 217–18.

88 Ibid., 218.

89 Ibid., 222.

90 Ibid.

91 Ibid.

92 Crapanzano 1995, 108.

93 Durkheim 1995 [1912], 223.

94 Turner 1995 [1969], 93.

95 Shore 1989, 143.

96 Marx 1977 [1867], 164–65.

97 Durkheim 1995 [1912], 222.

98 Ibid., 425.

99 Wagner 1981 [1975], 46.

100 Ibid., 231.

101 Durkheim 1973c [1898].

102 In *The Division of Labour in Society*, Durkheim turns a piously practical face toward what he clearly saw as the malingering aesthetes of his generation: "We do not cling to very much when we have no very determined objective, and, consequently, we cannot very well elevate ourselves beyond a more or less refined egotism. On the contrary, he who gives himself over to a definite task is, at every moment, struck by the sentiment of common solidarity in the thousand duties of occupational morality" (Durkheim 1973b [1893b], 140). One imagines how Lukács, Simmel, and even Weber would have cringed at the brisk philistinism of these words.

103 Durkheim 1995 [1912], 209.

104 Graham 2007, 33; see also Crapanzano 1995.

105 Thanks to Crapanzano (1995) for pointing me to this reference in Lukes.

106 Mauss, quoted in Lukes 1972, 338–39n71.

107 Durkheim 1995 [1912], 222.

108 Ibid.

109 The Replacements, *Pleased to Meet Me* (Sire Records, 1987).

110 As Goldenweiser rightly observed in an early review of *The Elementary Forms*: "We hear nothing of the effect on the individual of the cultural type of the group, of the tribal or national or class patterns of thought and action, and even emotion, patterns developed by history and fixed by tradition" (Goldenweiser 1915a, 728).

111 Quoted in Steiner 1995, 60.

112 Durkheim 1995 [1912], 158.

113 See Dolar 1993 for an excellent discussion of the forced choice of ideological interpellation.

114 Turner 1967, 30.

115 Ibid., 305.

116 Mauss 2001 [1902–3], 30.

117 Ibid., 38.

118 See, for example, Bell 1997; Bloch 1986; Cole 2001; Comaroff 1985; Engelke 2007; Herdt 2006; Kelly and Kaplan 1990; Sahlins 1981, 1985; Stasch 2011; Taussig 1987; Turner 1995 [1969]; Wagner 1984.

119 Malinowski 1948 [1925], 58.

120 Others have complained that Durkheim's entirely social explanation of the religious misses the importance of revelations that happen under conditions of seclusion, isolation, and silence. See, for example, Goldenweiser's objections: "A crowd-psychological situation may intensify or even transform a religious thrill, but it can not create one" (Goldenweiser 1917, 123) and the pithier "the gods live not by ritual alone" (Goldenweiser 1915a, 731). Durkheim's valiant defenders might here point to the need to explore the structural relation—rather than just the empirical coincidence—between solitary illuminations and collective ritual.

121 De Martino 1988 [1948], 65–154.

122 As Valerio Valeri puts it, summarizing Keesing's argument: "Mana is, in a sense, the efficacy of a system or relations personified by an individual (for instance a chief): it is the notion that the system 'works'" (Valeri 1985, 97).

123 Ibid., 90.

124 Wagner 1981, 35.

125 Ibid., 105.

126 De Martino 1988 [1948], 124.

127 Ibid., 107.

128 Codrington 1891.

129 De Martino 1988 [1948], 73.

130 Ibid., 74.

131 Laclau 1999, 86.

132 Žižek 1989; see also Boyer 2013; Boyer and Yurchak 2010; Mazzarella 2015; Yurchak 2006; Wedeen 1999.

133 De Martino 1988 [1948], 68.

Chapter Three

1 Sloterdijk 2011 [1998], 484.

2 Mladen Dolar invokes Kaja Silverman's notion of "entrapment" to describe the anxiety triggered by a voice that evokes that "first" voice that enabled one's emergence as a subject: "the voice which was both the first nest and the first cage" (quoted in Dolar 2006, 41).

3 Fredric Jameson suggests something along these lines in his *Valences of the Dialectic*: "the tendency to dismiss all of manipulated mass culture as false consciousness then leaves unused and deprives of their very reason for being the very rich instruments of formal analysis also developed by Adorno, which in his work only come to find their fullest application in the decipherment and deconcealment of the formal contradictions at work in the monuments of high culture" (2009, 334). I would only add: yes, but the challenge is not only to extend the reach of Adorno's tools; the problem is also to understand the work that his own prohibition on extending them does.

4 Adorno 1997 [1970], 243.

5 Sloterdijk 2011 [1998], 261. See also During 2002, 15.

6 Applbaum 2003; Marchand 2001; Strasser 2003 [1989].

7 Acland 2012; Lemov 2015; Masco 2014; Melley 2011.

8 Debord 1977 [1967]; Dorfman and Mattelart 1975 [1971]; Goffman 1979; Haug 1986 [1971]; Williamson 1978.

9 Horkheimer and Adorno 2002 [1944], 109.

10 Ibid., 111.

11 Ibid., 96, 119.

12 Ibid., 124.

13 Ibid., 100.

14 Ibid., 106.

15 Adorno 2005 [1951], 204-5.

16 Horkheimer and Adorno 2002 [1944], 116.

17 Adorno 2005 [1951], 201.

18 Fiske 1989; Hebdige 1979; see also Brooker and Jermyn 2002; Morley 1992; G. Turner 1990.

19 Ghosh 2001, 447.

20 Mazzarella 2004.

21 Foucault 1978 [1976], 48.

22 Miller 1997; Moeran 1996; see also Kemper 2001; Mazzarella 2003b; Moeran and Malefyt 2003.

23 Quoted in Wiggershaus 1994 [1986], 457.

24 Butler 1999, 28.

25 Schudson 1984. Others have attributed the saying to Lord Leverhulme (William Lever, the founder of Lever Brothers) and to legendary British adman David Ogilvy.

26 "AdWords PPC Resolves . . ." 2013.

27 Sunstein 2001, 8, 9. Peter Sloterdijk, who came of age during the collectivist political and intellectual ferment of the late 1960s, inimitably describes the prospect of our brave new consumerist world in terms of "the heightened individualism characterizing the current thrust of telematic abstraction, as well as the aestheticistic neo-isolationism of postmodern lifestyle propaganda" (Sloterdijk 2011 [1998], 231). Given how much and how deeply I draw on Sloterdijk in the pages that follow, I am more than willing to forgive him this moment of grandstanding glibness that, after all, contains its own enjoyment!

28 Seaver 2012.

29 Dooley 2012, 65.

30 Horkheimer and Adorno 2002 [1944], 22.

31 Charlie Kaufman, dir. 2008; Sony Pictures Classics.

32 Peters 2010, 124.

33 Malefyt and Morais 2012, 127, 129.

34 Thanks to Mary Robertson for bringing this piquant phrase to my attention.

35 Howe 2009; Surowiecki 2005.

36 Latour 1993.

37 Couliano 1987 [1984], 95–96.

38 Ibid., 97.

39 McCarthy 2015, 77.

40 Ibid., 133–34.

41 Ibid., 133.

42 Ibid., 23.

43 Hassin, Uleman, and Bargh 2006; Mlodinow 2012. For overviews of the classic literature on subliminal communication, see Dixon 1971, 1981.

44 Mlodinow 2012, 194.

45 Shatz quoted in Dooley 2012, 55.

46 See, e.g., Lende and Downey 2012.

47 Mlodinow 2012, 16, 17. See, however, Mark Solms's (2015) provocative attempts to reintegrate neuroscience and psychoanalysis.

48 Canetti 1984 [1960], 108.

49 Dooley 2012, 174. Ironically, in the context of my discussion here, Dooley uses mimesis to explain magical stagecraft. Magicians, he says, scratch their noses and ruffle their hair—everyday gestures to which our mimetic impulses are helplessly attracted—so as to distract us from their sleights of hand.

50 Walvis 2010, 203.

51 Ibid., 205. Dooley makes the same point with less finesse: "If neuro-marketing techniques are used properly, we'll have better ads, better products, and happier customers" (Dooley 2012, xiv).

52 Žižek 1999d, 53–54. Žižek reprises the discussion, with audiovisual illustration, in *The Pervert's Guide to Ideology* (dir. Sophie Fiennes, 2012).

53 In that regard it seems a bit curious that Žižek inserts a footnote (note 55 on page 54), where he says that the question of justifiable paranoia must remain open in the case of actual subliminal advertising. But is this not precisely the problem: that by bringing the subliminal above board, as it were, the heralds of the new unconscious have made it less possible to reassure ourselves, as we could in the old days, that "actual" instances of subliminal messaging were far less common than the paranoiac popular discourse would have us believe?

54 Zwick and Cayla 2011, 7.

55 Malefyt and Morais 2012, 132.

56 Ibid., 129.

57 Wegner 2005, 30, 31.

58 Žižek 1999a, 104.

59 Wagner 1981, 62–63.

60 The literature on magic frequently emphasizes that faith is crucial to magical efficacy. In the sixteenth century Giordano Bruno writes: "Faith is the strongest bond, the chain of chains [*vinculum vinculorum*]" (quoted in Couliano 1987 [1984], 93). Perhaps one of the casualties of the primitive settlement is a difficulty, when it comes to the analysis of non-Western peoples, in distinguishing between faith and belief.

61   Wagner 1981, 63, 66.

62   See Taussig 1999 on the auratic powers of defacement.

63   Knausgård 2013 [2011], 474, my translation.

64   Jean Pouillon: "it is the unbeliever who believes that the believer believes" (1982 [1979], 4).

65   Baudrillard 1996 [1968], 194.

66   Lévi-Strauss 1952, 12.

67   Quoted in Taussig 2006b, 145. See also Gable 2002.

68   Žižek 1993.

69   Schudson 1984.

70   Siegel 2006, 47.

71   Tylor 1874 [1871], 89.

72   Goldenweiser 1915a, 729.

73   Evans-Pritchard notes that Van Der Leeuw appears to have been the main influence on Freud here, although one would have to add that such associations were widespread at the time. Summarizing Van Der Leeuw's argument, Evans-Pritchard gives it the expected intellec-tualist twist: "Magicians believe that by words, spells, they can alter the world, and so they belong to that noble category of people who place an overemphasis on thought: children, women, poets, artists, lovers, mystics, criminals, dreamers, and madmen. All attempt to deal with reality by the same psychological mechanism" (Evans-Pritchard 1965, 41).

74   Durkheim 1995 [1912], 385.

75   See, e.g., Clifford 1988; Goldwater 1986; Rubin 1984.

76   Lévi-Strauss 1987 [1950], 63. Jeremy MacClancy suggests that it is pre-cisely the fact that mana is a floating signifier that has made it so his-torically durable, as both an etic "theoretical" and an emic "folk" con-cept (MacClancy 1986, 149).

77   Horkheimer and Adorno 2002 [1944], 25.

78   Adorno 1997 [1970], 228.

79   Ibid., 241.

80   Horkheimer and Adorno 2002 [1944], 13–14.

81 Ibid., 14.

82 Miriam Hansen's (2012) extended discussion of the category of aura in Benjamin is, to my mind, the single finest exposition of the roots, variations, and internal tensions of this infamously slippery yet infinitely suggestive (i.e., quite mana-like) notion.

83 Benjamin 1999d [1933], 720.

84 Adorno 1973 [1966], 183, see also Adorno 1998 [1969].

85 Sloterdijk 1987 [1983], 360. See also Mitchell 2005.

86 Horkheimer and Adorno 2002 [1944], 9.

87 Girard 1977 [1972], 34.

88 Adorno 1998 [1969], 254. I am reminded of the lamentable slogan that the Chicago Museum of Contemporary Art adopted for some years in a bid to look user friendly: Fear No Art. In that regard, the slogan in use at New York's Metropolitan Museum of Art as I write this is far preferable: Yield to the Art.

89 Horkheimer and Adorno 2002 [1944], 10–11.

90 I would especially recommend Buck-Morss 1977, 1989, 2000; Hansen 2012; Jay 1973, 1984; Wiggershaus 1994; Zuidervaart 1991.

91 Adorno 1991 [1938], 57.

92 Benjamin 1999b [1932].

93 Benjamin 2002b [1936], 128n23.

94 Ibid., 124n10.

95 Almost thirty years after Benjamin's death, Adorno was still arguing with what he saw as his friend's undialectical take on aura/mana: "Aura is not only — as Benjamin claimed — the here and now of the artwork, it is whatever goes beyond its factual givenness, its content; one cannot abolish it and still want art" (Adorno 1997 [1970], 45).

96 Ibid., 228.

97 Benjamin 2002b [1936], 104–5.

98 Horkheimer and Adorno 2002 [1944], 14.

99 Adorno 1973 [1966], 25.

100 Ibid., 52.

101 Adorno 1997 [1970], 333.

102 Hegel 1977 [1807], 32.

103 Adorno 1973 [1966], 27.

104 Adorno 1997 [1970], 353.

105 Adorno 1973 [1966], 27–28.

106 Ibid., 38.

107 Ibid., 39.

108 Ibid., 330.

109 Adorno 1997 [1970], 259.

110 Ibid., 17.

111 Bourdieu 1984 [1979], 1993.

112 Adorno 1997 [1970], 6, 8.

113 Adorno 1997 [1970], 2. And: "In formal terms, independent of what they say, [artworks] are ideology in that a priori they posit something spiritual as being independent from the conditions of its material production and therefore as being intrinsically superior and beyond the primordial guilt of the separation of physical and spiritual labour" (ibid., 227).

114 Horkheimer and Adorno 2002 [1944], 114.

115 Sahlins 1976, 149.

116 Adorno 1999a [1935], 113.

117 Adorno 1973 [1966], 191.

118 Mazzarella 2013a.

119 Adorno 1997 [1970], 17.

120 Horkheimer and Adorno 2002 [1944], 26.

121 Adorno 1997 [1970], 10.

122 Ibid., 254. Adorno was writing with one eye on the then-vital radical student movement whose leaders, by the second half of the 1960s, were satirizing Adorno and his allies as repressed old fuddy-duddies who understood nothing of pleasure. In response, Adorno lashed out at their cult of desublimation, which he saw as disastrously indiscriminate and complicit with an authoritarian agenda: "Their most recent trick, which was admittedly already practiced by Fascism, revalorizes ego-weakness, the incapacity for sublimation, as a superior quality and sets a moral premium on the line of least resistance. . . . Although their constant refrain is concreteness, they judge abstractly and summarily, blind to the unsolved tasks and possibilities that have been repressed by the most recent aesthetic actionism" (ibid., 251). In return for his critique, some female students famously flashed Adorno at the lecture podium in the summer of 1969. He died of a heart attack while on holiday weeks later.

123 Ibid., 12.

124 Ibid., 234.

125 Ibid., 339.

126 Mazzarella 2013b.

Chapter Four

1 For Horkheimer and Adorno, the relation between Odysseus—tied up but hearing—and the crew—laboring at the oars and not hearing—functions as an allegory of a primal class division: between those who agree to practical impotence as the price to be paid for aesthetic experience and those who, cut off from their "higher" senses, must channel their practical activity into instrumental labor.

2 Homer 1996, 276.

3 Povinelli 2006.

4 Berlant 2011, 16.

5 Žižek 2006, 7.

6 Habermas 1989 [1962]. Habermas is drawing on the pathbreaking work done by Marcuse (2007 [1937]) and other members of the Frankfurt collective on the ambiguous autonomy of the private sphere—parallel as it is to the ambiguous autonomy of the aesthetic—in bourgeois life.

7 Norbrook 1996, 331.

8 Mazzarella 2009.

9 Quoted in Claussen 2008, 15.

10 Quoted in Benjamin 2002a, 442.

11   Malefyt and Moeran 2003, 9.

12   Denny and Sunderland 2009.

13   Sahlins 1976, 1996.

14   Sahlins 1976, 217.

15   For a bracing discussion of such appropriations in the domain of marketable ethnic identification, see Comaroff and Comaroff 2009.

16   Again, Marshall Sahlins has, more eloquently than most, repeatedly deconstructed *Homo economicus* by showing its sociohistorical determinants. See, especially, Sahlins 1996.

17   Lévi-Strauss 1966 [1962], 20.

18   Mauss 2001 [1902-3], 155.

19   Ibid., 156.

20   Benjamin 1999c [1933], 721.

21   Frazer 1922 [1890].

22   Hansen 2012, 147, 148.

23   Benjamin 2002a, 442, 721. And Dolar: "this doxa of our times that 'in the beginning was Saussure' (a very particular kind of Word) is rather dubious" (2006, 17). See also Benjamin 1996a [1916].

24   Benjamin 2002a, 442, 722.

25   See also, in this connection, Benjamin's discussion of correspondences and their relation to experience in Baudelaire and Proust (Benjamin 2003 [1940]).

26   Bracken 2007, 147.

27   Hansen 2012, 214.

28   This, again, is why the antipsychological critique, by the anthropologists of the empiricist settlement, of what Evans-Pritchard misleadingly but symptomatically called "emotionalist" theories of religion and magic, does not exhaust their value for us today (see my discussion in chapter 2). For a finely detailed discussion of the roots and dimensions of Benjamin's use of innervation as a concept, see Hansen (2012, 132-46).

29   Canetti 1984 [1960], 108.

30   Hansen 2012, 91.

31   Benjamin 2002 [1936], 124n10.

32   Banks 2009, 16.

33   Couliano 1987 [1984], xviii.

34   In ancient Greek myth, Anne Carson reminds us, the same goddess, Peitho, is in charge of both rhetorical persuasion and the arts of seduction (Carson 2014 [1986], 108).

35   Ibid., 87. Mana, like pneuma, at points appears in the ethnographic archive as breath. Valerio Valeri, analyzing "ancient" Hawaiian kingship ritual, notes that here mana could be transmitted by breathing or spitting into another's mouth:

> This mode of transmission also gives clues to what kind of "substance" mana is: it seems to be connected with speech, with which spit, breath, and mouth are obviously associate[d]. Moreover, breath is connected with life: . . . thus we may deduce that mana is a sort of life in speech and life-giving power in speech. That this power may be transmitted through the anterior fontanel is interesting in view of the identification of that part of the head with an aspect of the "soul" having to do with feelings, affections, sympathy, and dispositions. . . . This seems to imply that a man's speech having mana can become another man's speech having mana by affecting the seat of his feelings, sympathies, and dispositions. (Valeri 1985, 99)

36   Plato 2009.

37   Sloterdijk 2011 [1998], 239.

38   Ibid., 207.

39   Ibid., 31.

40   Ibid., 45.

41   Quoted in Hansen 2012, 127.

42   Sloterdijk 2011 [1998], 222.

43   Ibid., 247.

44   Lacan 2002 [1949], 6.

45   Sloterdijk, 2011 [1998], 525.

46   Ibid., 12.

47   Ibid., 13.

48 Murdoch 1973, 198.

49 Carson 2014 [1986], 87.

50 Tarde 1903 [1890], 78.

51 Quoted in Starobinski 2003 [1999], 315.

52 Žižek 2012, 213, 231.

53 Dolar 1993, 83.

54 Quoted in Fox 1985, 308.

55 Simmel 1971b [1908], 147.

56 Žižek 2012, 213.

57 Keesing 1984, 149. Similarly, as William Murphy notes, Weber suggested that charisma was a matter of actualized "proofs" that would, retroactively, affirm the charisma of the person who apparently managed to bring about a result: "The attribute of 'proofs' shifts the emphasis from charisma as a personality trait to charisma as manifested in special public acts and effects in the world, which are culturally defined as extraordinary" (Murphy 1998, 571).

58 Not everyone is convinced of the value of charisma as an analytical term. Fredric Jameson, for example, insists (in a manner not wholly unlike the empiricist anthropologists' abjection of mana—see chapter 1) that "charisma is . . . an utterly useless pseudo-concept or pseudo-psychological figment: it simply names the problem to be solved and the phenomenon to be explained" (Jameson 2009, 300).

59 Weber makes the connection in his sociology of religion between charisma and "extraordinary powers that have been designated by such special terms as 'mana,' 'orenda,' and the Iranian 'maga'" (Weber 1968a [1920], 400). Riesebrodt (1999) suggests that Marett was the key influence on Weber in connecting charisma to mana.

60 Weber quoted in Tiryakian 1995, 272.

61 Shils 1958, 4; see also Apter 1968.

62 Eisenstadt 1968, xl, emphasis added.

63 Feuchtwang 2008, 94.

64 Tarde 1903 [1890], 51.

65 Sloterdijk 2011 [1998], 524.

66 Quoted in Hocart 1914, 98.

67 Lévi-Strauss 1966 [1962], 5.

68 Taussig 2006b, 155.

69 Hansen 2012, 148.

70 Sloterdijk 2011 [1998], 220.

71 Shils 1958, 207.

72 Ibid., 201.

73 Ibid., For Shils as for Lévi-Strauss, *order as such* promises therapeutic results. Observe, in the following quotations, both the repetition of the idea that charisma is normatively attached to order, and, within that repetition, the incantatory repetition of the word *order* itself: "The need for order and the fascination of disorder persist, and the charismatic propensity is a function of the need for order. The generator or author of order arouses the charismatic responsiveness"; "the disposition to attribute charisma is intimately related to the need for order. The attribution of charismatic qualities occurs in the presence of order-creating, order-disclosing, order-discovering power as such; it is a response to great ordering power"; "great power announces itself by its power over order; it discovers order, creates order, maintains it, or destroys it."

Shils seems, with an intensity bordering on desperation, to be attempting, at the level of sociological theory, the same charismatic gesture of order-giving that he asserts as a universal principle of social life. He notes in passing, as he must, "the fascination of disorder" and the fact that charisma is just as tightly related to the destruction as to the production of order. But it is as if, just as in the Durkheimian ritual scenario inherited by generations of anthropologists, the incitement of unruly energies is no sooner acknowledged as a crucial constitutive moment of social life than it has to be contained—tightly mediated by and through a symbolic order.

74 Durkheim 1995 [1912], 220.

75 Ibid., 221.

76 See Mellor 1998 and Schiermer 2016 for related arguments.

77 Falco 1999, 74.

78 Ibid., 76.

79 Ibid., 77.

80 Kantorowicz 2016 [1957].

81 Santner 2011, 2015. Here, Santner is at once developing and contesting Claude Lefort's (1991 [1988]) argument in *Democracy and Political Theory* that the democratic revolution, by dispensing with the body of the king, installed an "empty place" at the heart of sovereignty. Both Santner and Lefort are, in turn, developing and contesting Kantorowicz's classic study.

82 Shils 1965, 200. One might, perhaps, easily suppose that Shils was describing nothing so much as the routinized ennui of American postwar suburbia on the cusp of the counterculture. But Shils was also, like so many Euro-American social scientists in the 1950s and 1960s, preoccupied with the emergence of new nations in the wake of decolonization and especially the prospects and problems associated with charismatic leadership as a kind of short circuit between tradition and modernity (Shils 1958).

83 Riesebrodt 1999 argues that Weber paved the way for this double notion of charisma as at once centralized and distributed by an inconsistent use of the term: centralized in his political sociology, distributed in his sociology of religion. My own sense is that Weber's theory of elective affinities suggests how the two conceptions can be imagined as dialectically related.

84 Shils 1965, 206n10.

85 Jowitt 1992.

86 Spadola 2014, 23.

87 Schiermer 2016, 133. Schiermer also usefully reminds us that Durkheim mistrusted the more ephemeral, commodified mediations of modern life. In *Suicide* he speaks of them in passing as "morbid effervescence" (Durkheim 2002, 335–36).

88 Berlant 2011, 85.

89 See, for example, Alexei Yurchak's splendidly sensitive interpretation of the persistence of Lenin's body (Yurchak 2015).

90 Sloterdijk 1987 [1983], 147. I gather, from German-speaking friends, that to speak of the "chocolate side" of something is a not unusual German idiom. Still, for an English-language reader, Sloterdijk's phrase is an eloquent example of just how much may be gained in translation.

91 Klein n.d., 30, 3.

92 Eagleton 1990, 28.

93 Quoted in Foster 2007, 714.

94 Ibid.

95 Ibid., 718. Foster is drawing on Coombe 1998.

96 Ibid., 726.

97 Berlant 2011, 15.

98 Ibid., 97.

99 Zupančič 2006, 165.

100 In a passage that deserves far more attention than it has received, Horkheimer and Adorno remark: "While the mechanism is to all appearances planned by those who serve up the data of experience, that is, by the culture industry, it is in fact forced upon the latter by the power of society, which remains irrational, however we may try to rationalize it; and this inescapable force is processed by commercial agencies so that they give an artificial impression of being in command" (Horkheimer and Adorno 1972 [1944], 124–25). This same passage appears rather differently in the 2002 English translation: "Although the operations of the mechanism appear to be planned by those who supply the data, the culture industry, the planning is in fact imposed on the industry by the inertia of a society irrational despite all its rationalization, and this calamitous tendency, in passing through the agencies of business, takes on the shrewd intentionality peculiar to them" (Horkheimer and Adorno 2002 [1944], 98).

101 "'The Trump campaign is not a bad campaign,' James Carville, who managed Bill Clinton's 1992 campaign, told me. 'It's not a messed-up campaign. It's not a dysfunctional campaign. There *is* no campaign.' Carville continued, 'Everybody that's done this for a living and got paid to do it is, like, "Oh, my gosh, suppose this works. We're all rendered useless. He will have destroyed the entire profession"'" (Widdicombe 2016, 24).

102 Dolar 1993, 92.

103 Foucault 1986 [1967].

104 Eagleton 1990, 90.

105 Kafka 1971, 431.

106 Ibid., 432.

107 Ibid., 431.

108 Ibid., 432.

109 Ibid., 431.

110 Dolar 2006, 172.

111 Kafka 1971, 430.

112 Žižek's formulation resonates here: "the subject's ultimate and radical *freedom*, the freedom whose space is sustained by the Other's inconsistency and lack" (Žižek 1999b, 258).

113 Benjamin 1994, 509.

114 Benjamin 1996b [1924-25], 298.

References

Acland, Charles. 2012. *Swift Viewing: The Popular Life of Subliminal Influence*. Durham, NC: Duke University Press.

Adorno, Theodor. 1973 [1966]. *Negative Dialectics*. New York: Bloomsbury Academic.

———. 1991 [1938]. "The Fetish Character of Music and the Regression of Listening." In *The Culture Industry: Selected Essays on Mass Culture*, edited by J. M. Bernstein, 29–60. London: Routledge.

———. 1997 [1970]. *Aesthetic Theory*. Minneapolis: University of Minnesota Press.

———. 1998 [1969]. "On Subject and Object." In *Critical Models: Interventions and Catchwords*, 245–58. New York: Columbia University Press.

———. 1999 [1935]. Letter number 39 in *Theodor Adorno and Walter Benjamin: The Complete Correspondence, 1928–1940*, edited by Henri Lonitz, 104–14. Cambridge, MA: Harvard University Press.

———. 2005. [1951]. *Minima Moralia: Reflections on a Damaged Life*. New York: Verso.

"AdWords PPC Resolves: 'Half the money I spend on advertising is wasted.'" 2013. http://www.stratoserve.com/2013/06/adwords-ppc-resolves-half-the-money-i-spend-on-advertising-is-wasted.html, accessed January 13, 2015.

Althusser, Louis. 2008 [1970]. "Ideology and Ideological State Apparatuses: Notes Toward an Investigation." In *On Ideology*, 1–60. New York: Verso.

Anton, Ted. 2013 [1997]. *Eros, Magic, and the Murder of Professor Culianu.* Evanston, IL: Northwestern University Press.

Applbaum, Kalman. 2003. *The Marketing Era: From Professional Practice to Global Provisioning.* London: Routledge.

Apter, David. 1968. "Nkrumah, Charisma, and the Coup." *Daedalus* 97 (3): 757–92.

Banks, Iain M. 2009. *Transition.* New York: Orbit.

Baudrillard, Jean. 1996 [1968]. *The System of Objects.* New York: Verso.

Bell, Catherine. 1997. *Ritual: Perspectives and Dimensions.* Oxford: Oxford University Press.

Benedict, Ruth. 1938. "Religion." In *General Anthropology*, edited by Franz Boas, 627–65. Boston: D. C. Heath.

Benjamin, Walter. 1994. *The Correspondence of Walter Benjamin, 1910–1940.* Chicago: University of Chicago Press.

———. 1996a [1916]. "On Language as Such and on the Language of Man." In *Walter Benjamin: Selected Writings*, vol. 1, edited by Marcus Bullock and Michael Jennings, 62–74. Cambridge, MA: Harvard University Press.

———. 1996b [1924–25]. "Goethe's Elective Affinities." In *Walter Benjamin: Selected Writings*, vol. 1, edited by Marcus Bullock and Michael Jennings, 297–360. Cambridge, MA: Harvard University Press.

———. 1999a. *The Arcades Project.* Cambridge, MA: Harvard University Press.

———. 1999b [1932]. "Light from Obscurantists." In *Walter Benjamin: Selected Writings*, vol. 2, edited by Michael Jennings and Howard Eiland, 653–57. Cambridge, MA: Harvard University Press.

———. 1999c [1933]. "On the Mimetic Faculty." In *Walter Benjamin: Selected Writings*, vol. 2, edited by Michael Jennings and Howard Eiland, 720–27. Cambridge, MA: Harvard University Press.

———. 2002a. *Walter Benjamin: Selected Writings.* Vol. 3. Cambridge, MA: Harvard University Press.

———. 2002b [1936]. "The Work of Art in the Age of Its Technological Reproducibility." In *Walter Benjamin: Selected Writings*, vol. 3, edited by Howard Eiland and Michael Jennings, 101–33. Cambridge, MA: Harvard University Press.

———. 2003 [1940]. "On Some Motifs in Baudelaire." In *Walter Benjamin: Selected Writings*, vol. 4, edited by Howard Eiland and Michael Jennings, 313–55. Cambridge, MA: Harvard University Press.

Berlant, Lauren. 2008. *The Female Complaint: The Unfinished Business of Sentimentality in American Culture*. Durham, NC: Duke University Press.

———. 2011. *Cruel Optimism*. Durham, NC: Duke University Press.

Bhabha, Homi. 1984. "Of Mimicry and Man: The Ambivalence of Colonial Discourse." *October* 28 (Spring): 125–33.

Bloch, Maurice. 1986. *From Blessing to Violence: History and Ideology in the Circumcision Ritual of the Merina of Madagascar*. Cambridge: Cambridge University Press.

Blom, Philipp. 2008. *The Vertigo Years: Europe, 1900–1914*. New York: Basic.

Blust, Robert. 2007. "Oceanic Mana Revisited." *Oceanic Linguistics* 46 (2): 404–23.

Borch, Christian. 2013. *The Politics of the Crowd: An Alternative History of Sociology*. Cambridge: Cambridge University Press.

Bourdieu, Pierre. 1984 [1979]. *Distinction: A Social Critique of the Judgment of Taste*. Cambridge, MA: Harvard University Press.

———. 1993. *The Field of Cultural Production*. New York: Columbia University Press.

Boyer, Dominic. 2013. "Simply the Best: Parody and Political Sincerity in Iceland." *American Ethnologist* 40 (2): 276–87.

Boyer, Dominic, and Cymene Howe. 2015. "Portable Analytics and Lateral Theory." In *Theory Can Be More Than It Used to Be: Learning Anthropology's Method in a Time of Transition*, edited by Dominic Boyer, James Faubion, and George Marcus, 15–38. Ithaca, NY: Cornell University Press.

Boyer, Dominic, and Alexei Yurchak. 2010. "American *Stiob*: Or, What Late-Socialist Aesthetics of Parody Reveal about Contemporary Political Culture in the West." *Cultural Anthropology* 25 (2): 179–221.

Bracken, Christopher. 2007. *Magical Criticism: The Recourse of Savage Philosophy*. Chicago: University of Chicago Press.

Breckenridge, Carol, ed. 1995. *Consuming Modernity: Public Culture in a South Asian World*. Minneapolis: University of Minnesota Press.

Brooker, Will, and Deborah Jermyn, eds. 2002. *The Audience Studies Reader*. London: Routledge.

Buck-Morss, Susan. 1979 [1977]. *Origin of Negative Dialectics: Theodor W. Adorno, Walter Benjamin, and the Frankfurt School*. New York: Free Press.

———. 1989. *The Dialectics of Seeing: Walter Benjamin and the Arcades Project*. Cambridge, MA: MIT Press.

———. 2000. *Dreamworld and Catastrophe: The Passing of Mass Utopia in East and West*. Cambridge, MA: MIT Press.

Buehler, Arthur. 2012. "The Twenty-First-Century Study of Collective Effervescence: Expanding the Context of Fieldwork." *Fieldwork in Religion* 7 (1): 70–97.

Burke, Edmund. 2006 [1789–90]. *Reflections on the Revolution in France*. Mineola, NY: Dover.

Butler, Judith. 1999. "Restaging the Universal: Hegemony and the Limits of Formalism." In *Contingency, Hegemony, Universality: Contemporary Dialogues on the Left*, edited by Judith Butler, Ernesto Laclau, and Slavoj Žižek, 11–43. New York: Verso.

Canetti, Elias. 1984 [1960]. *Crowds and Power*. New York: Farrar, Straus and Giroux.

Carson, Anne. 2005. *Decreation: Poetry, Essays, Opera*. New York: Vintage Contemporary.

———. 2014 [1986]. *Eros the Bittersweet*. Champaign, IL: Dalkey Archive.

Claussen, Detlev. 2008. *Theodor W. Adorno: One Last Genius*. Cambridge, MA: Harvard University Press.

Clifford, James. 1988. *The Predicament of Culture: Twentieth-Century Ethnography, Literature, and Art*. Cambridge, MA: Harvard University Press.

Clifford, James, and George Marcus, eds. 1986. *Writing Culture: The Poetics and Politics of Ethnography*. Berkeley: University of California Press.

Codrington, Robert. 1891. *The Melanesians: Studies in Their Anthropology and Folklore*. Oxford: Clarendon Press.

Cole, Jennifer. 2001. *Forget Colonialism? Sacrifice and the Art of Memory in Madagascar*. Berkeley: University of California Press.

Comaroff, Jean. 1985. *Body of Power, Spirit of Resistance: The Culture and History of a South African People*. Chicago: University of Chicago Press.

Comaroff, Jean, and John Comaroff. 2009. *Ethnicity, Inc*. Chicago: University of Chicago Press.

———. 2012. *Theory from the South; Or, How Euro-America Is Evolving toward Africa*. Boulder, CO: Paradigm.

Coombe, Rosemary. 1998. *The Cultural Life of Intellectual Properties: Authorship, Appropriation, and the Law*. Durham, NC: Duke University Press.

Couliano, Ioan. 1987 [1984]. *Eros and Magic in the Renaissance*. Chicago: University of Chicago Press.

Crapanzano, Vincent. 1995. "The Moment of Prestidigitation: Magic, Illusion, and Mana in the Thought of Emile Durkheim and Marcel Mauss." In *Prehistories of the Future: The Primitivist Project and the Culture of Modernism*, edited by Elazar Barkan and Ronald Bush, 95–113. Stanford, CA: Stanford University Press.

Da Col, Giovanni, and David Graeber. 2011. "Foreword: The Return of Ethnographic Theory." *HAU: Journal of Ethnographic Theory* 1 (1): vi–xxxv.

Darnton, Robert. 1968. *Mesmerism and the End of the Enlightenment in France*. Cambridge, MA: Harvard University Press.

Debord, Guy. 1977 [1967]. *Society of the Spectacle*. Detroit, MI: Black and Red.

Deleuze, Gilles. 2001 [1995]. "Immanence: A Life." In *Pure Immanence*, 25–33. New York: Zone.

Deleuze, Gilles, and Félix Guattari. 1994 [1991]. *What Is Philosophy?* New York: Columbia University Press.

De Martino, Ernesto. 1988 [1948]. *Primitive Magic: The Psychic Powers of Shamans and Sorcerers*. Bridport, Dorset: Prism Press.

Denny, Rita, and Patricia Sunderland. 2009. *Doing Anthropology in Consumer Research*. Walnut Creek, CA: Left Coast Press.

Derrida, Jacques. 1981 [1972]. *Dissemination*. Chicago: University of Chicago Press.

Dolar, Mladen. 1993. "Beyond Interpellation." *Qui Parle* 6 (2): 75–96.

———. 2006. *A Voice and Nothing More*. Cambridge, MA: MIT Press.

Dooley, Roger. 2011. *Brainfluence: 100 Ways to Persuade and Convince Consumers with Neuromarketing*. Hoboken, NJ: Wiley.

Dorfman, Ariel, and Armand Mattelart. 1975 [1971]. *How to Read Donald Duck: Imperialist Ideology in the Disney Comic*. New York: International General.

Duclos, Vincent. forthcoming. "At Home in the Outer World? Peter Sloterdijk, Ontological Anthropology in the Monstrous."

During, Simon. 2002. *Modern Enchantments: The Cultural Power of Secular Magic*. Cambridge, MA: Harvard University Press.

Durkheim, Émile. 1966 [1895]. *The Rules of Sociological Method*. New York: Free Press.

———. 1973a [1893a]. "Progressive Preponderance of Organic Solidarity." In *Emile Durkheim on Morality and Society*, edited by Robert Bellah, 63–85. Chicago: University of Chicago Press.

———. 1973b [1893b]. "Division of Labour in Society: Conclusion." In *Emile Durkheim on Morality and Society*, Robert Bellah 134–48. Chicago: University of Chicago Press.

———. 1973c [1898]. "Individualism and the Intellectuals." In *Emile Durkheim on Morality and Society*, edited by Robert Bellah, 43–57. Chicago: University of Chicago Press.

———. 1973d [1914]. "The Dualism of Human Nature and Its Social Conditions." In *Emile Durkheim on Morality and Society*, edited by Robert Bellah, 149–63. Chicago: University of Chicago Press.

———. 1974. *Sociology and Philosophy*. New York: Free Press.

———. 1995 [1912]. *The Elementary Forms of Religious Life*. New York: Free Press.

Durkheim, Émile, and Marcel Mauss. 1963 [1903]. *Primitive Classification*. Chicago: University of Chicago Press.

Dussel, Enrique. 1995 [1992]. *The Invention of the Americas: Eclipse of the "Other" and the Myth of Modernity*. New York: Continuum.

Eagleton, Terry. 1990. *The Ideology of the Aesthetic*. Oxford: Blackwell.

Eisenstadt, S. N. 1968. "Introduction—Charisma and Institution Building: Max Weber and Modern Sociology." In *Max Weber on*

Charisma and Institution Building, edited by S. N. Eisenstadt, ix–lvi. Chicago: University of Chicago Press.

Engelke, Matthew. 2007. *A Problem of Presence: Beyond Scripture in an African Church*. Berkeley: University of California Press.

Esposito, Roberto. 2011. *Immunitas: The Protection and Negation of Life*. Cambridge: Polity.

Evans-Pritchard, E. E. 1929. "The Morphology and Function of Magic: A Comparative Study of Trobriand and Zande Ritual and Spells." *American Anthropologist* 31: 619–41.

———. 1965. *Theories of Primitive Religion*. Oxford: Clarendon.

Falco, Raphael. 1999. "Charisma and Tragedy: An Introduction." *Theory, Culture, and Society* 16 (3): 71–98.

Feuchtwang, Stephan. 2008. "Suggestions for a Redefinition of Charisma." *Nova Religio: The Journal of Alternative and Emergent Religions* 12 (2): 90–105.

Firth, Raymond. 1940. "The Analysis of *Mana*: An Empirical Approach." *Journal of the Polynesian Society* 49 (4): 483–510.

Fiske, John. 1989. *Understanding Popular Culture*. London: Routledge.

Foster, Robert. 2007. "'The Work of the New Economy: Consumers, Brands, and Value Creation." *Cultural Anthropology* 22 (4): 707–31.

———. 2013. "Things to Do with Brands: Creating and Calculating Value." *HAU: Journal of Ethnographic Theory* 3 (1). http://www.haujournal.org/index.php/hau/article/view/hau3.1.004/720.

Foucault, Michel. 1986 [1967]. "Of Other Spaces." *Diacritics* 16 (1): 22–27.

———. 1978 [1976]. *The History of Sexuality*. Vol. 1, *An Introduction*. New York: Vintage.

Fox, Stephen. 1985. *The Mirror Makers: A History of American Advertising and Its Creators*. New York: Vintage.

Frazer, James. 1922 [1890]. *The Golden Bough*. Abr. ed. New York: Collier.

Freedberg, David. 1989. *The Power of Images: Studies in the History and Theory of Response*. Chicago: University of Chicago Press.

Freud, Sigmund. 1959 [1921]. *Group Psychology and the Analysis of the Ego*. New York: W. W. Norton.

———. 1990 [1913]. *Totem and Taboo*. New York: W. W. Norton.

Gable, Eric. 2002. "Beyond Belief? Play, Skepticism, and Religion in a West African Village." *Social Anthropology* 10 (1): 41–56.

Gandhi, Leela. 2014. *The Common Cause: Postcolonial Ethics and the Practice of Democracy.* Chicago: University of Chicago Press.

Geertz, Clifford. 1973. *The Interpretation of Cultures.* New York: Basic.

Gell, Alfred. 1988. "Technology and Magic." *Anthropology Today* 4 (2): 6–9.

Geschiere, Peter. 2003. "On Witch Doctors and Spin Doctors." In *Magic and Modernity: Interfaces of Revelation and Concealment,* edited by Birgit Meyer and Peter Pels, 159–82. Stanford, CA: Stanford University Press.

Ghosh, Amitav. 2001. *The Glass Palace.* New York: Random House.

Girard, René. 1977 [1972]. *Violence and the Sacred.* Baltimore: Johns Hopkins University Press.

Godelier, Maurice. 1999 [1996]. *The Enigma of the Gift.* Chicago: University of Chicago Press.

Goffman, Erving. 1979. *Gender Advertisements.* New York: Harper and Row.

Goldenweiser, A. A. 1915a. Book review of Émile Durkheim's *Elementary Forms of Religious Life. American Anthropologist,* n.s., 17 (4): 719–35.

———. 1915b. "Spirit, Mana, and the Religious Thrill." *Journal of Philosophy, Psychology, and Scientific Methods* 12 (23): 632–40.

———. 1917. "Religion and Society: A Critique of Émile Durkheim's Theory of the Origin and Nature of Religion." *Journal of Philosophy, Psychology, and Scientific Methods* 14 (5): 113–24.

Goldwater, Robert. 1986. *Primitivism in Modern Art.* Cambridge, MA: Belknap Press.

Graeber, David. N.d. Endorsement for *Hau.* http://www.haujournal.org/index.php/hau/pages/view/endorsements, accessed May 25, 2015.

———. 2004. *Fragments of an Anarchist Anthropology.* Chicago: Prickly Paradigm Press.

———. 2011. *Revolutions in Reverse: Essays on Politics, Violence, Art, and Imagination.* New York: Autonomedia.

———. 2013. *The Democracy Project: A History, a Crisis, a Movement.* New York: Spiegel and Grau.

Graham, E. Tyler. 2007. "The Danger of Durkheim: Ambiguity in the Theory of Social Effervescence." *Religion* 37: 26–38.

Gregg, Melissa, and Gregory Seigworth, eds. 2010. *The Affect Theory Reader*. Durham, NC: Duke University Press.

Habermas, Jürgen. 1989 [1962]. *The Structural Transformation of the Public Sphere: An Inquiry into a Category of Bourgeois Society*. Cambridge, MA: MIT Press.

Handy, E. S. Craighill. 1927. *Polynesian Religion*. Bernice P. Bishop Museum Bulletin 34.

Hannerz, Ulf. 1992. *Cultural Complexity: Studies in the Social Organization of Meaning*. New York: Columbia University Press.

Hansen, Miriam Bratu. 2012. *Cinema and Experience: Siegfried Kracauer, Walter Benjamin, and Theodor W. Adorno*. Berkeley: University of California Press.

Hardt, Michael, and Antonio Negri. 2000. *Empire*. Cambridge, MA: Harvard University Press.

———. 2004. *Multitude: War and Democracy in the Age of Empire*. New York: Penguin.

———. 2009. *Commonwealth*. Cambridge, MA: Harvard University Press.

Harrison, Jane Ellen. 1921. *Epilegomena to the Study of Greek Religion*. Cambridge: Cambridge University Press.

Hassin, Ran, James S. Uleman, and John A. Bargh, eds. 2006. *The New Unconscious*. Oxford: Oxford University Press.

Haug, Wolfgang Fritz. 1986 [1971]. *Critique of Commodity Aesthetics*. Minneapolis: University of Minnesota Press.

———. 1987 [1986]. "Towards the Dialectics of the Aesthetic." In *Commodity Aesthetics, Ideology, and Culture*, 103–20. New York: International General.

Hebdige, Dick. 1979. *Subculture: The Meaning of Style*. London: Routledge.

Hegel, G. W. F. 1977 [1807]. *Hegel's Phenomenology of Spirit*. Translated by A. V. Miller. Oxford: Oxford University Press.

———. 1998a [1817]. "Encyclopaedia Logic: Preliminary Conception." In *The Hegel Reader*, edited by Stephen Houlgate, 139–74. Oxford: Blackwell.

———. 1998b [1835]. "Aesthetics." In *The Hegel Reader*, edited by Stephen Houlgate, 419–92. Oxford: Blackwell.

Herdt, Gilbert. 2006. *The Sambia: Ritual, Sexuality, and Change in Papua New Guinea*. Belmont, CA: Wadsworth.

Hewitt, J. N. B. 1902. "Orenda and a Definition of Religion." *American Anthropologist* 4 (1): 33–46.

Hirschkind, Charles. 2006. *The Ethical Soundscape: Cassette Sermons and Islamic Counterpublics*. New York: Columbia University Press.

Hocart, A. M. 1914. "Mana." *Man* 14: 97–101.

Hogbin, H. Ian. 1936. "Mana." *Oceania* 6 (3): 241–74.

Holbraad, Martin. 2006. "The Power of Powder: Multiplicity and Motion in the Divinatory Cosmology of Cuban Ifa (or mana, again)." In *Thinking through Things: Theorizing Artefacts Ethnographically*, edited by Amiria Henare, Martin Holbraad, and Sari Wastell, 189–225. Abingdon: Routledge.

Homer. 1996. *The Odyssey*. Translated by Robert Fagles. New York: Penguin.

Horkheimer, Max, and Theodor Adorno. 1972 [1944]. *Dialectic of Enlightenment*. New York: Continuum.

———. 2002 [1944]. *Dialectic of Enlightenment: Philosophical Fragments*. New York: Columbia University Press.

Howe, Jeff. 2009. *Crowdsourcing: Why the Power of the Crowd Is Driving the Future of Business*. New York: Crown Business.

Howe, Richard. 1978. "Max Weber's Elective Affinities: Sociology within the Bounds of Pure Reason." *American Journal of Sociology* 84 (2): 366–85.

Hume, David. 2000 [1739–40]. *A Treatise of Human Nature*. Oxford: Oxford University Press.

Hutton, J. H. 1938. *A Primitive Philosophy of Life*. Oxford: Clarendon Press.

Immergut, Matthew, and Mary Kosut. 2014. "Visualizing Charisma: Representations of the Charismatic Touch." *Visual Studies* 29 (3): 272–84.

Jameson, Fredric. 2009. *Valences of the Dialectic*. New York: Verso.

Jay, Martin. 1973. *The Dialectical Imagination: A History of the Frankfurt School and the Institute of Social Research, 1923–1950*. Berkeley: University of California Press.

———. 1984. *Adorno*. Cambridge, MA: Harvard University Press.

Jones, Graham. 2010. "Modern Magic and the War on Miracles in

French Colonial Culture." *Comparative Studies in Society and History* 52 (1): 66–99.

Jonsson, Stefan. 2000. *Subject without Nation: Robert Musil and the History of Modern Identity*. Durham, NC: Duke University Press.

———. 2013. *Crowds and Democracy: The Idea and Image of the Masses from Revolution to Fascism*. New York: Columbia University Press.

Jowitt, Ken. 1992. *New World Disorder: The Leninist Extinction*. Berkeley: University of California Press.

Kafka, Franz. 1971. *The Complete Stories*. New York: Schocken.

Kant, Immanuel. 1991 [1786]. "Conjectures on the Beginning of Human History." In *Kant: Political Writings*, edited by H. S. Reiss, 221–34. Cambridge: Cambridge University Press.

———. 1996 [1798]. *Anthropology from a Pragmatic Point of View*. Carbondale: Southern Illinois University Press.

———. 1999 [1784]. "What Is Enlightenment?" In *Immanuel Kant: Philosophical Writings*, edited by Ernest Behler, 263–69. New York: Continuum.

———. 2009 [1790]. *Critique of Judgment*. Oxford: Oxford University Press.

Kantorowicz, Ernst. 2016 [1957]. *The King's Two Bodies: A Study in Mediaeval Political Theology*. Princeton, NJ: Princeton University Press.

Keesing, Roger. 1984. "Rethinking 'Mana.'" *Journal of Anthropological Research* 40 (1): 137–56.

Kelly, John, and Martha Kaplan. 1990. "History, Structure, and Ritual." *Annual Review of Anthropology* 19: 119–50.

Kemper, Steven. 2001. *Buying and Believing: Sri Lankan Advertising and Consumers in a Transnational World*. Chicago: University of Chicago Press.

King, John. 1892. *The Supernatural: Its Origin, Nature, and Evolution*. London: Williams and Norgate.

Klein, Naomi. 1999. *No Logo*. New York: Picador.

———. 2002. *Fences and Windows: Dispatches from the Front Lines of the Globalization Debate*. New York: Picador.

———. 2007. *The Shock Doctrine: The Rise of Disaster Capitalism*. New York: Picador.

Klein, Steven. N.d. "Between Charisma and Domination: On Max

Weber's Critique of Democracy." Manuscript, forthcoming in *Journal of Politics*.

Kohn, Eduardo. 2015. "Anthropology of Ontologies." *Annual Review of Anthropology* 44: 311–27.

Knausgård, Karl-Ove. 2013 [2011]. *Min Kamp, del 6* (Swedish-language version). Stockholm: Norstedts.

Kracauer, Siegfried. 1995. *The Mass Ornament: Weimar Essays*. Edited by Thomas Levin. Cambridge, MA: Harvard University Press.

Lacan, Jacques. 2002 [1949]. "The Mirror Stage as Formative of the *I* Function, as Revealed in Psychoanalytic Experience." In *Écrits*, 3–9. New York: Norton.

Laclau, Ernesto. 1999. "Identity and Hegemony: The Role of Universality in the Constitution of Political Logics." In *Contingency, Hegemony, Universality: Contemporary Dialogues on the Left*, edited by Judith Butler, Ernesto Laclau, and Slavoj Žižek, 44–89. New York: Verso.

Latour, Bruno. 1993. *We Have Never Been Modern*. Cambridge, MA: MIT Press.

———. 2005. *Reassembling the Social: An Introduction to Actor-Network Theory*. Oxford: Oxford University Press.

Leach, Edmund. 1985. "Anthropology of Religion: British and French Schools." In *Nineteenth Century Religious Thought in the West*, vol. 3, edited by Ninian Smart, John Clayton, Patrick Sherry, and Steven T. Katz, 215–62. Cambridge: Cambridge University Press.

Lears, T. Jackson. 1994. *Fables of Abundance: A Cultural History of Advertising in America*. New York: Basic.

Le Bon, Gustave. 2002 [1895]. *The Crowd: A Study of the Popular Mind*. Mineola, NY: Dover.

Lefort, Claude. 1991 [1988]. *Democracy and Political Theory*. Cambridge: Polity.

Lehmann, Chris. 2003. *Revolt of the Masscult*. Chicago: Prickly Paradigm Press.

Lemov, Rebecca. 2005. *World as Laboratory: Experiments with Mice, Mazes, and Men*. New York: Hill and Wang.

Lende, Daniel, and Greg Downey, eds. 2012. *The Encultured Brain: An Introduction to Neuroanthropology*. Cambridge, MA: MIT Press.

Lévi-Strauss, Claude. 1952. *Race and History*. Paris: UNESCO.

———. 1963a [1949a]. "The Sorcerer and His Magic." In *Structural Anthropology*, 167–85. New York: Basic.

———. 1963b [1949b]. "The Effectiveness of Symbols." In *Structural Anthropology*, 186–205. New York: Basic.

———. 1966 [1962]. *The Savage Mind*. Chicago: University of Chicago Press.

———. 1987 [1950]. *Introduction to the Work of Marcel Mauss*. London: Routledge and Kegan Paul.

Lévy-Bruhl, Lucien. 1966 [1910]. *How Natives Think*. New York: Washington Square Press.

Leys, Ruth. 2011. "The Turn to Affect: A Critique." *Critical Inquiry* 37 (3): 434–72.

Lukács, Georg. 1971 [1923]. "Reification and the Consciousness of the Proletariat." In *History and Class Consciousness: Studies in Marxist Dialectics*, 83–222. Cambridge, MA: MIT Press.

Lukes, Steven. 1972. *Emile Durkheim: His Life and Work*. New York: Harper and Row.

MacClancy, Jeremy. 1986. "Mana: An Anthropological Metaphor for Island Melanesia." *Oceania* 57 (2): 142–53.

Mahmood, Saba. 2004. *Politics of Piety: The Islamic Revival and the Feminist Subject*. Princeton, NJ: Princeton University Press.

Malefyt, Timothy de Waal, and Brian Moeran. 2003. "Introduction: Advertising Cultures—Advertising, Ethnography, and Anthropology." In *Advertising Cultures*, edited by Timothy de Waal Malefyt and Brian Moeran, 1–34. Oxford: Berg.

Malefyt, Timothy de Waal, and Robert Morais. 2012. *Advertising and Anthropology: Ethnographic Practice and Cultural Perspectives*. New York: Bloomsbury Academic.

Malinowski, Bronislaw. 1922. *Argonauts of the Western Pacific: An Account of Native Enterprise and Adventure in the Archipelagoes of Melanesian New Guinea*. London: Routledge and Kegan Paul.

———. 1935. *Coral Gardens and Their Magic*. Vol. 2, *The Language of Magic and Gardening*. London: George Allen and Unwin.

———. 1948 [1925]. "Magic, Science, and Religion." In *Magic, Science, and Religion*. Garden City, NY: Doubleday Anchor.

Mann, Thomas. 1996 [1924]. *Magic Mountain*. New York: Vintage.

Marchand, Roland. 2001. *Creating the Corporate Soul: The Rise of*

Public Relations and Corporate Imagery in American Big Business. Berkeley: University of California Press.

Marcus, George, and Michael Fischer, eds. 1986. *Anthropology as Cultural Critique: An Experimental Moment in the Human Sciences.* Chicago: University of Chicago Press.

Marcuse, Herbert. 2007 [1937]. "The Affirmative Character of Culture." In *The Essential Marcuse,* edited by Andrew Feenberg and William Leiss, 201-32. Boston: Beacon Press.

Marett, R. R. 1914a [1908]. "The Conception of Mana." In *The Threshold of Religion,* 99-121. London: Methuen.

———. 1914b [1910]. "The Birth of Humility." In *The Threshold of Religion,* 169-202. London: Methuen.

Marx, Karl. 1977 [1867]. *Capital.* Vol. 1. New York: Vintage.

Masco, Joseph. 2014. *The Theater of Operations: National Security Affect from the Cold War to the War on Terror.* Durham, NC: Duke University Press.

Massumi, Brian. 2002. "The Autonomy of Affect." In *Parables for the Virtual: Movement, Affect, Sensation,* 23-45. Durham, NC: Duke University Press.

———. 2015. *Politics of Affect.* Cambridge: Polity Press.

Mauss, Marcel. 2001 [1902-3]. *A General Theory of Magic.* With Henri Hubert. New York: Routledge.

Mazzarella, William. 2003a. "Critical Publicity/Public Criticism: Reflections on Fieldwork in the Bombay Ad World." In *Advertising Cultures,* edited by Timothy DeWaal Malefyt and Brian Moeran, 55-74. Oxford: Berg.

———. 2003b. *Shoveling Smoke: Advertising and Globalization in Contemporary India.* Durham, NC: Duke University Press.

———. 2004. "Culture, Mediation, Globalization." *Annual Review of Anthropology* 33: 345-67.

———. 2005. "Public Culture, Still." *Biblio: A Review of Books* 10 (9-10).

———. 2009. "Affect: What Is It Good For?" In *Enchantments of Modernity: Empire, Nation, Globalization,* edited by Saurabh Dube, 291-309. London: Routledge.

———. 2010. "The Myth of the Multitude, or, Who's Afraid of the Crowd." *Critical Inquiry* 36 (4): 697-727.

———. 2013a. *Censorium: Cinema and the Open Edge of Mass Publicity*. Durham, NC: Duke University Press.

———. 2013b. "Why Is Adorno So Repulsive?" In *Beyond the Aesthetic and the Anti-Aesthetic*, edited by James Elkins and Harper Montgomery, 190-94. University Park: Pennsylvania State University Press.

———. 2015. "Totalitarian Tears: Does the Crowd Really Mean It?" *Cultural Anthropology* 30 (1): 91-112.

McCarthy, Tom. 2015. *Satin Island*. New York: Knopf.

McCreery, John. 1995. "Malinowski, Magic, and Advertising: On Choosing Metaphors." In *Contemporary Marketing and Consumer Behaviour: An Anthropological Sourcebook*, edited by John Sherry, 309-29. New Delhi: Sage.

McDougall, William. 1908. *An Introduction to Social Psychology*. London: Methuen.

McKinnon, Andrew. 2010. "Elective Affinities of the Protestant Ethic: Weber and the Chemistry of Capitalism." *Sociological Theory* 28 (1): 108-26.

Meillassoux, Quentin. 2008. *After Finitude: An Essay on the Necessity of Contingency*. New York: Continuum.

Melley, Timothy. 2011. "Brain Warfare: The Covert Sphere, Terrorism, and the Legacy of the Cold War." *Grey Room* 45 (Fall): 19-41.

Mellor, Philip. 1998. "Sacred Contagion and Social Vitality: Collective Effervescence in *Les forms élémentaires de la vie religieuse*." *Durkheimian Studies*, n.s., 4: 87-114.

Meyer, Birgit. 2015. "How to Capture the 'Wow': R. R. Marett's Notion of Awe and the Study of Religion." *JRAI*, n.s., 22: 7-26.

Miller, Daniel. 1997. *Capitalism: An Ethnographic Approach*. Oxford: Berg.

Miller, Jacques-Alain. 2008. "Extimity." *The Symptom 9*. http://www.lacan.com/symptom/?p=36, accessed May 21, 2015.

Mitchell, W. J. T. 2005. *What Do Pictures Want? The Lives and Loves of Images*. Chicago: University of Chicago Press.

Mlodinow, Leonard. 2012. *Subliminal: How Your Unconscious Mind Rules Your Behaviour*. New York: Vintage.

Moeran, Brian. 1996. *A Japanese Advertising Agency*. Honolulu: University of Hawai'i Press.

Moeran, Brian, and Timothy de Waal Malefyt, eds. 2003. *Advertising Cultures*. Oxford: Berg.

Mondragón, Carlos. 2004. "Of Winds, Worms, and Mana: The Traditional Calendar of the Torres Islands, Vanuatu." *Oceania* 74 (4): 289–308.

Morley, David. 1992. *Television, Audiences, and Cultural Studies*. London: Routledge.

Murdoch, Iris. 1973. *The Black Prince*. New York: Penguin.

Murphy, William. 1998. "The Sublime Dance of Mende Politics: An African Aesthetic of Charismatic Power." *American Ethnologist* 25 (4): 563–82.

Musil, Robert. 1996 [1952]. *The Man without Qualities*. Vol. 1, *A Sort of Introduction and Pseudo Reality Prevails*. New York: Vintage.

Nakassis, Constantine. 2012. "Brand, Citationality, Performativity." *American Anthropologist* 114 (4): 624–38.

———. 2013. "Brands and Their Surfeits." *Cultural Anthropology* 28 (1): 111–26.

Needham, Rodney. 1967 [1963]. Introduction to Émile Durkheim and Marcel Mauss, *Primitive Classification*, edited and translated by Rodney Needham, vii–xlviii. Chicago: University of Chicago Press.

———. 1976. "Skulls and Causality." *Man*, n.s., 11 (1): 71–88.

Norbrook, David. 1996. "The Emperor's New Body? *Richard II*, Ernst Kantorowicz, and the Politics of Shakespeare Criticism." *Textual Practice* 10 (2): 329–57.

Nye, Robert. 1995. "Savage Crowds, Modernism, and Modern Politics." In *Prehistories of the Future: The Primitivist Project and the Culture of Modernism*, edited by Elazar Barkan and Ronald Bush, 42–55. Stanford, CA: Stanford University Press.

Packard, Vance. 1957. *The Hidden Persuaders*. New York: D. McKay.

Paine, Thomas. 1998 [1791]. "Rights of Man, &c, &c." In *Rights of Man, Common Sense, and Other Political Writings*, 83–197 New York: Oxford University Press.

Pauchant, Thierry. 1991. "Transferential Leadership: Towards a More Complex Understanding of Charisma in Organizations." *Organization Studies* 12: 507–27.

Pels, Peter. 2003. "Introduction: Magic and Modernity." In *Magic and Modernity: Interfaces of Revelation and Concealment*, edited by Birgit Meyer and Peter Pels, 1–38. Stanford, CA: Stanford University Press.

Peters, John Durham. 2001. *Speaking into the Air: A History of the Idea of Communication*. Chicago: University of Chicago Press.

———. 2010. "Broadcasting and Schizophrenia." *Media, Culture, and Society* 32: 123–40.

———. 2015. *The Marvelous Clouds: Toward a Philosophy of Elemental Media*. Chicago: University of Chicago Press.

Pickering, W. S. F. 1984. *Durkheim's Sociology of Religion: Themes and Theories*. London: Routledge and Kegan Paul.

Pinney, Christopher. 2001. "Introduction: Public, Popular, and Other Cultures." In *Pleasure and the Nation: The History, Politics, and Consumption of Public Culture in India*, edited by Rachel Dwyer and Christopher Pinney, 1–34. New Delhi: Oxford University Press.

———. 2004. *"Photos of the Gods": The Printed Image and Political Struggle in India*. London: Reaktion.

Plato. 2009. *Symposium*. Oxford: Oxford University Press.

Pouillon, Jean. 1982 [1979]. "Remarks on the Verb 'To Believe.'" In *Between Belief and Transgression: Structuralist Essays in Religion, History, and Myth*, edited by Michel Izard and Pierre Smith, 1–8. Chicago: University of Chicago Press.

Povinelli, Elizabeth. 2006. *The Empire of Love: Toward a Theory of Intimacy, Genealogy, and Carnality*. Durham, NC: Duke University Press.

Pratt, Mary Louise. 1992. *Imperial Eyes: Travel Writing and Transculturation*. London: Routledge.

Radin, Paul. 1937. *Primitive Religion: Its Nature and Origin*. New York: Viking.

———. 1957 [1927]. *Primitive Man as Philosopher*. New York: Dover.

Riesebrodt, Martin. 1999. "Charisma in Max Weber's Sociology of Religion." *Religion* 29 (1): 1–14.

Rivers, W. H. R. 1918. *Dreams and Primitive Culture*. Manchester: Longmans, Green.

Rubin, William, ed. 1984. *"Primitivism" in 20th Century Art: Affinity of the Tribal and the Modern*. New York: Museum of Modern Art.

Sahlins, Marshall. 1976. *Culture and Practical Reason*. Chicago: University of Chicago Press.

————. 1981. *Historical Metaphors and Mythical Realities: Structure in the Early History of the Sandwich Islands Kingdom*. Ann Arbor: University of Michigan Press.

————. 1985. *Islands of History*. Chicago: University of Chicago Press.

————. 1996. "'The Sadness of Sweetness: The Native Anthropology of Western Cosmology." *Current Anthropology* 37 (3): 395–428.

————. 2012. "J. Prytz Johansen: Kant among the Maori." Introduction to the new edition of *The Maori and His Religion in Its Non-Ritualistic Aspects*. Chicago: Hau Books.

Santner, Eric L. 2011. *The Royal Remains: The People's Two Bodies and the Endgames of Sovereignty*. Chicago: University of Chicago Press.

————. 2015. *The Weight of All Flesh: On the Subject-Matter of Political Economy*. New York: Oxford University Press.

Saunders, George. 2016. "Trump Days: Up Close with the Candidate and His Crowds." *New Yorker*, July 11 and 18, 50–61.

Scannell, Paddy. 2000. "For-Anyone-as-Someone Structures." *Media, Culture, and Society* 22 (1): 5–24.

Schiermer, Bjørn. 2013. "Aura, Cult Value, and the Postmodern Crowd: A Durkheimian Reading of Walter Benjamin's Artwork Essay." *Distinktion: Scandinavian Journal of Social Theory* 14 (2): 191–210.

————. 2016. "On the Ageing of Objects in Modern Culture: Ornament and Crime." *Theory, Culture, and Society* 33 (4): 127–50.

Schmitt, Carl. 2006 [1922]. *Political Theology: Four Chapters on the Concept of Sovereignty*. Chicago: University of Chicago Press.

Schnapp, Jeffrey, and Matthew Tiews, eds. 2006. *Crowds*. Stanford, CA: Stanford University Press.

Schudson, Michael. 1984. *Advertising, the Uneasy Persuasion: Its Dubious Impact on American Society*. New York: Basic.

Seaver, Nick. 2012. "Algorithmic Recommendations and Synaptic Functions." *Limn* (March). http://limn.it/algorithmic-recommendations-and-synaptic-functions/, accessed September 28, 2016.

Shaviro, Steven. 2014. *The Universe of Things: On Speculative Realism*. Minneapolis: University of Minnesota Press.

Shils, Edward. 1958. "The Concentration and Dispersion of Charisma: Their Bearing on Economic Policy in Underdeveloped Countries." *World Politics* 11 (1): 1-19.

————. 1965. "Charisma, Order, and Status." *American Sociological Review* 30 (2): 199-213.

Shirokogoroff, Sergei. 1935. *The Psychomental Complex of the Tungus.* London: Kegan Paul, Trench, Trubner.

Shore, Bradd. 1989. *"Mana* and *Tapu."* In *Developments in Polynesian Ethnology,* edited by Alan Howard and Robert Borofsky. Honolulu: University of Hawai'i Press.

Siegel, James. 2006. *Naming the Witch.* Stanford, CA: Stanford University Press.

Simmel, Georg. 1971a. *Georg Simmel: Individuality and Social Forms.* Edited by Donald Levine. Chicago: University of Chicago Press.

————. 1971b [1908]. "The Stranger." In *Georg Simmel: Individuality and Social Forms,* edited by Donald Levine, 143-49. Chicago: University of Chicago Press.

————. 1997 [1918]. "The Conflict of Modern Culture." In *Simmel on Culture,* edited by David Frisby and Mike Featherstone, 75-89. London: Sage.

————. 2010 [1918]. *The View of Life: Four Metaphysical Essays with Journal Aphorisms.* Chicago: University of Chicago Press.

Sloterdijk, Peter. 1987 [1983]. *Critique of Cynical Reason.* Minneapolis: University of Minnesota Press.

————. 2011 [1998]. *Spheres.* Vol. 1, *Bubbles—Microspherology.* New York: Semiotext(e).

————. 2013 [2009]. *You Must Change Your Life.* Cambridge: Polity.

Smith, Adam. 1984 [1759]. *The Theory of Moral Sentiments.* Indianapolis, IN: Liberty Fund.

Smith, Jonathan Z. 2004. "Manna, Mana Everywhere and /⌣/⌣/." In *Relating Religion: Essays in the Study of Religion,* 117-44. Chicago: University of Chicago Press.

Solms, Mark. 2015. *The Feeling Brain: Selected Papers on Neuropsychoanalysis.* London: Karnac.

Spadola, Emilio. 2014. *The Calls of Islam: Sufis, Islamists, and Mass Mediation in Urban Morocco.* Bloomington: Indiana University Press.

Stambach, Amy. 2000. "The Rationality Debate Revisited." *Reviews in Anthropology* 28 (4): 341-51.

Starn, Orin, ed. 2015. *Writing Culture and the Life of Anthropology.* Durham, NC: Duke University Press.

Starobinski, Jean. 2003 [1999]. *Action and Reaction: The Life and Adventures of a Couple.* New York: Zone.

Stasch, Rupert. 2011. "Ritual and Oratory Revisited: The Semiotics of Effective Action." *Annual Review of Anthropology* 40: 159–74.

Steiner, Wendy. 1995. *The Scandal of Pleasure: Art in an Age of Fundamentalism.* Chicago: University of Chicago Press.

Stewart, Kathleen. 2007. *Ordinary Affects.* Durham, NC: Duke University Press.

Stocking, George. 1968. *Race, Culture, and Evolution: Essays in the History of Anthropology.* Chicago: University of Chicago Press.

———. 1995. *After Tylor: British Social Anthropology, 1888–1951.* Madison: University of Wisconsin Press.

Strasser, Susan. 2003 [1989]. *Satisfaction Guaranteed: The Making of the American Mass Market.* Washington, DC: Smithsonian Institution Press.

Sunstein, Cass. 2001. *Republic.com.* Princeton, NJ: Princeton University Press.

Surowiecki, James. 2005. *The Wisdom of Crowds.* New York: Anchor.

Tambiah, Stanley Jeyaraja. 1990. *Magic, Science, and the Scope of Rationality.* Cambridge: Cambridge University Press.

Tarde, Gabriel. 1903 [1890]. *The Laws of Imitation.* New York: Henry Holt.

———. 1969 [1901]. "The Public and the Crowd." In *Gabriel Tarde on Communication and Social Influence,* edited by Terry Clark, 277–96. Chicago: University of Chicago Press.

Taussig, Michael. 1987. *Shamanism, Colonialism, and the Wild Man: A Study in Terror and Healing.* Chicago: University of Chicago Press.

———. 1991. *The Nervous System.* London: Routledge.

———. 1993. *Mimesis and Alterity: A Particular History of the Senses.* London: Routledge.

———. 1999. *Defacement: Public Secrecy and the Labour of the Negative.* Stanford, CA: Stanford University Press.

———. 2006a. "Viscerality, Faith, and Skepticism: Another Theory of Magic." In *Walter Benjamin's Grave.* Chicago: University of Chicago Press.

————. 2006b. *Walter Benjamin's Grave*. Chicago: University of Chicago Press.

————. N.d. "Mooning Texas." Unpublished manuscript.

Tiryakian, Edward. 1995. "Collective Effervescence, Social Change, and Charisma: Durkheim, Weber, and 1989." *International Sociology* 10 (3): 269–81.

Tomlinson, Matt. 2006. "Retheorizing Mana: Bible Translation and Discourse of Loss in Fiji." *Oceania* 76 (2): 173–85.

Trouillot, Michel-Rolph. 2003 [1991]. "Anthropology and the Savage Slot: The Poetics and Politics of Otherness." In *Global Transformations: Anthropology and the Modern World*, 7–28. London: Palgrave Macmillan.

Turner, Edith. 2011. *Communitas: The Anthropology of Collective Joy*. New York: Palgrave Macmillan.

Turner, Graeme. 1990. *British Cultural Studies: An Introduction*. London: Routledge.

Turner, Victor. 1967. *The Forest of Symbols*. Ithaca, NY: Cornell University Press.

————. 1995 [1969]. *The Ritual Process: Structure and Anti-Structure*. New Brunswick, NJ: Aldine Transaction.

Tylor, Edward Burnett. 1874 [1871]. *Primitive Culture: Researches into the Development of Mythology, Philosophy, Religion, Language, Art, and Custom*. New York: Henry Holt.

Urban, Greg. 2015. "Symbolic Force: A Corporate Revitalization Video and Its Effects." *Signs and Society* 3, no. S1: S95–S124.

Valeri, Valerio. 1985. *Kingship and Sacrifice: Ritual and Society in Ancient Hawaii*. Chicago: University of Chicago Press.

Viveiros de Castro, Eduardo. 2013. "The Relative Native." *HAU: Journal of Ethnographic Theory* 3 (3): 473–502.

Wagner, Roy. 1981 [1975]. *The Invention of Culture*. Chicago: University of Chicago Press.

————. 1984. "Ritual as Communication: Order, Meaning, and Secrecy in Melanesian Initiation Rites." *Annual Review of Anthropology* 13: 143–55.

Walvis, Tjaco. 2010. *Branding with Brains: The Science of Getting Customers to Choose Your Company*. London: Financial Times.

Warner, Michael 2002. "Publics and Counterpublics." *Public Culture* 14 (1): 49–90.

Weber, Max. 1968a [1920]. "Religious Groups (The Sociology of Religion)." In *Economy and Society: An Outline of Interpretive Sociology*, edited by Guenther Roth and Claus Wittich, 399–421. Berkeley: University of California Press.

———. 1968b [1922]. "The Types of Legitimate Domination." In *Economy and Society: An Outline of Interpretive Sociology*, edited by Guenther Roth and Claus Wittich, 212–301. Berkeley: University of California Press.

———. 2002 [1905]. *The Protestant Ethic and the Spirit of Capitalism*. New York: Penguin Classics.

Webster, Hutton. 1913. Review of Emile Durkheim, *Les forms élémentaires de la vie religieuse*. *American Journal of Sociology* 18 (6): 843–46.

Wedeen, Lisa. 1999. *Ambiguities of Domination: Politics, Rhetoric, and Symbols in Contemporary Syria*. Chicago: University of Chicago Press.

———. 2007. *Peripheral Visions: Publics, Power, and Performance in Yemen*. Chicago: University of Chicago Press.

Wegner, Daniel. 2005. "Who Is the Controller of Controlled Processes?" In *The New Unconscious*, edited by Ran Hassin, James Uleman, and John Bargh, 19–36. New York: Oxford University Press.

Widdicombe, Lizzie. 2016. "Family First." *New Yorker*, August 22, 24–30.

Wiggershaus, Rolf. 1994 [1986]. *The Frankfurt School: Its History, Theories, and Political Significance*. Cambridge, MA: MIT Press.

Wilder, Gary. 2015. *Freedom Time: Negritude, Decolonization, and the Future of the World*. Durham, NC: Duke University Press.

Williams, Raymond. 1980 [1962]. "Advertising, the Magic System." In *Problems in Materialism and Culture: Selected Essays*, 170–95. New York: Verso.

Williamson, Judith. 1978. *Decoding Advertisements: Ideology and Meaning in Advertising*. London: Boyars.

Wilson, Bryan, ed. 1991 [1970]. *Rationality*. Oxford: Blackwell.

Yurchak, Alexei. 2006. *Everything Was Forever until It Was No More: The Last Soviet Generation*. Durham, NC: Duke University Press.

———. 2015. "Bodies of Lenin: The Hidden Science of Communist Sovereignty." *Representations* 129: 116–57.

Žižek, Slavoj. 1989. *The Sublime Object of Ideology*. New York: Verso.

———. 1999a. "Class Struggle or Postmodernism? Yes, Please!" In *Contingency, Hegemony, Universality: Contemporary Dialogues on the Left*, by Judith Butler, Ernesto Laclau, and Slavoj Žižek, 90–135. New York: Verso.

———. 1999b. "Da Capo Senza Fine." In *Contingency, Hegemony, Universality: Contemporary Dialogues on the Left*, by Judith Butler, Ernesto Laclau, and Slavoj Žižek, 213–62. New York: Verso.

———. 1999c. "Questions from Slavoj Žižek." In *Contingency, Hegemony, Universality: Contemporary Dialogues on the Left*, by Judith Butler, Ernesto Laclau, and Slavoj Žižek, 9–10. New York: Verso.

———. 1999d. *The Ticklish Subject: The Absent Center of Political Ontology*. New York: Verso.

———. 2006. *The Parallax View*. Cambridge, MA: MIT Press.

———. 2012. "Is It Still Possible to Be a Hegelian Today?" In *Less Than Nothing: Hegel and the Shadow of Dialectical Materialism*, 193–240. London: Verso.

Zuidervaart, Lambert. 1991. *Adorno's Aesthetic Theory: The Redemption of Illusion*. Cambridge, MA: MIT Press.

Zupančič, Alenka. 2006. "When Surplus Enjoyment Meets Surplus Value." In *Jacques Lacan and the Other Side of Psychoanalysis: Reflections on* Seminar XVII, edited by Justin Clemens and Russell Grigg, 155–78. Durham, NC: Duke University Press.

———. 2008. *The Odd One In: On Comedy*. Cambridge, MA: MIT Press.

Zwick, Detlev, and Julien Cayla. 2011. *Inside Marketing: Practices, Ideologies, Devices*. Oxford: Oxford University Press.

Index

Lacan, Jacques (*continued*)
50–51, 151; on mirror stage, 152–
53; on subjectivity, 150–51
lack in human beings, 24–25, 50–51,
151
latent resources, 8–9, 35, 63, 64, 147
Latour, Bruno, 10, 62, 110
Leach, Edmund, 45, 47
Lévi-Strauss, Claude: on barbarians,
118–19; denunciation of Mauss,
61, 66, 77, 80–82; on floating
signifiers, 121; on mana as dark
matter, 51; on science of the concrete, 76–77, 158; on shamanic
practice, 67; on signs, 144
Lévy-Bruhl, Lucien: on fascinations,
54; on lure of vitalism, 43–44; on
primitive/modern culture, 72–
74; on primitive thought, 77–78,
146, 151
"Life as Transcendence" (Simmel),
65
life/form, 64–65
love. *See* eros/nomos
Lukács, Georg, 16–17, 84
Lukes, Steven, 52

magical practices: and advertising,
33–34; and aesthetics, 120–22;
alter egos in, 94–95; endurance
of, 36–37; and eros, 35, 148–49;
extimacy of, 57–58, 121; of language, 34; as manipulation, 119;
of mass publicity, 33–35, 41, 126,
134–35, 140, 148–49; vs. modernity, 70; participation in, 146;
persistence of, 71–72; and religious ritual, 90–91; and scientific
thought, 75; and skill, 158; sympathetic, 146; as world making,
92
Magic Mountain, The (Mann), 44
magnetizer, 57, 158
Malefyt, Timothy, 109, 115–16, 143
Malinowski, Bronislaw: on advertising as modern savagery, 57, 72,
120, 141, 153; on collective energies, 34; on crowd effervescence,
93; fieldwork paradigm of, 41,
46; on magical language, 34; on

magic and advertising, 33–34, 37;
on mana, 37, 40
mana: and charisma, 4, 156–57,
203n59; and collective effervescence, 80–81, 85, 160; constitu-
tive/destitutive work of, 24; in
consumer branding, 2, 3–4, 162,
164; as dark matter, 51–55; defined, 1, 19, 33, 38–40; as electricity, 51–54; emergent properties of, 4; as European invention,
52–53; as extimate, 3–4, 14, 15,
19–20, 23, 50, 59, 84, 90, 160,
164; fractalized, 159–61, 162;
immanence/transcendence of,
39–40, 58, 66, 169; macro-forms/
micro-dimensions in, 3; as magic
of persuasion, 37; Melanesian,
39–40; as moral power, 60; order
in, 4; as primitive potentiality,
10; sacred/profane in, 160–61; in
social theory, 2–4; sovereignty
of, 125; as symptom of encounter,
38, 50; use of term, 46–47; vitality of, 49, 55, 61–62, 66, 77, 102;
as world making, 20, 27, 65–66,
81–82, 92. *See also* mass publicity,
mana of; mass society, mana of
mana moment, 37, 41–44; aesthetic
settlement in, 120–21, 136; afterlife of, 48, 49, 62, 71; atavism in,
42; crowd theory, 79, 114; empiricist settlement in, 44–45, 47, 51,
55, 61–62; end of, 44–45, 61–62,
75, 157, 171; enlightenment in,
122; era of, 25–26, 41, 43; imperialism, end of, 171; metaphorics
of, 52–54; as participation/repre-
sentation, 35; primitivism in, 43,
71, 73, 74, 75, 78, 89, 119; racist
assumptions in, 72; reenchantment in, 44
mana workers, 33, 104, 138, 148, 153,
168
Mann, Thomas, 44
Man without Qualities, The (Musil),
41–42
Maori mana talk, 46
Marcus, George, 143
Marcuse, Herbert, 142

modernity (*continued*)
    magic, 70; masses in, 41; vs.
    primitivism, 26-27, 37-38, 42,
    72-73, 102, 119, 157
modern savagery: compared to
    primitive, 42, 47; mass publicity
    as, 47, 72, 120, 123, 141, 153; and
    primitivism, 34; of urban crowds,
    42-43, 54
Moeran, Brian, 106, 143
Morais, Robert, 109, 115-16
Moses, 80-81
Murdoch, Iris, 153
Murphy, William, 203n57
Musil, Robert, 41

narrowcasting, 108
Needham, Rodney, 52
Negative Dialectics (Adorno), 129
neovitalism, 68, 129-30
neuromarketing, 108, 112-14, 196n51
Newton, Isaac, 62
nomos. *See* eros/nomos
nonsensuous similarity, 145-46, 149,
    158
Norbrook, David, 174n26
Northern Tribes of Central Australia
    (Spencer/Gillen), 82-83
Nye, Robert, 42

object-ethics, 15, 21-22, 102, 123
objects: encounters, 101-2; erotic
    principle of, 124; primacy of, 28,
    123-26, 128-31, 146. *See also* aes-
    thetic autonomy
Occupy movements, 2
Odysseus and Sirens (Greek my-
    thology), 27-28, 82, 101, 103, 127,
    134-36, 137, 140, 165, 169-70
Odyssey (Homer), 101
olon, 97
orenda, 70-71

Packard, Vance, 104
Paine, Thomas, 63-64
participation/representation, 27, 35,
    44, 73-74, 78, 91, 96, 111, 119, 122,
    125, 138-39, 164
pathology and vitality, 44
Pauline Christian community, 161

pause, 74-75
Pels, Peter, 70
perfect addressability, agony of,
    108-9, 115, 117, 134
Peters, John Durham, 24-25, 109
Phenomenology of Spirit (Hegel), 129
Pickering, W. S. F., 79-80
picture-thinking, 76
Plato, 149
Plotinus, 44
pneuma concept, 61, 149
Polynesian mana-tapu complex, 67-
    68
Polynesian religion, 52, 67-68, 84,
    179n52
Polynesian Religion (Handy), 52
Povinelli, Elizabeth, 139
power: chocolate side of, use of
    term, 165, 166; and constitutive
    resonance, 165; and desire, 24;
    and difference, 24, 169; mana
    as moral, 60; and pleasure, 106;
    weakness of, 167-68
pragmatic aesthetics, use of term, 42
Prikonsky, V. L., 97
Primitive Classification (Durkheim/
    Mauss), 74
Primitive Culture (Tylor), 48, 75
Primitive Magic (de Martino), 92
primitive settlement, 10, 27, 70-74,
    96, 102
primitivism: fascination with, 43;
    mana theorists on, 51, 89; meta-
    phors, 141; vs. modernism, 26-27,
    37-38, 72-73, 102, 119, 157; and
    modern savagery, 34, 141; and
    potentiality, 10; and savagery, 42;
    survival/revival of, 71; thought
    in, 46, 72, 74-78, 96, 182n85;
    use of term, 70. *See also* magical
    practices; ritual assemblies
prosumption, 168
provocation, 5-7, 11, 36, 50, 135
psychoanalysis, 44, 61, 96, 113

Radin, Paul, 179n52
Reich, Wilhelm, 61
religion: collective effervescence
    in, 93; vital basis of, 79. *See also*
    magical practices

CPSIA information can be obtained
at www.ICGtesting.com
Printed in the USA
LVHW01s1012180118
562879LV00002B/3/P